RESEARCH ON EDUCATIONAL INNOVATIONS

SECOND EDITION

Arthur K. Ellis
Jeffrey T. Fouts

EYE ON EDUCATION
6 DEPOT WAY WEST, SUITE 106
LARCHMONT, NY 10538
(914) 833–0551
(914) 833–0761 fax

ISBN

Library of Congress Cataloging-in-Publication Data

```
Ellis, Arthur K.
   Research on educational innovations / Arthur Ellis and Jeffrey
Fouts. -- 2nd ed.
     p.   cm.
   Includes bibliographical references and index.
   ISBN 1-883001-41-2
   1. Education--United States--Experimental methods.  2. Educational
innovations--United States.  3. Education--Research--United States.
I. Fouts, Jeffrey T.  II. Title.
LB1027.3.E45  1997
371.3'9--dc21                                             97-10151
                                                              CIP
```

10 9 8 7 6 5 4

Editorial and production services provided by Richard H. Adin Freelance Editorial Services, 9 Orchard Drive, Gardiner, NY 12525 (914–883–5884)

ABOUT THE AUTHORS

Arthur K. Ellis is Professor of Education at Seattle Pacific University. Previously, he taught in public school and at the University of Minnesota. He is the author of nine published books and numerous journal articles. He consults to numerous government agencies and to various school systems in the United States and abroad.

Jeffrey T. Fouts is Professor of Education at Seattle Pacific University. Previously, he taught in public school in the State of Oregon. He is the author of three published books and has done research on classroom environments, as well as consulting work in the United States and in other countries.

TABLE OF CONTENTS

PREFACE

Just as in agriculture the operations that come before the planting, as well as the planting itself, are certain and easy; but as soon as the plant comes to life, there are various methods and great difficulties in raising it; so it is with humans: little industry is needed to plant them, but it is quite a different burden we assume from the moment of their birth, a burden full of care and fear—that of training them and bringing them up.

Michel de Montaigne

Welcome to the second edition of Research on Educational Innovations. We appreciate the favorable reception and many positive reviews, citations, and adoptions given the first edition. Our purpose in this edition remains constant: to bring to your attention such fundamentals as definitions, descriptions, theoretical and empirical bases, critical analyses, and conclusions. We do this in the spirit of inquiry, inviting you to inquire along with us. Our focus is upon major educational innovations, by which we mean programs and curriculums that have achieved widespread influence. Because the influx of new ideas into our profession is continuous, we are forced to be selective about the innovations we can reasonably include in this book. Specific practices and programs come and go. Our criteria for a program's inclusion are that the program be one of the most dominant in the literature, that it often appears as a topic of professional meetings, that it is widely used in school settings, and that it is emphasized in teacher education, both preservice and inservice. Our attempt is to be dispassionate and to avoid either promoting or disparaging any given innovation simply out of hand. Basing our case on the evidence we are able to find, we prefer, to paraphrase Michelangelo, to let the chips fall.

Since the first edition was published, major restructuring efforts have dominated the educational agenda. The call for reform seems as urgent at it ever was, perhaps more so. As a result, interest in innovative practice remains high. We have included four new chapters in this volume: Self-Esteem Programs, Teaching for Intelligence, Direct Instruction, and Alternative/Authentic Assessment. School restructuring, the emergence of new research, and changing political perspectives in the field have made it possible for us to take a fresh look at many of those innovations which we examined in the previous edition but which remain in the forefront today.

We are fascinated by the new: new cars, new fashions, new insights, and so on. There is something exciting and motivating about newness. Think about it: new hope, new beginnings. In recent American political history, we have had both the New Deal and the New Frontier. Our desire to try something new is often based on a wish to break with the past and the present, especially where feelings of discontent exist. In some sense, the new brings to mind utopian images and dreams of a better world. The researcher Thomas Guskey, appraising this phenomenon, has made insightful reference to our "infatuation" with innovations.

American schools have become seedbeds of discontent in recent times. We read everywhere about the loss of confidence in our schools on the part of the public. Anyone who follows the story line has heard talk of a golden era in American public education. Our current efforts are placed alongside those of a mythical past and are found wanting. And even for those who don't spend a lot of time longing for the golden days of yesteryear, there is always the desire to improve, to do better. We set our goals not at levels of mediocrity, but at the far reaches of excellence.

So the search for what is new and good continues. The dream of every teacher and administrator is of new heights of achievement, civic participation, and personal fulfillment for the next generation. Much hope exists for the young. We see that hope at the PTA meeting when so many parents of kindergarten and first grade children show up. And we see the hope turn to reality, for better or for worse, as children find their way through the school years.

Like pilgrims in quest of the Holy Grail, we look for the curriculum or method that will get us where we want to go, to the land of excellence. And with great perseverance and un-

flagging good cheer, we are willing to try this or that innovation, hoping that at last we have something better than we've
ever had before. We hear about cooperative learning, and we
agree to try it because maybe it will improve the social fabric of
classroom life and raise achievement at the same time. We hear
about self-esteem programs and wonder what role we could
play toward making kids feel better about themselves. And we
read an article on brain-based learning and find ourselves
agreeing that, of course, the little three-pound organ called the
human brain has unlimited capabilities.

So the quest continues. Each year, it seems, new ideas about
improving the system are brought to our attention, often with
great fanfare. Some of them literally scream for our attention,
reminding the more reflective among us of the centuries-old
words of the writer Baltasar Gracian, who noted that a brand-
new mediocrity is thought more of than accustomed excellence.

One of the things we wish to accomplish in this book is to
help you separate the "brand-new mediocrities" from that
which is excellent, whether old or new. To do this we had to set
up a screen, much in the way someone panning for gold in a
mountain stream uses a screen to dip into the rushing waters.
The screen allows what is not valuable to return to the creek
while the rich ore is retained. It's not a perfect system, whether
you are seeking gold ore or golden educational ideas. But if
you are persistent, and we were, you will find some nuggets.

Our screen is published research. We use it for two reasons.
The first is that virtually everyone has access to published research through the readily available journals in education. This
is not true of unpublished research. It is often nearly impossible to access. Much of the time we know about it only because
someone touting an innovation refers to certain glowing results
without showing us the conditions, the controls, the design,
and the analysis.

The second reason for our setting this standard is that published research has undergone levels of careful scrutiny that
unpublished research never experiences. Does this mean that
unpublished research is necessarily bad? No, we think not; but

we can tell you that we have carefully examined much unpublished research. Most of the time it simply does not meet the standards that you would knowingly demand if you were about to spend much time, energy, and money on a particular innovation. Research published in such journals as the *Review of Educational Research* or the *Journal of Educational Psychology* is carefully reviewed by knowledgeable jurors before acceptance, or, in most cases, before rejection. In other words, you never even see the faulty research because it doesn't appear in these journals. It is not a perfect system, but we prefer it to the alternatives that come to mind.

We are excited about sound educational innovation, and we hope that you are also. But there is no point in becoming excited about so-called improvements that really give us no proof of their goodness. Nothing is gained in the name of innovation when we find ourselves in the very same circumstance as that of the ancient King Pyrrhus, who said, "One more such 'victory' and we are undone." Our role is that of messengers, and we are fully aware that in ancient times messengers were often thrown into a well when they brought bad tidings, and merely taken for granted when the news they brought was good. We accept this in good humor, hoping the metaphor is not pushed too far. So be prepared—some of the tidings we bring are good and some are less than that.

Let us all agree that we seek progress and not merely change. We respect your judgment, and it is in that spirit that we bring you this information about educational innovations. We ask only that you review our findings as well as those of others and reach your own conclusions. We have gone to original sources, and we encourage you to do the same. It was observed long ago that one's judgment is only as good as one's information, and our goal is to inform you.

1

THE NATURE OF EDUCATIONAL INNOVATION

*One doesn't discover new lands without consenting
to lose sight of the shore for a very long time.*
André Gide

Each generation must answer anew a set of age-old questions. Those questions go to the heart of our existence. They are questions of purpose, of being, of destiny. They are questions of justice, of relationships, of goodness. The fact that previous generations have grappled with the same questions is helpful but not sufficient. The questions are so basic that we must address them; we ignore them at our peril. Others cannot answer them for us, although they can give us insights, and we can benefit from their experience. We must seek our own answers, however different or similar to those arrived at by our predecessors. This is so because the search is as important as the outcome and because situations change over time. It is the process of arriving at answers, however tentative or even deficient, which makes us human.

Just as we seek answers to life's larger questions, we seek answers within the frames of our professional existence, in this case teaching and learning. As teachers and administrators, we seek answers to questions about the nature of knowledge, the nature of learning, and the nature of teaching. We ask ourselves if there is a better way to organize teaching, a better way to present ideas to young people, a better way to assess learning. We grapple with such dualisms as control vs. freedom, cooperation vs. independence, time-on-task vs. creativity. As

1

practical people working in school settings with all the complexities one finds in such socially contrived environments as
playgrounds and lunchrooms, and such academically contrived environments as high school physics laboratories and
primary reading classes, we wonder what to teach, how best to
teach it, and even if what we teach has lasting value. These
questions tend to deplete our energy, especially when we are
continually reminded by the popular press that American
schools are doing a poor job of preparing the nation's young
for an increasingly complex future.

At the same time, the educational literature is filled with
ideas and strategies for innovation: mastery learning, whole
language learning, interdisciplinary curriculum, learning
styles, developmentally-appropriate practice, cooperative
learning, effective teaching, school restructuring, site-based
management, and the list goes on. Each of these innovations is
touted by its proponents as the key to an improved school experience for teachers and students. Administrators read about
a given innovation and wonder whether it could be the answer
for their school. A teacher attends a workshop where the pre-
senter makes a compelling case for some "new paradigm."
Like wandering nomads in search of the next oasis, we move
from fad to fad in search of the next wellspring with the vague
hope that we might find a permanent place to settle. Of course,
we never do.

Still, the waves of innovation are received with mixed re-
actions. What is the source of our ambivalence toward innovation in education? On the one hand, we seem ready, as educational historian Herbert Kliebard has pointed out, to grasp at
anything so long as it is *new*. There is a feeling, almost a fear,
that our school could be left behind. On the other hand, those
teachers and administrators who have been around for awhile
have seen so many "innovations" come and go that a certain
degree of cynicism sets in when they are told at fall meetings,
"we are going to adopt a site-based management approach," or
whatever.

In this book, we have attempted to provide teachers, administrators, counselors, and other school personnel with in-

sights to a carefully selected set of innovations. The innovations chosen to appear in these pages have nationwide (if not international) impact. They have application across a range of grade and subject levels. And they have considerable staying power. As you read about them, you should gain knowledge not only of certain specific innovations, but insights into the nature of innovation itself and how and to what extent a particular innovation, perhaps one that is yet to appear, is not merely new, but worthwhile.

At this point a cautionary note must be sounded. No new idea, no matter how well researched, is worthwhile outside a context of purpose. For example, if we were asked, "Is an interdisciplinary curriculum a good idea for my school," we would be forced to respond by asking, "What is the purpose of your school?" No one can answer that question meaningfully except the people who have a genuine interest in your school. Now this may seem rather simplistic and even obvious to everyone. But the history of failure and disappointment in educational innovation starts with confusion of purpose. It inevitably leads to cynicism and the "we tried that" syndrome.

So somewhere in the matrix of your individual and school goal structures you must measure any new educational idea's worth. The more meaningful question is not, "Is it the latest trend," but "Is it good for us?" Each educator, each school faculty, and each school community must face the same basic questions:

+ What does our school stand for?
+ What should students learn?
+ What are the best conditions for learning?
+ What experiences enhance learning?
+ How should classes and schools be organized?
+ How can we know if we are attaining our goals?

...and so on. The questions are endless because:

+ Teaching is as much an art as a science.
+ Learning is a poorly understood process.

- Students are diverse and they respond differentially.
- Societal needs and demands change.
- Local and site-specific needs differ considerably.

WHAT IS AN INNOVATION?

Innovation and *novelty* come from the same Latin root. They both imply that something is new. The idea that something is "new" is dear to our hearts. We have been conditioned by advertisers and promoters to associate "new" with "improved," whether the product is a detergent or a curriculum. The *Oxford English Dictionary* defines the *innovation* as "the introduction of novelties." "Innovation" is a noun related to the verb "to innovate," first found in print in 1561 in T. Norton's *Calvin's Instructions*, in which the sentence appears, "A desire to innovate all things moveth troublesome men." So, the term appears to have reached through to the emotions, negative and positive, from that time to this day.

In the school-based world of teaching and learning, innovation seems to be all-important. School people often express a desire to be on the "cutting edge" of things, to know the latest trends, to avoid being old-fashioned or out-of-date. The teacher workshop/inservice training business, which employs educational innovations as its stock-in-trade, is a multimillion-dollar industry in the United States and Canada.

WHERE ARE THEY NOW?

A generation ago, a series of innovations entered the world of education. Depending on your age or your powers of recollection, you may recognize some of them. They included team teaching, career education, values clarification, multicultural education, human relations training, open schools, competency-based education, peace education, back to the basics, bilingual education, and a few others. Where are they now? The answers vary. Some disappeared without a trace. Some are the forerunners of present-day reform efforts. Some are still around in one form or another. This will always be the case. Today's trend is often tomorrow's forgotten dream. Some of the innovations that sweep through the school scene are nothing more than fads. Some have greater staying power. Let's look at why this might be so.

RESEARCH-BASED?

A common claim of most educational innovations is that they are "research-based." The intent, apparently, is to give school personnel cause to think that a particular program is valid and reasonable for them to use because it will yield improved results. The term *research-based* lends almost mystical qualities to the innovation, making it difficult if not impossible for the average teacher, administrator, or school board member to challenge the claims made in behalf of the innovation. Who among us, after all, is going to challenge RESEARCH? The fact is that many school personnel simply do not understand the arcane procedures of educational research with its language of statistical analysis, control groups, experimental designs, etc. As a result, they are left to the mercy of persuasive arguments by "experts" who tell them what the research says and what they should therefore do. We will demystify the process.

To begin, it is useful to consider examples of research from the field of natural science because science has served as the paradigm for most social science research, of which educational research is a subset. We begin with the idea of theory. Theories are *tentative* ways of explaining and predicting phenomena. A theory represents a carefully considered set of ideas about something. The development of a theoretical model is the quest of persons doing pure or basic (as opposed to applied) research. While working in the field of physics, Albert Einstein developed his theory of relativity, a theory that stated that all motion must be defined relative to a frame of reference. In other words, space and time are relative, not absolute, concepts. They take on meaning in relation to their context. Einstein proposed his ideas as a theoretical model to be tested, not as a fact. Other physicists conducted research on the theory, finding much supportive evidence for it. Today the theory of relativity serves as a useful model for the explanation and prediction of the behavior of matter and energy. However, as a theory it is subject to new interpretation, and in time it may well be modified considerably in the light of new knowledge.

Most often, scientific theory emerges as the result of some preliminary research in a particular field. When Charles Darwin sailed aboard H.M.S. *Beagle* to the Galapagos Islands and to the South Pacific in the 19th century, he made careful, systematic observations of certain animals and their unique characteristics. From his data collecting, he advanced the hypothesis that changes in the physical characteristics of animals were the result of an ongoing, evolutionary process. More than a century later, his theory of evolution remains the object of scientific study, although it has itself evolved considerably over time. Many questions have been answered, but far more questions, remain so research on the topic continues.

Our first two examples are about the behavior of matter and energy and adaptive change in the physical characteristics of animals. As complex as those issues are, they seem pure and uncomplicated when compared to theories advanced within the frame of the social sciences. The theories of Sigmund Freud and Karl Marx, for example, were social theories. Freud developed a theory of personality based on research with patients who were mainly institutionalized, sexually abused women. In time, he built a huge amount of scaffolding around his observations, and his ideas became so pervasive that whole terminologies entered the vocabulary of the middle class (e.g., "Freudian slip," "ego") as a result of his work. To many, his ideas seemed more like solid findings than theories, and they found their way into literature, film, and everyday life, not to mention introduction to psychology classes. Today his ideas seem rather quaint, and unlike Darwin's or Einstein's, they are not really the basis for advancements in the field of psychological research.

The theories of Karl Marx were tried out on about half the world's population under the name of communism. They still prevail in one form or another in certain countries. Marx theorized a leadership of the working class and a utopian society unfettered by religion, private ownership, competition, and other traditional forms of thought and practice. One might argue whether Marx's pure theory was in fact what was institutionalized in the former USSR, its satellites, and so forth. As bizarre and ugly as the socialist "experiment" called Marxism was, it does serve to make a point to consumers of educational research: Theories of human behavior have real, lasting consequences when we try them out on human beings, so we had better be careful when we consider applying them to our classrooms and schools. The leap from theory to practice is often quite a jump and one fraught with imminent peril.

HOW EDUCATIONAL THEORIES DEVELOP

Basic or pure research findings from psychology and other fields are often used to develop theoretical models of teaching and learning. Those theoretical models are then used to derive implications for education. A specific school program emerges when certain educational implications are in turn developed into a coherent set of teaching strategies, materials, learner activities, and classroom or school structural changes. Therefore, the developer exhorts us, change what you are doing presently and adopt this innovation. Why? Because it is better, and the "research" shows that to be true or we would not ask you to do it.

Three steps are involved along the way to your classroom or school: (1) pure research; (2) educational implications; and (3) suggested classroom or school practice. Let's examine the steps one at a time using a specific example, *cooperative learning*.

LEVEL I

In the 1940s and 1950s, social psychologist Morton Deutsch used his research findings to develop a theory of social interdependence. Like most good scientific researchers, Deutsch was familiar with prior research, especially, in this case, the work of Kurt Lewin in the 1930s. Lewin had developed an idea called field theory which said in essence that a group is actually a "dynamic whole" rather than a mere collection of individuals. What Lewin meant by that is that the behaviors of members in a group are interactive, thereby creating the potential for greater outcomes than one might get merely by adding the sum of the parts of a group. "Deutsch theorized that social interdependence exists only when the goals of individuals in a group are affected, for better or worse, by the others." It was the "better" that intrigued him. Building on Lewin's insights to motivation, inclusion, and democratic processes, Deutsch theorized that when people with common goals worked with each other in cooperative fashion, something better happened than when they either worked alone or competed with each other. Deutsch went on to theorize that the process is enhanced when individuals *perceive* that they can reach their goals only if other members of their group can also reach their goals. In repeated experiments, Deutsch found that his theory seemed to hold up. He published his results, thus allowing others to support, extend, or challenge his findings in the free marketplace of intellectual endeavor. Others, of course, contributed to the theoretical construct. One can, for example, readily trace its origins to Gestalt theory which emerged in 19th-century Austria and which became noted for its pioneering studies in perception. Gestalt theory took issue with reductionist, atomistic processes popular at the time. The Gestalt theorem that "the whole of anything is greater than the sum of its parts" is fundamental to cooperative learning.

LEVEL II

In time educational researchers began to show interest in the theory of social interdependence. They reasoned that what worked in small groups and workplace settings where the theory had originally been field-tested might also work in classrooms. School classrooms seemed like a logical place to apply the theory of social interdependence since a typical room has about 30 kids who traditionally each work alone, or who, even when placed in groups, may not have the skills to identify and achieve a common goal. Also, because of tradition, amongst other things, most students (and often their parents) probably do not *perceive* that they can better attain their academic goals if other students improve as well. It almost seems contrary to common sense. The research studies in classrooms, of which there have been many, were driven by questions of increased achievement, increased motivation to learn, and attitude toward school, attitude toward fellow students, as well as by other outcomes. Among the leading Level II researchers are Robert Slavin of Johns Hopkins University, and David and Roger Johnson of the University of Minnesota, who, in collaboration with their associates, have conducted numerous empirical studies of the effects of cooperative learning in school settings. As the efficacy of cooperative learning became increasingly clear, especially its beneficial effects in conceptual and problem-solving tasks, the argument for teachers and administrators to use it in classrooms became compelling.

LEVEL III

Efficacious outcomes for cooperative learning were increasingly reported at professional meetings and in research in education journals throughout the 1970s, 1980s, and 1990s. Many of the reported studies had been conducted in school classrooms across a range of grade and subject matter levels. The word began to spread. It was at this point that schools of education began to incorporate cooperative learning methods into teacher education courses, and workshops, sometimes conducted by the researchers themselves, sprang up around the country. Any teacher or administrator interested in applying cooperative learning in the classroom or school had little trouble finding workshops, institutes, retreats, classes, or "practical" articles in such magazines as *Instructor* and *Learning*. In short, cooperative learning was sweeping through the educational community like wildfire. The workshops, institutes, retreats, classes, and articles were mainly focused on practical applications of the theory and were available in both initial and advanced forms. Teachers and parents wanted an-swers to such questions as, "How do I know the slower stu-dents won't just copy the ideas of better students?" "How do I measure individual achievement?" "What do I do if a kid won't cooperate with other members of the group?" "How is this different from just assigning kids to committees?" "Won't this slow down higher achievers?" Out of these excellent, practical questions came new educational research studies, journal articles, and books such as David and Roger Johnson's *Leading the Cooperative School* (1989).

Thus, more than 50 years after the theory of social interde-pendence began to crystallize, and more than a century since the origins of Gestalt psychology, the ongoing refinement of school and classroom applications of cooperative learning con-tinues. At this point, more than 300 research studies conducted in classroom settings and school districts are available. Liter-ally thousands of policy articles can be found on the topic. And all of this is completely necessary simply because it's a long leap from a theory of social interdependence formulated by social psychologists in the 1930s to a third-grade science class near the turn of the 21st century.

A final note is in order. A theory exists in relatively pure form. Its empirical test comes when researchers try it out under controlled conditions. These tests make it possible to accept, modify, or reject the theory in specific settings. However, the fact that a theory tests well under controlled conditions does not guarantee that it will survive the inevitable distortions that come with real-world applications by individuals and groups who choose it or are told to use it. These insights have been enriched through the rise of the qualitative research movement where life in classrooms is chronicled on the basis of careful observations, interviews, and so forth. In summary, Level I is theory building, or pure research, or both; Level II is empirical research, either quantitative, qualitative, or a combination thereof; and Level III is program evaluation where it becomes possible to learn the extent to which a program or curriculum is successful when its implementation becomes widespread in schools or entire districts.

We selected cooperative learning as a case study in the nature of educational innovation because it strikes us as a positive example of the gradual unfolding of the process of how a theory germinates and how it ultimately finds its way to classroom practice. If the theory has real promise, it will interact with classroom practice in such a way as to cause further refinement of the theory. Thus, the process is cyclical rather than linear. If it were linear, we would simply impose the finished product on a classroom. This has been done with disastrous consequences. The exciting aspect of the teacher's role or that of the administrator is that they can be a fundamental part of the process. This is so because they are key figures in the ongoing refinement of an idea, not because they say an idea is good or not good. The practical application of ideas by teachers and students in real-world educational settings represents the best test of an idea's staying power.

CONCLUSION

Each of the educational innovations that we examine in this book began as a theory far removed from classroom life. Each has found its way into the classrooms and schools of America. We propose to examine how that happened. Our analysis of each raises a basic set of questions including:

- How good was the original theory on which the idea is based?

- How appropriate is the research that advocates the use of this theory in school settings?

- What does this theory purport to do that will improve life in schools and classrooms?

- What claims are made in behalf of the theory as a necessary component of the school curriculum?

- What are the requisite conditions of the theory for school success?

- Why would someone want to use the ideas that flow from this theory in school settings?

Classroom life unfolds within a complex set of conditions. The list of human and material variables is endless. No two individuals and no two classrooms are the same, just as no two schools or communities are the same. The presence or absence of one student in a classroom changes the circumstances. Each teacher's personal, practical sense of teaching and learning is different. The leadership is variable from one school to the next, ranging from dynamic to nil. The public's perception and support of schools in each community has much to do with a school's success or failure. And, of course, what happens in families matters even more than what happens at school.

As teachers and administrators, we are always trying to improve ourselves. We want our efforts to help young people to learn to be productive. Therefore, we seek the help of others who also care and who can help us. And that is what this book is about.

2

THE STRUCTURE OF EDUCATIONAL INNOVATION

*Out of every ten innovations attempted, all very splendid,
nine will end up in silliness.*

Antonio Machado

It can be argued that there is very little that is new in education. It can be argued, and has been, that there is nothing new under the sun. Most things have been tried before in some form. But our experiences are different from those of the previous generation because they are *our* experiences. As we consider the many problems of teaching and learning, new perspectives emerge and compete for our attention. In these times of sustained criticism of the educational system, new ideas, new terminology, and new reform programs are abundant simply because people sincerely want to improve things. It is as simple as supply and demand. In fact, the proliferation of new programs, which range from the well researched to something less than that, has reached a level of staggering proportions.

At this point it will serve us well to return to some of the ideas presented in Chapter 1. The chart presented in Figure 2.1 illustrates how innovative programs emerge and are developed. Early on someone identifies an idea or research which suggests the possibility of a theory about human behavior. The theory might emerge from insight into human behavior, thinking processes, or perceptions of reality, just to name a few examples. In any event, the theory may have implications for

13

FIGURE 2.1. DEVELOPMENT OF INNOVATIVE PROGRAMS

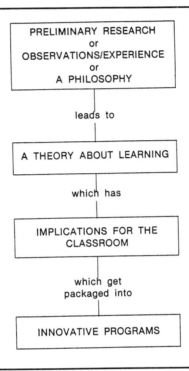

how teachers teach and under what conditions students learn best. Jean Piaget's theory of the development of the intellect, for example, clearly identified age-related stages through which one progresses. Further, the theory stated that persons in a particular stage of development are capable of certain intellectual activities and not capable of others, which must happen later. This theory intrigued a number of educational researchers who wished to apply Piaget's ideas to school settings, something Piaget had never done. Some researchers hypothesized that intellectual development could be accelerated with enriched programs. But to the best of our knowledge, this idea does not have anything close to sufficient empirical support. This line of thinking amused Piaget; he called it the "American question."

In any event, at some point someone in the education field thinks through the implications of a given theory and develops the ideas into a program or curriculum suitable for use in educational research. The program might be designed to change teacher behaviors, student behaviors, or classroom environments to conform to the ideal set of conditions on which the theory is predicated.

REAPING THE WHIRLWIND

What is the role of educational research in all of this? How is educational research different from systematic program evaluation? The claims are that many of these innovative programs are research-based. We must point out that there is a difference between saying that a program is research-based, and that research has shown a program to be effective under certain conditions. Unfortunately, many educators do not make this crucial distinction. **In fact, the best that many developers can claim is that the theory and resulting programs are developed from basic research, often in psychology, into programs for teaching and learning. Often, however, innovative programs are questionably based on theoretical models, with scant evidence to support or justify exactly how the program is truly a practical application of the theory.** This is the initial realm of question posing that educators should enter with those who tout a particular program.

Ideally, before expenditures of time and money are spent on the widespread implementation of educational innovations, those programs should be subjected to careful, unbiased investigation through the evaluation of pilot programs. Unfortunately, as educational researcher Robert Slavin has pointed out, this generally tends to happen *toward the end* of the cycle of the innovation, after the rush has died down, and educators have cynically moved on to some other new activity or program. Thus, we reap the whirlwind.

How did our profession get caught up in this succession of fad-driven spirals of innovation based not on goodness, but on newness? Slavin (1989), one of the most careful researchers in the educational community, has observed and examined this phenomenon over the years. His insights into the process are rather revealing. Slavin writes that, "generational progress does occur in education, but it is usually a product of changes in society, rather than changes in educational techniques themselves. For example, the clearly beneficial trend toward desegregation and more equal treatment of minorities represents true generational progress, but it arose from social and legal changes, not from educational innovation. More often, education resembles such fields as fashion and design, in which change mirrors shifts in taste and social climate, and is not usually thought of as true progress" (p. 752).

Slavin states further that, "one of the most important reasons for the continuing existence of the educational pendulum is that educators rarely wait for or demand hard evidence before adopting new practices on a wide scale. Of course, every innovator claims research support for his or her methods; at a minimum, there is usually a 'gee whiz' story or two about a school or district that was 'turned around' by the innovation. Alternatively, a developer may claim that, while the program itself has not been formally evaluated, the principles on which it is based are supported by research" (p. 753).

THE HUNTER MODEL:
"ONE MORE SUCH VICTORY AND WE ARE UNDONE"

Pyrrhus, King of ancient Epirus, left us the term "Pyrrhic Victory," an allusion to his battle field triumphs accompanied by horrendous causalities among his own troops. There are many such "victories" in the annals of education, but here is a recent example. Slavin examines in detail the Madeline Hunter model. He calls Hunter "perhaps the most popular educational trainer of our time" (p. 754). We have not included a chapter on Hunter's program because the movement itself appears to have faded. But it can serve as an excellent example of what happens in the name of educational innovation.

Since it seems almost inconceivable that there are educators today who have not heard of the Hunter program or model, we will give it only the briefest overview here. The model is sometimes called Instructional Theory Into Practice (ITIP) or Program for Effective Teaching (PET). It emerged in the early 1970s with a series of books and workshops by Madeline Hunter. Throughout the 1970s and well into the 1980s, schools, and oftentimes entire districts and states, provided inservice training in the Hunter model. Entire staff development programs and faculty evaluation procedures were based on it. District personnel officers would routinely quiz prospective teachers on their knowledge of the Hunter model. Courses for preservice and inservice teachers, where people actually got college credit for studying ITIP "theory," were offered throughout the land. Student teachers were expected to develop lesson plans and units that used the ITIP steps to effective teaching as a template. Teachers themselves were often divided over the program. Many became advocates and some were themselves trained as ITIP trainers, creating a multiplying effect. Some teachers shrugged it off as one more fad they had to endure. A few brave souls openly questioned the validity of the entire thing, but that took some courage in light of its overwhelming popularity and near-complete dominance. The amazing thing is that as it disappears, there are no apologies, seemingly no regrets. But the lesson to be learned by those who wish to profit from it is enormous. It draws out the danger present in what the philosopher Francis Bacon called, "The Idol of the Tribe." When the Idol of the Tribe is worshipped, few dare question events because, after all, everyone is doing it. It's the "in" thing to do. Basically, a mentality is created where criticism is not welcome, to say the least.

The ITIP or PET program itself is a method for analyzing the key elements of a lesson with suggested procedures for lesson development. It was purportedly based on educational and psychological theory and research. It focused on four elements: (1) teaching to an objective (generally a behavioral objective); (2) teaching at the correct level of (cognitive) difficulty; (3) monitoring and adjusting instruction (i.e., formative evaluation and reteaching, mastery learning); and (4) using established principles of learning (e.g., reinforcement, motivation, transfer, etc.).

The ITIP movement followed the "pendulum" swing described by Slavin. It serves as a classic example. The program was proposed in the early 1970s and implemented in a few school districts. Anecdotal claims of great success were made. The word spread rapidly that here at last was a research-based program that worked in real-world school settings. ITIP became *de rigueur* among staff developers. Schools of education incorporated it into their teacher training programs. By the late 1970s and early 1980s the movement had begun to sweep the country, even though there were no quality studies that showed the program was at all effective in increasing student learning. Complaints by researchers and other critics were either ignored or thought of as sour grapes. Anecdotal stories proliferated to verify the program's success.

The program's originator, Madeline Hunter, appeared at conventions, wrote books and articles, and consulted with school districts directly. Where she was unavailable, surrogates took her place. Thousands of teachers and administrators attended workshops at beginning and advanced levels. It became generally expected that anyone who was "current" knew the ITIP protocols. At its peak, the Hunter program was being used, and in many cases enforced by district officers, in all 50 states. Its popularity exceeded any phenomenon in modern school practice history.

By the mid-to-late 1980s interest in the program began to wane as staff developers moved on to other topics such as learning styles and outcome-based education. They did this not because the latter were proven to be any better, but because they had become the latest fad. At about this time, evaluation results of ITIP programs showed that the program had impact that was no more positive on student learning than random efforts by teachers. The research results mattered little because by the time they weighed in, ITIP had pretty much run its course. New fads had taken its place.

IN RETROSPECT

What was touted as an educational program based on "research" was actually a classic example of the process of implementation we described earlier. Many of the elements of ITIP *were* based on psychological research and learning theory. But the implementation of the program itself had not been evaluated with quality research to determine its effectiveness in increasing student learning. For example, reinforcement was identified as one of the key components of ITIP. Psychological research has, in fact, clearly shown that positive reinforcement of learning predictably results in increased learning. Similarly, psychological research has also shown that the immediacy of feedback, another ITIP protocol, can serve as a motivating factor in learning. Both of these are elements of ITIP that have a substantiated research base. Other elements of ITIP, such as the correct level of difficulty, were based on theoretical models; in this instance, Benjamin Bloom's taxonomy of educational objectives in the cognitive domain, a model the very vocabulary of which raises fundamental questions.

In this manner, then, ITIP was presented as a research-based model of teaching and learning. And in one sense it was. Certain individual elements were based on psychological research in the area of learning. In other words, specific elements of the program may have been sound in and of themselves under given conditions. But when the entire package was put together as a unified model, that is, when individual research findings and theories were combined to form one unified construct (usually in the form of lesson plans) called ITIP, it was no longer actually correct to say that ITIP was research-based. The very act of conceptualizing ITIP resulted in a new construct consisting of many divergent research findings and theories. It was, therefore, a new entity that as such had not been researched at all. And in retrospect, that may be giving ITIP too much credit. Actually, the German educator Johann Herbart had conceptualized an almost identical scheme in the 19th century, one that identified five points in effective teaching. It, too, swept across our landscape like a prairie fire! Today, only a handful of educators have even heard of it or of Herbart. As the poet and philosopher George Santayana noted, "Those who cannot remember the past are condemned to repeat it."

Perhaps an analogy will serve us well in explaining the complex issue of validating an educational innovation, even one "based" on sound theories. We know from the laws of physics that a billiard ball struck at a certain angle by another billiard ball will behave in a predictable fashion, at least on a flat, well-made felt-covered billiard table where there are no competing, interfering variables such as an imperfectly shaped ball, a gale-force wind, a table with uneven legs, molasses poured on the surface, and so forth. But what happens to our billiard ball, even under optimum conditions, if the table is littered with a dozen other billiard balls? The answer is that the laws of physics still work, but the situation is quite complex because of the probable interactions of the other balls with the ball that is initially struck. So now we have balls going in all directions. Actually, a billiard table littered with billiard balls is a fairly simple situation compared to a classroom filled with 30 students. Thus, a theory about motivation developed under controlled conditions during psychological experiments has only limited predictive validity in the seemingly random, infinitely complex world of classroom life. The theory itself may indeed be valid, but now the theory no longer stands in the splendid isolation of controlled laboratory conditions. It interacts with and becomes a mere part of an infinitely more complex situation. Our point is not to disparage educational or psychological research. On the contrary, we find it quite helpful when it is done well. It is the misapplication and over-reaching of research findings that bother us. It is the misapplication and over-reaching of research findings that should bother you. What we wish to say is that the claims made by someone who says, "the research shows…" must be carefully considered before we enter into wholesale policy or curriculum change.

The business of teaching and learning in school settings is a very serious trust. All of us involved in the work of schools must do our best to honor that trust. We know that all is not well in the world of teaching and learning in America. As educators, we are very vulnerable to new nostrums and fixes that will make things right at last. Change is a necessary condition of progress, and it behooves us to make the most meaningful changes possible. Our hope is that as you examine the various attempts at innovation found in this book, you will learn to ask the right questions and that you will find useful answers.

REFERENCES

Slavin, R. (1989). PET and the pendulum: fadism in education and how to stop it. *Phi Delta Kappan, 70,* 752–758.

3

"THE RESEARCH SAYS..."

There aren't any embarrassing questions—just embarrassing answers.
Carl Rowan

Have you ever found yourself at a meeting or conference listening to a speaker who pauses dramatically and states in august tones, "Well, the research says...?" Everyone, including you, quickly puts pen to paper in anticipation of some significant pronouncement that will change school life forevermore. If we only had a nickel for each time an education hustler has used such a phrase! If only it were as significant a statement as it appears to be to the uninitiated. The only appropriate response that comes to mind in the midst of such confusion is, "What research?"

In fact, the claim of virtually all innovators or purveyors of innovation is that research has in some strategic way played an important part in the evolution and development of their ideas, programs, or materials. And in some sense, the claim is generally true, but often misleading. For example, if someone claims his or her program for elementary children is based in part on learning transfer, we may be impressed. After all, the concept of transfer of learning is well documented in the annals of psychological research. But the leap from research in a laboratory setting to classroom application is long and difficult.

WHAT "KIND" OF RESEARCH?

We will show you a classification system that should prove helpful as you attempt to sort out different kinds of research. With this knowledge you will be able to determine for yourself what is behind the statement, "the research says...."

The term "research" has become so generic that it can and does refer to a wide range of activities. For example, you may "research" the cost of an airline ticket by checking on prices from five different airlines. To a freshman, a "research" paper is often little more than a collection of what other people have said about a topic. There is the old story of the student who searched the library for ideas before reaching the insight that, to make his term paper truly meaningful, he needed to re-search the topic. To an advanced engineering student, research may mean mainly controlled experimental studies. We have "the teacher as researcher," model, often referred to as action research, which is typically a narrative of classroom events. This approach has led in some cases to collaborative research between teachers and university scholars. Currently, there is the ongoing debate over the relative value of two research paradigms—quantitative and qualitative. The origins of the debate are profoundly philosophical, and the nature of the de-bate is at times quite heated, with each side claiming to do re-search that is more valid. Others, searching perhaps for the golden mean, cite the necessity of doing both.

In spite of these problems of definition, we believe that it is helpful to conceptualize educational research in the following manner. We propose a model of research with three levels, each of which has different, but related, implications for edu-cational innovation. The first is basic or pure research done theoretically and in "laboratory" settings; the second is applied research done under controlled conditions in school settings; and the third is evaluation research applied to school programs once they have been implemented. Each is quite different from the others, and each yields its own unique types of conclusions (see Fig. 3.1).

LEVEL I RESEARCH

Level I research is basic or pure research on learning and behavior. It is most commonly conducted in experimental or laboratory settings by psychologists, learning theorists, lin-guists, and others. Its purpose is to establish a theoretical

FIGURE 3.1. THE THREE LEVELS OF EDUCATIONAL RESEARCH

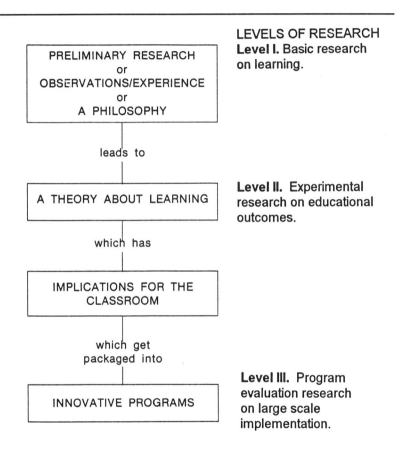

construct or idea as having some validity. For example, Jean Piaget constructed a theory of stages of intellectual development through which children pass on their way to adult thought (Piaget, 1960). Jerome Bruner constructed a theory of the structure of knowledge that included alternative ways by which knowledge of some reality could be represented to learners (Bruner, 1966, 1996). And Howard Gardner has constructed a theory of multiple intelligences which essentially broadens the definition of the term "intelligence" (Gardner, 1986).

The research from which a theory emerges may come from controlled studies employing traditional empirical methods, or from qualitative, subjective observations, or from both. Invariably, it also takes into account prior contributions to the topic, modifying or possibly even rejecting them. This type of theory development is referred to as "grounded theory." It is a process of deriving constructs and theories directly from immediate data that the researcher has collected. However, the usefulness of the constructs and theories grounded in the specific data must be validated with further research.

It is important to note that not all educational theories are derived from such research. It is possible for a learning theory to emerge out of a philosophical or religious belief, which may or may not have empirical support. For example, if a person is convinced of the inherent goodness of human beings, that person may quite readily propose that children's learning and their accompanying desire to learn would increase in a supportive, nonrestrictive, open environment. For the theory to be taken seriously, of course, it would need to have a well-established rationale. Such examples of theory building based on philosophical positions probably account for as many or more theories than do theories grounded in empirical data. More often, a well-grounded theory contains elements of both.

Although Level I research can serve as a foundation for curriculum development, it is not designed to answer applied educational questions directly. Piaget claimed on the basis of his research that most 8-year-olds are in a stage of concrete operations, leading many builders of innovative curriculum packages to put together mathematics and science activities that involved manipulative materials. And, rightly or wrongly, they did that on the assumption that the message from pure research could be applied to groups of 25 or 30 children learning together in a classroom setting. The extent to which it is reasonable to do this becomes a function of Level II research.

LEVEL II RESEARCH

Level II research involves studies whose purpose is to determine the efficacy of particular programs or instructional methods in *educational* settings. Educational researchers who are interested in applying theories and procedures developed at the pure or basic level generally conduct such studies. For example, an educational researcher might attempt to set up controlled conditions in several classrooms for the purpose of comparing, say, cooperative learning in social studies with independent student learning. The experimental conditions might call for randomly assigning students and teachers to different treatment modes or conditions where the same material is studied. Pre- and posttests may be administered to all participants and comparisons made to determine whether a statistically significant difference occurred between or among treatments.

Level II research is applied research because (1) it is conducted in the same or similar settings that are actually found in schools, and (2) it makes no attempt to develop a theory, but rather attempts to make instructional or curricular applications of a given theory. At its best, Level II research provides practical insights that cannot be derived directly from pure research. Thus, even though we all can agree that reinforcement has been shown to be a powerful psychological concept by pure researchers, it remains for the Level II researcher to demonstrate how it might be advantageous to apply reinforcement in teaching in classroom settings.

Level II research is crucial to the process of validation of programs or methods of instruction. But time and time again, this step is simply ignored or poorly crafted as program developers or purveyors urge teachers and administrators to adopt a particular product. To return to the ITIP or PET "theory into practice" model for a moment, in retrospect we can see that it claimed its validity on the basis of such pure or basic research constructs as reinforcement, transfer, retention, and so forth, which are real enough. But it was almost totally lacking in any proof of what happens when one takes those constructs and "packages" them as a template for use by teachers in classroom settings. The same thing can be said for a number of other programs that have swept the country such as "Assertive Discipline," "TESA," and higher level thinking strategies.

One of the best sources for school personnel to search at Level II is the journal, *Review of Educational Research*, published by the American Educational Research Association (AERA). This journal carries reviews and meta-analyses of various programs, projects, and packages. Doing so will give you insight into the quantity and nature of applied research that has been conducted in a given area.

A final point about Level II research is that each study, even if it represents good research, is severely limited in its generalizability. If, for example, a study were conducted of teaching methods of reading and literature with fourth grade inner-city children, then whatever the results, it would be unwise to generalize them to, for example, rural eighth grade students. This is why large numbers of good investigations about a given program should be carried out before school districts jump on this or that bandwagon. Cooperative learning, to cite an example where this has been done, has been and continues to be investigated in such a wide variety of school-based settings that its Level II foundation is quite secure, especially compared to most other innovations. Level II research in education is invariably improved by carefully crafted replication studies, something that is all too rare in our field.

LEVEL III RESEARCH

Level III research is evaluation research designed to determine the efficacy of programs at the level of school or district implementation. It is by far the least likely of the three types to be carried out in any systematic way, and because of this, programs (good, bad, or indifferent) usually go through phases from initial enthusiasm to gradual abandonment, replaced by the next fad.

Examples of Level III research include evaluation studies that examine the overall effects on teachers and students of a particular district- or schoolwide innovation. If a district changes, for example, from basal reading instruction to whole language learning, it is the job of evaluation researchers to determine exactly what changes were brought about and what the results of those changes were. This might involve interviews with teachers, students, and parents, the application of classroom environmental scales and observations to determine student perceptions of whole language learning, assessments of the amount and nature of support for the innovation, and analyses of achievement data over time.

It is important to note that an educational theory may have sound research support at Levels I and II, and yet still may not be successful when implemented on a larger scale. This could happen for a number of reasons. For example, Level II research may have been conducted with highly trained teachers or with teachers who were quite supportive of the new program and who volunteered for the Level II research. When the program was implemented on a districtwide scale, however, there may well have been many teachers who were skeptical of it, who were reluctant to participate, who were poorly trained, or who decided on their own to make certain adaptations to the program. The availability of strategic and tactical support in the form of administrative and inservice leadership, as well as parental reaction, also represent factors which become known only over time. These and other variables make it crucial that Level III research or program evaluation be conducted.

A generation ago when the New Math swept the country, it had a pretty firm foundation at Levels I and II, but what little evidence we did gain at Level III showed us that many teachers were actually subverting the New Math, preferring to teach traditional arithmetic in its place whenever they could. Mixed to negative parental reaction was seriously underestimated to say the least. And even the more farsighted of developers probably underestimated the drumbeat of criticism that arose in the popular press. So, even if you are convinced that the theory behind some new program is sound, and even if you have seen published evidence of controlled studies in classroom settings that are supportive of the theory's application, you're still not home-free until you have seen the results of evaluation studies that indicate that this program really works in large numbers of regular classrooms.

Now you may be thinking that this represents quite a few gates for a new program to have to open before it proves its worth. And that is exactly the point! If we are to become less susceptible to fads, then it will be because we have become more deliberate and cautious along the way to adopting new programs.

Figure 3.1 illustrates the process that ideally unfolds in the cycle of educational innovation. We begin with theories derived from pure or basic research. We then test the theory under experimental or quasiexperimental conditions in school settings. And we move from there to the program evaluation stage where assessment is made based on data from real classrooms which operate under typical day-to-day conditions.

We realize that these levels are somewhat arbitrary, and we certainly do not maintain that there is necessarily a linear flow from pure to applied to evaluation research. Sometimes there is, but more often the situation is more chaotic than that. In some cases, the theoretical construct is less the source of energy than is the simple fact that something is available for educational use that was not available previously. Computers and calculators are obvious examples of this.

SUMMARY

In the world of prescription medications, the Food and Drug Administration (FDA) subjects new medicines to a long and exhaustive review prior to allowing them to be prescribed by doctors and dispensed by pharmacists. And even this process is a far cry from releasing a product to over-the-counter sales. Some critics of this system have pointed out that in many cases it takes years from the time we read about an experimental drug in the newspapers and that drug's availability to the public. The role of the FDA is to play gatekeeper as tests are conducted, effects examined, potential drug interactions investigated, and so on. As a result, some drugs never make it to the marketplace and some do after a period of time.

With respect to educational innovations, however, we have no counterpart to the FDA. Therefore, programs can be rushed into the schools with little or no testing at any stage of the game. This may please those who are in a hurry to jump on the latest bandwagon, but it disadvantages those who would prefer to be consumers of thoughtfully tested and refined programs. In so many instances, whole districts have adopted particular curriculums and teaching procedures that had basically no research foundation. This renders our profession vulnerable to criticisms that are difficult to refute.

In this chapter, we suggested that research be conducted at three distinctly different levels along the way to validating or invalidating educational innovations. Those three levels are (1) basic or pure research, (2) applied research in school settings, and (3) evaluation research where the effects of the large-scale implementation of an innovation are studied. All of this takes time, and rightly so. We think that the only way to improve educational practice is to approach educational innovation with such a deliberate, measured sense of its worth.

Of course, schools adopt new ideas on the basis of something more than educational research. Economic, political, and cultural considerations will always play a role in this process. We have no problem with that. That is part of your reality and ours. But where we can be more thoughtful about change on the basis of a thorough examination of the merits of a given change, we ought to proceed cautiously.

Years ago there was a radio show called, "It Pays to Be Ignorant." The theory behind the show was that people could win cash prizes and major household appliances by proving to the world, or at least to the huge nationwide radio audience, that they really were ignorant when it came to answering questions put to them by the genial host of the show. It was a great concept and a successful program. But we wish to say as clearly as possible that it doesn't pay to be ignorant when it comes to spending the public's tax dollars on educational innovations that really haven't proven themselves.

THE FOLLOWING CHAPTERS

In this book we have attempted to provide teachers, administrators, district inservice personnel, preservice and graduate students, and other interested persons with a brief overview and analysis of current innovations in education. In the process of selecting these topics, we looked carefully at a wide variety of state and school district inservice offerings, college and university courses, and staff development institutes. During this process it became obvious to us that many of the offerings were simply variations of a more limited number of basic ideas or concepts. It is these basic concepts, or golden threads, which are the focus of the following chapters. Of course, we recognize that the manifestation of the concepts may differ somewhat from one region of the country to another, or from one packager to another. We, however, focus only on programs that have truly nationwide impact, whatever their regional calling cards happen to be.

For each of the following chapters we have constructed a common format for our presentation of the topic under review. We begin each chapter with an overview of the concept in an attempt to clarify exactly what is being talked about. We have depended heavily on primary sources for these sections. At times, this has required synthesizing the writing and ideas of numerous authors because for many of these topics there is no single developer who speaks for or represents the entire area. For example, the *brain research* movement in education is not dependent on the work of one person; rather, it represents a compilation of ideas from numerous investigators and promoters. Even in the instances where one individual is clearly identified with the topic, for example, Madeline Hunter for the "Hunter Model," we have expanded our discussions past that individual to include descriptions of the programs as they are being implemented and expanded by others. We have identified the "main players" in each particular field of endeavor; that is, those most closely associated with the topic and related programs. While we may refer to various individuals and their programs as examples, the interpretations and descriptions of the concepts and programs are ours alone.

We have also provided specific examples of the structural effects these programs have, or would have, if implemented, in the schools. For example, a teacher who adopts a whole language approach for the classroom will organize (1) the classroom, (2) the curriculum, and (3) instruction differently from a teacher following, say, a basal-reader approach. Similarly, a school following an outcome-based education model will have a different focus and decision-making process from that found in a goal-free approach to schooling. In each of these chapters, we show in specific terms what changes might occur if you implement a given program. In other words, ideas have consequences when they become reality, and we wish to be clear about that with you.

Included in each chapter is a critique of the given topic. It is fair to say that the work of the proponents of these ideas and programs is not above criticism, and we are not at all reluctant to do just that. Some programs have been carefully developed and come complete with a sound research foundation. Others are "faddish" and are lacking both a theoretical and research base. In some cases, certain programs are antithetical to one another and the attempt to adopt both or to blend them will lead only to a confusion of purpose. We will be clear about the cautionary notes that are necessary before wholesale changes in an educational system are undertaken. Who knows, but what you are presently doing may be better than what will happen if you implement a certain highly touted program.

We also examine proponents' claims about the degree to which the programs are "research based." The term "research-based" can be a little like the term "low fat" found on product labels. It can be rather misleading. At the very least, one must know how to interpret it.

We conclude each chapter with a brief bibliography for those who wish to pursue the issues further.

REFERENCES

Bruner, J. (1966/96). *Toward a theory of instruction.* Cambridge, MA: Harvard University Press.

Gardner, H. (1986). *Frames of mind.* New York: Basic Books.

Piaget, J. (1960). *The child's conceptions of the world.* Atlantic Highlands, NJ: Humanities Press, Inc.

4

SELF-ESTEEM PROGRAMS

There is within this movement an implicit (and increasingly explicit) intuition, an assumption—a faith, if you will—that an essential and operational relationship exists between self-esteem and responsible human behavior, both personal and social.

John Vasconcellos

There is no getting around the fact that most educators who speak earnestly about the need to boost students' self-esteem are unfamiliar with the research that has been conducted on this question....Very few people in the field seem to have any feel for the empirical literature as a whole—what the evidence really says and how meaningful it is.

Alfie Kohn

We who served on the task force were determined that our findings would be grounded in the most current and valid research available...Many of us on the task force are convinced that a sizable number of practitioners in functioning programs are well ahead of academic researchers in their appreciation of self-esteem's central role in the social problems that plague our society.

California Task Force on Self-Esteem

...[C]ultural beliefs regarding self-esteem and its influence on individual behavior provide a powerful counterbalance to academic knowledge claims on the topic. This cultural commitment leads to widespread support for self-esteem despite the consistent failure of sympathetic researchers to demonstrate a causal connection between it and various forms of pro-social behavior.

Joseph Kahne

If you search for a more strongly held belief within the American school system than the belief in the importance of self-esteem to school success—and indeed to success in general—you won't find one. It is a type of "cultural belief" that permeates nearly every facet of teaching and curriculum.

Indeed, the notion that positive self-esteem promotes achievement is widely accepted as fact. Trying to convince certain teachers that it might not be so is like trying to convince them the sun rises in the west. This causal relationship theory is so prevalent and strong that Barbara Lerner (1996) has suggested that, "Many teachers will be hard pressed to think of a contrasting theory. The self-esteem theory of educational development has been the reigning orthodoxy for so long that they were never taught anything else"(p. 10). There are rival theories, as we shall see, but they are given little credence in education circles.

WHAT IS SELF-ESTEEM?

Psychologists, counselors, and educators use a range of terms to capture the elusive concept of self-esteem. Generally speaking, however, "self-concept," "self-esteem," and "self-image" are used interchangeably by educators, and all refer to how we view ourselves, our abilities, our appearance, our self-worth, and so on; in other words, one's perception of oneself. The idea is that, for each of us, our self-measure can vary considerably, both quantitatively and qualitatively. On a continuum, we see ourselves as valued, or not valued, capable or less so, worthwhile or not, and so on. The idea that self-esteem is a viable construct and one worth considering from an educational point of view is a fairly recent one, and one for which the case to be made is problematic at best.

It is instructive to consider some of the instruments that purport to measure self-esteem. For better or worse, they furnish us with operational definitions. For example, the *Coopersmith Self-Esteem Inventory* (Coopersmith, 1987) defines self-esteem as "the evaluation a person makes and customarily maintains of him- or herself; that is an expression of approval or disapproval, indicating the extent to which a person believes him- or herself competent, successful, and significant and worthy." The *Culture-Free Self-Esteem Inventories* (Battle, 1992) define self-esteem as "a composite of an individual's feelings, hopes, fears, thoughts, and views of who he is, what she is, what he has been, and what she might become." And the *Piers-Harris Children's Self-Concept Scale* (Piers & Harris, 1984) defines self-concept as a "relatively stable set of self-attitudes reflecting both a description and an evaluation of one's own behavior and attitudes." Although the word choice varies somewhat, you will note that the definitions are more similar than different. This, then, is at least a place to start.

In pursuit of further clarification, three ideas should be noted. First, psychologists have differentiated between *global* and *narrow* constructs of self-esteem. For example, one might have an overall high opinion of oneself but could hold oneself in very low esteem as an athlete. One might score very high on an academic self-esteem inventory, but low on a musical one. This suggests that self-esteem is not a broad construct at all, but that each of us has multiple constructs of self-esteem. Thus, one's self-esteem may be dependent on the area of life in question. However, this distinction is at odds with the view of those educators who consider self-esteem as a unified, global construct.

Second, the construct is also convoluted by the tendency to equate self-esteem with human dignity, thereby rendering it an entitlement of personhood in a civil society. Keep in mind, however, that because all people are of equal worth, it does not follow that they can perform all tasks with equal skill. The doctrine of equal value as human beings is certainly a broad construct of self-esteem. But it confuses attempts to get at the more narrow constructs of self-esteem in specific areas of endeavor. Perhaps it is useful in this regard to separate the idea of "being" from that of "doing." That, however, is much easier to propose than to carry out.

Third, there is the issue of perceptions of reality. The broad construct of self-esteem (equal value as human beings) should not necessarily cause a problem here, but the narrow constructs can because some people's views of themselves are so far removed from reality that it does them a disservice. In fact, they may be better or worse at certain things than they think they are. Here is an example. In a five-nation comparison of mathematical abilities of 10-year-olds made in 1989, American children finished last in mathematics achievement and South Korean children finished first. However, the American children had the highest self-estimate of their mathematical abilities, and the South Korean children had the lowest.

It has been estimated that there have been more than 10,000 research studies done on self-esteem (Kohn, 1994). As of January 1997 there are over 8,000 citations in the ERIC data base alone. Whether the construct is real or imagined, it is, nonetheless, a part of American culture, and it is a major focus of attention among educators and educational researchers.

THE CLAIMS AND THE PROGRAMS

At the heart of the matter are the claims made by educators and psychologists, basically humanistic psychologists, that feeling good about oneself is important for constructive life choices and helps prevent destructive behaviors. Basically, the idea is that people who view themselves favorably are able to work and learn more effectively. It is claimed that self-esteem and academic achievement are positively associated, that there is a causal relationship between the two (in the esteem-achievement direction), and, therefore, to increase achievement, we should try and raise students' self-esteem. Consider the following comment in Carl Rogers' classic book, *Freedom to Learn* (1969). Rogers quotes a teacher with whom he was working at the time as saying, "I cannot explain exactly what happened, but it seems to me, that when their [the students] self-concept changed, when they discovered they *can*, they did! These 'slow learners' became 'fast learners'; success built upon success" (p. 22).

The strength of these beliefs runs deep, and as Lerner pointed out, it is so ingrained that teachers cannot even come up with a rival theory. The cause-and-effect theory, however, goes well beyond achievement. In the late 1980s, legislation was passed which created the California Task Force on Self-Esteem. With a $700,000 budget the task force was to place self-esteem at the center of a social science research agenda, with the intent of ameliorating the pressing social issues of welfare dependency, drug and alcohol abuse, school failure, child abuse, and teenage pregnancy. John Vasconcellos, who created the legislation, stated:

> As we approach the twenty-first century, we human beings now—for the first time ever—have it within our power to truly improve our human condition. We can proceed to develop a social vaccine. We can outgrow our past failures—our lives of crime and violence, alcohol and drug abuse, premature pregnancy, child abuse, chronic dependence on welfare, and educational failure. (California Task Force, 1990, p. ix)

What Jonas Salk had achieved in the crusade against polio, the California Task Force would achieve in the crusade against low self-esteem.

The California Task Force proposed to vaccinate children against a disease that had plagued students for years. After all, nothing is as powerful as an idea whose time has come. As the belief that self-esteem, and therefore achievement and other things, could be boosted by informed teachers became more widespread, two concurrent developments emerged. First, educational practices in general began to change in an attempt to alleviate any "damage" being done to students by traditional practices and to promote more self-esteem that is positive by the use of different strategies and curriculum. Practices dropped, or at least attacked, included various grading procedures in which students failed, tracking of students by ability, negative reinforcement, the monocultural curriculum, competition, and autocratic procedures in general. These were replaced by positive reinforcement from teachers, grade inflation, self-talk, identifying personal strengths, opportunities to study one's own culture, counseling, creative spelling, ebonics, and so on. Obviously, this coincided with many other developments that led to more "progressive" educational practices, but the self-esteem movement was evident in virtually all of them.

The second development was the use of prepackaged self-esteem curriculum programs which germinated, quickly sprouted, and which continue to flower to this day. It is a big business. Examples include *Esteem Builders, Power of Positive Students* (POPS), *Phoenix Curriculum,* and even the *DARE* program for drug prevention. These are merely a few of the better-known programs. All focus, variably, on the activities mentioned in the preceding paragraph. The philosophies behind two of these programs are presented in Figure 4.1.

Consider for a moment the following excerpt from *Bridges: A Self-Esteem Activity Book for Students in Grades 4–6* (McGuire & Heuss, 1994). The activity in question is titled "How to Develop a High Self-Esteem."

> How does a person who has low self-esteem go about raising it? Well, the best way is to change his thought patterns. It's true—we feel the way we THINK we feel! The more positive you are, the better you'll feel. And the better you feel, the higher your self-esteem will be. GO FOR IT! (p. 59)

This use of teacher and student time away from such real issues as character formation, academic achievement, and hard work, with its focus on feeling good, is presented by the authors as though "raising" one's self-esteem were a simple matter of doing this and the many other activities found in the program. In economic theory, the concept of "opportunity cost" suggests that choosing to do one thing also means giving up certain others. What is the opportunity cost of spending time in these activities? The school day contains only so many hours. The reader is informed on the book's back cover that the authors' "mission" is to promote positive self-esteem, but nowhere in the activity book is there a shred of theory, research, documented findings, or linkages between self-esteem and anything else beyond feeling good about oneself.

We should also mention that some advocates have adopted the causation theory as a useful explanation of why certain minority groups continue to lag academically. Indeed, many multicultural curricula are designed to promote students' self-esteem based on their ethnic identity and on the idea that all cultures are worthwhile and have made valuable contributions (e.g., Vann & Kunjufu, 1993).

FIGURE 4.1. DESCRIPTIONS OF TWO SOCIAL VACCINE–SELF-ESTEEM PROGRAMS USED NATIONWIDE

The Phoenix Curriculum*

The goal of the Phoenix Curriculum is to help teenagers gain an understanding of their potential and an appreciation of themselves. The curriculum consists of a 10-module program for grades 6, 7, and 8, divided into three units focusing on self-esteem, getting along with others, and goal setting and achievement; and a 20-module program for high school divided into five units focusing on self-esteem, personal relationships, responsibility, happiness and success, and goal setting and achievement.

The Phoenix Curriculum provides an organized, well-focused approach to overcome boredom, negativity and defeatism. The real strength of the program is that, as students learn about goal setting and personal choice, it allows them to take more and more responsibility for themselves and for learning. Students learn to trust themselves and to take pride in who they are. Once they have that self-confidence--the belief that they can achieve whatever they set their minds to--teachers can proceed with the traditional part of their job: providing opportunities for learning.

The Power of Positive Students**

We accept, and research supports, the relationship between self-concept and achievement in school. Because the school experience is a primary influence on how students perceive themselves, and because students with a positive self-concept are more effective learners, self-esteem must be a major concern of those who plan and implement the school curriculum. The psychological, social, emotional and moral development of a child is not incidental to education but the foundation on which it is built. Building self-esteem as part of the curriculum is a worthy end in itself.

Our plan, however, goes beyond pedagogic reform. The purpose is to modify the total instructional environment to sustain the positive feelings that most children have about themselves when they enter school....Any effective plan requires the cooperation of all persons who compose a child's human environment.

Sample techniques and strategies employed:

- To achieve a positive climate, and a positive self-concept, we repeated in endless variations, morning , noon, and night, the message, "You can succeed if you want to," and "Everybody is somebody."

- We held district wide programs...to see and hear nationally known personalities who credit their success to positive thinking.

- We thoroughly briefed members of the community, and enlisted their support for the program.

- We informed our central administrative staff of the theoretical base, aims, and methodology of the plan, and kept them current through weekly meetings.

- We deliberately surrounded children with assurances of their self-worth.

- We held slogan contests.

- We looked for ways to introduce positive thinking into our topics.

* Source: Youngs, B.B. (1989). The Phoenix curriculum. *Educational Leadership, 46*(5), 24.

** Source: Mitchell, W. H., and McCollum, M.G. (1983). The power of positive students. *Educational Leadership, 40*(5), 48–51.

THE CRITICS

In recent years, the critics of these strategies and programs have become more and more vociferous. The attacks have come from a wide range of sources on either side of the political spectrum. They have come largely from the popular press, but also from some conservative essentialist writers in education. The daily cartoons *Calvin and Hobbes* and *Doonesbury* have lampooned the efforts and programs by educators in this area. There have been editorials by nationally syndicated columnists such as Charles Krauthammer, George Will, and John Leo, blasting the ludicrousness of it all, and generously citing the more bizarre examples to be found. Some see it as simply the latest incarnation of the long-standing emphasis on positive thinking and self-help.

Most of the critics are in basic philosophical disagreement with the causation theory, and, as we shall see, are quite aware of the almost total lack of empirical data to support that theory. For example, Thomas Sowell (1993, p. 97), a senior fellow at the Hoover Institution stated that, "The very idea that self-esteem is something *earned*, rather than being a prepackaged handout from the school system, seems not to occur to many educators." Alfie Kohn (1994, p. 277) stated that, "the whole enterprise could be said to encourage a self-absorption bordering on narcissism," and that the programs are superficial, consisting of such drivel as, "I am special because...," essays "all about me, " and chanting hollow phrases like, "I think" and "I feel."

It is more difficult to find critics within the educational establishment, but there are a few. For example, Elizabeth McPike (1996), the editor of *American Educator,* the journal of the American Federation of Teachers (AFT), wrote: "...[W]ell-intentioned but misguided notions about self-esteem have become, if anything, even more deeply embedded in the culture of many, many schools. These notions get played out in various ways and constitute one of the most serious threats to the movement to raise academic and disciplinary standards and improve the learning opportunities and life chances of our nation's children"(p. 9). Roy Baumeister (1996) goes even further, advising educators to "beware the dark side" of teaching self-esteem and advises schools to "forget about self-esteem, and concentrate on self-control." And, as we shall see, a number of researchers are also quite troubled by the claims of causation, and even relationship, between self-esteem and achievement and prosocial behaviors. But these critics within the profession are rare. Even more rare are those who challenge the multi-cultural claims about self-esteem and students' success as have O'Donnell and O'Donnell (1995).

LEVEL I RESEARCH

It is best to think of the Level I research in two separate ways: First, we consider theoretical models, and second, we look at empirical studies examining the relationship between self-concept and achievement and pro-social behaviors.

In Chapter 3, we discussed how educational theories often derive from a variety of sources: philosophy, experience, observations, and basic research (often done in other fields, such as psychology). Consider two scenarios. First, someone may conduct exploratory research—collecting data on a variety of people, analyzing them statistically looking for relationships between variables. Then, on the basis of those relationships, either a theory of causation—that is, that one variable has a directing influence on the other variable—or a theory of relationship—that is, that where one variable is found, the other(s) probably will be also—is developed. For example, an economist may find a positive correlation or relationship between a person's amount of education and income. The data show that as the amount of a person's education increases, his or her income also increases. One might theorize a cause-and-effect relationship between the two variables: education determines income. This makes a certain amount of sense. Educated people in our society can usually demand a higher salary than those less educated.

However, the nature of correlation is sometimes confusing. In this case, one could just as easily have theorized that income drives education, because people with money are more likely to be able to afford to go to college. This theory also seems plausible. But, it is just as plausible that both variables are driven by something else. The German social scientist, Max Weber, advanced a theory in the late 19th century of the relationship between Protestantism and success in capitalist ventures. Weber had noted a significant statistical correlation between the two variables. His critics, however, have pointed out that highly developed capitalist enterprises existed prior to the advent of Protestantism and can also be found in Asian cultures where Protestantism is hardly present. Weber was well aware that other preconditions, material and psychological, are often present for the development of successful capitalism, and even he admitted that a cause-and-effect relationship is tentative at best.

The second scenario develops somewhat differently. Based on a philosophical or worldview of human nature, one might develop a theory independent of much empirical data. At this point, it is a theory with little or no evidence. It becomes the work of empirical researchers to see if the theory fits "reality," that is, whether there is reason to think it is true or workable in certain circumstances. Sometimes evidence is gathered to a degree that the theory is accepted as "true" or valid. And sometimes the evidence is lacking and the theory is rejected as insufficient to explain reality. A celebrated example of this is the phenomenon known as "phrenology." The theory of phrenology, conceptualized by the Austrian doctor Franz-Joseph Gall around the turn of the 18th century, posited that the conformation of the skull is indicative of mental faculties and character traits. Phrenology enjoyed popular appeal until well into the 20th century when it became discredited for lack of scientific evidence. As a field, education is replete with such examples, the most recent of which is the Instructional Theory into Practice (ITIP) model referred to earlier.

Self-esteem theory appears to have developed in this second way. Scheirer and Kraut (1979) concluded that many of the self-esteem ideas can be traced back to early humanist psychologists. They state:

> Professional psychologists as early as William James emphasized that a person's beliefs about himself will influence his decisions and actions. The forefathers of American social psychology, C.H. Cooley and George Herbert Mead, described the self as a social entity formed by appraisal reflected from other persons. Following Mead and Cooley, symbolic interactionists hypothesized that a positive self concept will lead to constructive, socially desirable behavior, and conversely that a distorted self concept will lead to deviant, socially inadequate behaviors. (p. 131)

Thus a correlation between self-esteem and prized behaviors, not to mention a cause-and-effect relationship, was hypothesized early on. What is noteworthy here is that these things were *theorized* as ways to explain human failure and "deviant, socially inadequate behaviors." One might just as easily have theorized the opposite, that people's socially inadequate behavior leads them to feeling bad about themselves. Or, a third hypothesis is that the causative agents sit somewhere outside the correlation.

Earlier we mentioned that Lerner (1996) noted that self-esteem theory has been the reigning orthodoxy for so long that, "Many teachers will be hard pressed to think of a contrasting theory." What many educators have never even thought of is that there are rival theories to this orthodoxy. For example, Lerner contrasts the orthodoxy with the ideas of Alfred Binet (of Stanford-Binet fame), who theorized that:

> ...[A] self-critical stance was at the very core of intelligence, its sine qua non and seminal essence....[H]e saw self-criticism as the essence of intelligence, the master key that unlocked the doors to competence and excellence alike....[H]is view on the natural inclinations [one of egotism] of children [was] not novel at all,... that egotism was the natural state of childhood. Teachers who took this view saw it as their job to help children overcome their egotism... and [learn] to see themselves and their accomplishments in a realistic perspective in order to take realistic steps toward excellence. (p. 10)

Lerner calls this "earned self-esteem" as opposed to "feel-good–now self-esteem." In this contrasting theory, self-esteem is earned. "It is not a precondition for learning but a product of it"(p. 10). This point of view, as well as the point of view of other rival theories, seems hardly to have been given serious consideration if one were to judge by the curricular artifacts available.

What empirical evidence exists to support the reigning self-esteem *theory*? Not much that we, or anyone else, apparently, have been able to find. In fact, the thousands of studies done on self-esteem in the past four decades have been reviewed numerous times (e.g., Scheirer & Kraut, 1979; Hansford & Hattie, 1982; Byrne, 1984; California Task Force on Self-Esteem, 1990; Skaalvic & Hagtvet, 1990; Kohn, 1994; Baumeister, Smart, & Boden, 1996) and the conclusions are always the same: The *relationship* between self-esteem and achievement and other related behaviors is minimal at best, and more likely nonexistent. And most of the researchers consistently point out that even with those factors for which a small relationship is found, it is usually so small as to have no practical significance. Additionally, these small correlations are in no way supportive of any type of cause-and-effect relationship.

Scheirer and Kraut (1979) examined the wealth of research and concluded that, "...little direct evidence exists in either psychological or sociological literature that self-concept has an independent influence on behavior" (p. 132). Regarding academic achievement in particular, they stated, "... the overwhelmingly negative evidence reviewed here for a causal connection between self-concept and academic achievement should create caution among both educators and theorists who have heretofore assumed that enhancing a person's feelings about himself would lead to academic achievement" (p. 145), and that, "...neither the internal needs model nor the identification with one's ethnic group model has stimulated an educational program with positive results linking self-concept with academic achievement" (p. 144)

Things had not changed much 25 years later when Alfie Kohn concluded:

- ◆ "...[T]he findings that emerge from this [self-esteem] literature are not especially encouraging for those who would like to believe that feeling good about oneself brings about a variety of benefits." (p. 273)

- ◆ "In sum, high self-esteem appears to offer no guarantee of inclining people toward pro-social behavior—or even of steering them away from antisocial behavior." (p. 275)

♦ "The implication is that the better the research, the less significant the connection it will find between self-esteem and achievement." (p. 275)

Among the more interesting developments in this intriguing realm are the actions of the California Task Force on Self-Esteem (1990). The Task Force was composed almost wholly of strong proponents of the self-esteem theory. The report of the Task Force stated, however, that, "We who served on the task force were determined that our findings would be grounded in the most current and valid research available" (p. 43). And what did they conclude?

> The associations between self-esteem and its expected consequences are mixed, insignificant, or absent. The nonrelationship holds between self-esteem and teenage pregnancy, self-esteem and child abuse, self-esteem and most cases of alcohol and drug abuse....If the association between self-esteem and behavior is so often reported to be weak, even less can be said for the causal relationship between the two. (Smelser, 1989, pp. 15, 17)

This did not stop advocates of the causal theory, however, who forged ahead with a wealth of new programs. How could this have happened, given the evidence? Joseph Kahne (1996), who studied this outcome from the California Task Force for Self-Esteem, noted that, "Findings that questioned the likelihood of ameliorating social problems by promoting self-esteem were ignored. More precisely,...they were overruled" (p. 12). Such is the strength of cultural beliefs, so much so that evidence itself seems not to matter and can simply be overruled by those who do not believe it. The task force itself offered this explanation: "... Many of us on the task force are convinced that a sizable number of practitioners in functioning [self-esteem] programs are well ahead of academic researchers in their appreciation of self-esteem's central role in the social problems that plague our society" (p. 43). So much for humility.

One other matter of note: From the decades of research on self-esteem, an interesting counter-theory has emerged, which suggests that self-esteem strategies may have detrimental effects. Wesley Burr (1992) suggested that out of this emphasis on self-esteem have emerged greater selfishness, excessive individualism, and processes that are undermining the health of families. Baumeister, Smart, and Boden (1996) have taken this charge a step further. Their examination of the research concluded that there is a lack of empirical evidence to support the idea that low self-esteem leads to antisocial behavior. They write, "The traditional view that low self-esteem is a cause of violence and aggression is not tenable in light of the present evidence" (p. 26). From the research, however, they have theorized, "that one major cause of violent response is threatened egotism, that is, a favorable self-appraisal that encounters an external and unfavorable evaluation.... In particular, unrealistically positive or inflated view of self, and favorable self-appraisals that are uncertain, unstable, or heavily dependent on external validation, will be especially vulnerable to encountering such threats" (p. 12). Finally, they theorize that, "An uncritical endorsement of the cultural value of high self-esteem may therefore be counterproductive and even dangerous" (p. 29).

In summary, what does the Level I research say? At the theoretical level, there are many plausible rival theories that most educators have never considered. At the empirical level, the theory has virtually no support.

LEVELS II AND III RESEARCH

Not surprisingly, the popular educational literature is replete with anecdotal stories that inform the reader of schools and students "turned around" by "innovative" school programs and practices designed to promote self-esteem. But we must agree with Alfie Kohn (1994), who concluded that, "Hard data to support the efficacy of such interventions [self-esteem programs] are...virtually nil." Even the sympathetic California Task Force on Self-Esteem reached similar conclusions. They concluded that, "There is no solid evidence that counseling and psychotherapy can increase self-esteem." If that type of intense treatment cannot change self-concepts, it seems improbable that slogans and other such efforts will have little effect on achievement and other pro-social behaviors.

However, there is one major Level II and Level III research study worth noting. The U.S. Office of Education initiated Project Follow Through, a comprehensive program in the primary grades of 170-plus communities (see Chapter 14). The largest and most expensive educational study ever conducted by the Office of Education, it involved research on a wide range of instructional approaches from open classrooms to very highly structured, teacher-controlled methodologies. Researchers (Stebbins et al., 1977) concluded that the models of instruction that produced the largest gains in self-esteem were those that assumed that *competence* enhanced self-esteem (Lerner's "earned self-esteem") and not the other way around. Those instructional programs concerned with affective outcomes and their causal influence on learning (Lerner's "feel-good–now self-esteem") produced minimal or even negative affective outcomes, as well as the lowest academic achievement. The sad note, however, is that given their popularity and the time and money spent on self-esteem programs, there is so little school-based evidence to support them.

CONCLUSION

We leave it to you to decide whether self-esteem programs in school settings are a worthwhile endeavor. Our advice is that little to no evidence exists at Levels I, II, and III to support their pursuit. We are reluctant, therefore, to advise you to go ahead. Recently, one of us had a conversation with a professor of education who works at another university. She is a staunch advocate of raising self-esteem in the classroom through strategies because this will lead, in her opinion, to higher achievement. To the remark that the evidence of that is lacking, she simply replied that the work is too important for us to be sitting around waiting for research results that may not be useful anyway. So, as Abraham Lincoln once observed, "People who like that kind of thing find that's just the kind of thing they like." And, apparently, many are sold on the idea. The question ultimately is not whether we all want young people to have a good opinion of themselves. Of course, we do. Rather, the question is how does that come about? Perhaps the answer is found in the pursuit of old-fashioned virtues such as helping others, showing courtesy and kindness, and applying ourselves diligently when it comes to hard work on serious matters. But that, too, is just a theory of ours waiting to be tested.

REFERENCES

Battle, J. (1992). *Culture-free self-esteem inventories* (2nd ed.). Austin, TX: PRO-ED, Inc.

Baumeister, R.F. (1996). Should schools try to boost self-esteem. *American Educator, Summer,* 14–19.

Baumeister, R.F., Smart, L., and Boden, J.M. (1996). Relation of threatened egotism to violence and aggression: the dark side of high self-esteem. *Psychological Review, 103*(1), 5–33.

Burr, W. (1992). Undesirable side effects of enhancing self-esteem. *Family Relations, 41,* 460–464.

Byrne, B.M. (1984). The general/academic self-concept nomological network: A review of construct validation research. *Review of Educational Research, 54*(3), 427–456.

California Task Force to Promote Self-esteem and Personal and Social Responsibility (1990). *Toward a state of esteem: the final report of the California Task Force to Promote Self-esteem and Personal and Social Responsibility.* Sacramento: California State Department of Education.

Coopersmith, S. (1987). *Coopersmith self-esteem inventory.* Palo Alto, CA: Consulting Psychologists Press, Inc.

Hansford, B.C., and Hattie, J.A. (1982). The relationship between self and achievement/performance measures. *Review of Educational Research 52*(1), 123–142.

Kahne, J. (1996). The politics of self-esteem. *American Educational Research Journal, 33*(1), 3–22.

Kohn, A. (1994). The truth about self-esteem. *Phi Delta Kappan, 76*(4), 272–283.

Lerner, B. (1996). Self-esteem and excellence: The choice and the paradox. *American Educator, Summer,* 9–13, 41–42.

McGuire, J., and Heuss, B. (1994). *Bridges: a self-esteem activity book for students in grades 4–6.* Boston: Allyn and Bacon.

McPike, E. (1996). Editor's introduction. In Lerner, B. (1996). Self-esteem and excellence: the choice and the paradox. *American Educator,* Summer, 1996, 9–13, 41–42.

Mecca, A.M., Smelser, N.J., and Vasconcellos, J. (Eds.) (1989). *The social importance of self-esteem.* Berkley: University of California Press.

Mitchell, W.H., and McCollum, M.G. (1983). The power of positive students. *Educational Leadership, 40*(5), 48–51.

O'Donnell, T.F., and O'Donnell, W.J. (1995). Multicultural myths. *American School Board Journal, 182*(7), 23–25.

Piers, E.V., and Harris, D.B. (1984). *Piers-Harris children's self-concept scale (The way I feel about myself).* Los Angeles: Western Psychological Services.

Rogers, C. (1969). *Freedom to learn.* Columbus, OH: Charles E. Merrill.

Scheirer, M.A., and Kraut, R.E. (1979). Increasing educational achievement via self-concept. *Review of Educational Research, 49*(1), 131–150.

Skaalvic, E., and Hagtve, K. (1990). Academic achievement and self-concept. *Journal of Personality and Social Psychology, 58*(2), 292–307.

Smelser, N.J. (1989). *Self-esteem and social problems: an introduction.* In Mecca, A.M., Smelser, N.J., and Vasconcellos, J. (Eds.) (1989). *The social importance of self-esteem.* Berkeley: University of California Press, pp. 1–25.

Sowell, T. (1993). *Inside American education: the decline, the deception, the dogmas.* New York: Free Press.

Stebbins, L., St. Pierre, R., Proper, E., Anderson, R., and Cerva, T. (1977). *Education as experimentation: A planned variation model (Vol. IVA–D)*. Cambridge, MA: Abt Associates.

Vann, K.R., and Kunjufu, J. (1993). The importance of an Afrocentric, multicultural curriculum. *Phi Delta Kappan, 74*(6), 490–491.

Walz, G.R., and Bleur, J.C. (1992). *Student self-esteem: a vital element of school success*. Alexandria, VA: American School Counselor Association.

Youngs, B.B. (1989). The Phoenix curriculum. *Educational Leadership, 46*(5), 24.

5

INNOVATIONS FROM BRAIN RESEARCH

Can a profession whose charge is defined by the development of an effective and efficient human brain continue to remain uninformed about that brain? If we do remain uninformed about the brain, we will become vulnerable to the pseudoscientific fads, generalizations, and programs that will surely arise from the pool of brain research.

Robert Sylwester

Over the past 20 years or more, neuroscientists have amassed a wealth of knowledge on the brain and its development from birth to adulthood. And they are beginning to draw some solid conclusions about how the human brain grows and how babies acquire language, sight and musical talents, and other abilities. The question now is: How much of these data can educators use? The answer is uncertain.

Debra Viadero

Take a moment to consider the following: structural and transportational cellular systems, glial cells, neurons, dendrites, amino acids, neurotransmitters, peptides, corpus callosum, and anterior commissure. These terms, which are a focus of brain research, have little meaning to most teachers and administrators. Yet, the research in this area may well have implications for how we should teach and how schools should be organized. Robert Sylwester, a leading figure in the field of brain research and school learning, points out that educators have stressed the environmental aspects of learning potential, largely without an understanding of how the brain actually works. However, medical research advances have made possible the startling recognition that the human brain is on the verge of understanding itself! In the light of this development, Sylwester concluded that, "Our profession has tended to think of the nurture side as dominant, but these new theories argue

55

that nature plays a far more important role than previously believed—or that the dichotomy itself is not an irrelevant issue. They also suggest that many current beliefs about instruction, learning, and memory are wrong" (1995, pp. 14–15).

The current love affair on the part of education with brain research flows from the belief that if we can figure out how the brain functions, that is, how information is received, stored, retrieved, and otherwise processed, we can then design educational programs based on that knowledge. Brain research represents for many the ultimate pedagogical frontier. Once this new territory is explored and mapped, the promise of maximizing the learning potential of each student will be realized. Sylwester's bold statement in the previous paragraph indicates that we may need to make fundamental changes in the ways we go about the business of school learning and teaching.

The basic research in this area began with Paul Broca's celebrated 19th-century theory of hemispheric dominance. Research into this and other areas of brain function has continued apace in the 20th century, and in 1981, Roger Sperry received the Nobel Prize for his split-brain research. In more recent years, medical research into brain function has expanded into a variety of areas to include brain development in childhood, short- and long-term memory, attention, emotions, gender differences, effects of aging, consciousness, creativity, sensory input, intelligence, sexuality, and others. It is all very technical and overwhelming for those outside the world of scientific investigation even to consider.

THE PENDULUM IS WELL INTO ITS SWING

It was not long after certain findings from brain research became publicized that educators jumped into the breach with ideas about how the findings should alter educational practices (Reiff, 1992; Carnine, 1990; Caine & Caine, 1990; Springer & Deutsch, 1989; Wittrock, 1981). A wide range of educational "theories" has emerged on the heels of medical investigations. More than 25 years ago, Robert Sylwester wrote, "The brain is the most magnificent three pounds of matter in the universe.

What we now know about the human brain and what we'll discover in the years ahead may well transform formal education" (Sylwester, 1981). Whether what we think we know about the brain will prove useful or not, educators have jumped on the bandwagon with article after article about the educational implications of medical research. Sylwester went on to say, ". . . but can we afford to wait until all problems are solved before we begin to study the education issues implicit in this research? When mass media begin to report discoveries, parents will expect us to respond" (Sylwester, 1981, p. 8).

In at least a comparative sense, Sylwester was cautious, believing that it was too early to implement curricular and instructional changes based on the medical research. He was no doubt well aware of the tendency of some educators to make wild claims and advocate unproven methodologies based on theories alone, and he remains cautious to this day. As he has more recently written, "We've already demonstrated our vulnerability with the educational spillover of the split-brain research: the right brain/left brain books, workshops, and curricular programs whose recommendations often went far beyond the research findings" (1995, p. 6).

Other educators were less restrained in their enthusiasm. It is fair to say that they have responded to the medical findings by developing activities and strategies designed to influence life in classrooms. The topic has become a common offering at conventions, workshops, and inservice meetings. Those who wish confirmation of our claim need only review the list of presentations found in the catalogues of major education conferences.

An example of learning implications derived from medical research is reflected in the work of Caine and Caine (1990, 1994). They write that they have developed "brain principles as a general theoretical foundation for brain-based learning. These principles are simple and neurologically sound. Applied to education, however, they help us to reconceptualize teaching by taking us out of traditional frames of reference and guiding us in defining and selecting appropriate programs and methodologies" (1990, p. 66). They go on to say: "If these principles are as sound as we believe they are, then they provide us with a framework for learning and teaching that moves us irrevocably away from the methods and models that have dominated education for more than a century" (1994, p. 87). Pretty heady stuff.

A summary of Caine and Caine's brain-based learning theory is presented in Figure 5.1. Each of the 12 learning principles has direct implications for teaching and learning. For example, Principle Two states that "brain-based teaching must fully incorporate stress management, nutrition, exercise, drug education, and other facets of health into the learning process" (p. 66). Principle Six states that "vocabulary and grammar are best understood and mastered when they are incorporated in genuine, whole-language experiences. Similarly, equations and scientific principles are best dealt with in the context of living science " (p. 67). These are interesting conclusions in any educational context, but to state that they are based on brain research gives them, one supposes, heightened credibility. At any rate, these assertions sailed past the editorial gatekeepers of *Educational Leadership*, a policy journal in the field of education.

The application of basic brain research to education has also resulted in an emphasis on learning styles, particularly among proponents of hemisphericity (right and left brain preference) in learning. It is worth noting that both learning styles advocates and brain research educators support a whole-brain approach to teaching. That is, they both claim that it is necessary to teach to both sides of the brain, thereby providing a wide and complementary range of strategies and activities to stimulate learners.

Berrnice McCarthy's 4MAT System (1987) is an example of a hybrid program that incorporates brain research and learning styles. McCarthy developed a comprehensive instructional approach to meeting individual needs by combining research on brain hemispheres with David Kolb's Learning Cycle (1985). The 4MAT System identifies the learning needs of four types of learners and accompanying strategies for the integration of both right and left brain processing skills.

FIGURE 5.1. CAINE AND CAINE'S BRAIN-BASED LEARNING PRINCIPLES AND TEACHING MODEL

Principles:

♦ Principle One: The Brain Is a Parallel Processor.

♦ Principle Two: Learning Engages the Entire Physiology.

♦ Principle Three: The Search for Meaning Is Innate.

♦ Principle Four: The Search for Meaning Occurs Through "Patterning."

♦ Principle Five: Emotions Are Critical to Patterning.

♦ Principle Six: Every Brain Simultaneously Perceives and Creates Parts and Wholes.

♦ Principle Seven: Learning Involves Both Focused Attention and Peripheral Perception.

♦ Principle Eight: Learning Always Involves Conscious and Unconscious Processes.

♦ Principle Nine: We Have Two Types of Memory: A Spatial Memory System and a Set of Systems for Rote Learning.

♦ Principle Ten: The Brain Understands and Remembers Best When Facts and Skills Are Embedded in Natural Spatial Memory.

♦ Principle Eleven: Learning is Enhanced by Challenge and Inhibited by Threat.

♦ Principle Twelve: Each Brain Is Unique.

Teaching Models:

	Traditional	*Brain-Based*
Source of Information	Simple. Two-way, from teacher to book, worksheet, or film to student	Complex. Social interactions, group discovery, individual search and reflection, role-playing integrated subject matter.

Figure 5.1 continues on the next page.

Classroom Organization	Linear. Individual work or teacher-directed.	Complex. Thematic, integrative, cooperative, workstations, individualized projects.
Classroom Management	Hierarchical. Teacher-controlled.	Complex. Designated status and responsibilities delegated to students and monitored by teacher.
Outcomes	Specified and convergent. Emphasis on memorized concepts, vocabulary, and skills.	Complex. Emphasis on reorganization of information in unique ways, with both predictable outcomes, divergent and convergent, increase in natural knowledge demonstrated through ability to use learned skills in variable contexts.

Source: Adapted from Caine, R.N. and Caine, G. (1994). *Making connections: teaching and the human brain.* Menlo Park, CA: Addison-Wesley.

Other educational implications cited by brain-based teaching advocates include:

♦ Balanced teaching in order to engage both hemispheres;

♦ Growth spurts and their implications for individualization, pacing, year-round schooling, acceleration, and failure policies;

♦ Matching structure and content of curricula, environments, activities, and interactions to cognitive abilities;

♦ Curriculum integration to provide meaningful contexts and connections among and between subjects;

♦ Schema theory, to furnish a learning environment that provides stability and familiarity as well as challenge and discovery;

♦ Wider ranges of contextual and sensory cues in learning in order to increase the number of links made with each new concept, thus leading to improved long-term memory and transfer.

RESEARCH ON EDUCATION AND THE BRAIN

The research at Level I is classic basic research into brain function. The researchers themselves admit that the research base is just developing and that it has barely scratched the surface. Sylwester (1995) identifies two approaches taken by scientists who study the brain: from the bottom up, and from the top down. The bottom up approach characterizes the work of neuroscientists who focus on the working of small units—individual cells or small systems of cells. The top-down approach focuses on complex cognitive mechanisms or functions, such as movement, language, and abstract analysis. These studies include the normal and abnormal functioning of single neurons, networks of neurons, and the factors that affect neuron activity. All of this (and much more) is accomplished through the use of CAT scans, EEGs, PETs, MRIs, and other tests. Some of this research is conducted on animals, as well as on people with brain damage or mental illness. Other studies are done in laboratory experiments with normal primates and humans, using brain imaging technology to determine chemical composition, electrical transmission, and blood flow patterns which occur normally and during the conduct of certain tasks. All of this sounds very technical, and it is.

A variety of theories and ideas have emerged from the basic research into brain function. Two of the earliest theories still prevalent in education circles coalesce around two major concepts: hemisphericity and growth spurts.

Sperry's research supports the idea that the two hemispheres of the brain serve differing but complementary functions. A person uses both hemispheres when learning or functioning, but one may dominate the other and determine a
person's style or preferred way of learning. Each hemisphere is
thought to contribute specialized functions to tasks. The left
hemisphere of the brain is associated with verbal, sequential,
analytical abilities. The right hemisphere is associated with
global, holistic, visual-spatial abilities. Two related ideas are
full *lateralization* and *parallel processing*. In lateralization, the left
hemisphere dominates in language expression while the right
hemisphere dominates in nonverbal processing. In parallel
processing, research indicates that the brain hemispheres perform many tasks simultaneously.

The concept of different functions for the two hemispheres
of the brain seems now to be widely accepted, with the left
brain controlling linear activity and the right brain controlling
global activity. Programs have emerged to teach to both sides
of the brain or to compensate for a weaker hemisphere. However, this conclusion is questioned by a number of researchers
and psychologists. For example, Zale, Sink, and Yachimowicz
(1992) concluded that "there is little empirical support for educational programs that supposedly train students to compensate for hemisphericity through teaching integrative process
techniques," and that "the notion of cerebral dominance has
limited theoretical or practical value for educators. . ." (pp. 55–
56).

Herman Epstein's medical research, done in the 1970s,
seems to indicate that the brain grows in spurts rather than in a
continual, uninterrupted process. This finding is often used to
support the Piagetian model of cognitive development.
Growth spurts in school age children often occur between the
ages of 6–8, 10–12, and 14–16. And they often occur in summer
when school is not in session. Myelination has to do with the
process of nerve fiber maturation, which occurs in stages that
seem to parallel Piagetian stages of cognitive growth and development. Connecting nerve systems are the last to myelinate

in childhood, indicating that a child could be said to have a "functionally split brain."

A number of other topics are currently the focus of investigation. Nobel Prize winner Gerald Edelman (1992) proposed a biological brain theory model based on evolutionary theory emergent from a type of jungle environment. He stresses the biological nature of learning and consciousness, which may have implications for the classroom, but it is not certain at this point what they might be. Another Nobel Prize winner, Francis Crick, has undertaken a biological search for the soul (or consciousness) within neural networks. His book, *The Astonishing Hypothesis: The Scientific Search for the Soul* (1994) has generated considerable interest. The implications of Crick's book for education are also unclear, but its nearly total focus on materialism certainly puts it at odds with many religious beliefs, a sure-fire prescription for controversy.

Exploration in the area of gender differences and brain function continues apace. For example, it has been well documented that males and females differ in the way they solve intellectual problems and experience emotions. Males generally perform better on certain spatial tasks and mathematical reasoning, while females typically outperform males on tasks of perceptual speed and verbal fluency. The extent to which these differences exist due to environmental factors or combinations of factors is problematic, but it is also theorized that they are due to different hormonal influences during brain development (Kimura, 1992).

Noteworthy are two other avenues of thought emerging from recent findings in brain research. Daniel Goleman (1995) has become famous with his construct of emotional intelligence, about which he cites research on the brain and emotion. His thesis is that individual success can be predicted better by emotional health than by standardized IQ tests. He says: "In a very real sense we have two minds, one that thinks and one that feels." And Peterson (1994) presents an interesting look at brain research and the idea of critical periods, that is, that certain periods of development are crucial if not vital to the development of specific cognitive and neurological functions.

Each of these has potential implication for how schools go about the business of teaching and learning.

There are a number of other areas of brain research that may well have educational implications, but they remain beyond our pedagogical grasp simply because the medical knowledge itself is still quite limited. These include endorphin molecules, memory, hyperactivity, attention span, creativity, and others. Just to cite an example, researchers at the UCLA Medical Center have discovered that children below the age of 10 have brain activity that is unusually rich in the secretion of theta waves, thought to be associated with creativity. Whether in the future this knowledge will stop teachers from handing out worksheet after worksheet to these naturally creative little characters remains speculative. The general opinion of experts is that we have barely scratched the surface in our knowledge of the human brain.

In our review of materials for this chapter, we came across scores of "research findings" and "implications" for education from brain research. Please recognize that the following list is only a sample of what educators and researchers are saying based on brain research. Our purpose is not to endorse these recommendations or even to suggest that ample evidence exist in their support.

- Critical periods exist for learning some skills.
- Early experience, education, and environment play a primary role in determining who we are.
- Research on hemisphericity is inconclusive.
- Emotion drives attention, and attention drives learning and memory.
- Music trains the brain for higher forms of thinking.
- Knowledge is retained longer if children connect not only aurally but also emotionally and physically to the material.

- Complex subjects such as trigonometry or foreign language should not wait for puberty to be introduced.

- Teens' biological clocks are set later than those of their fellow human beings and therefore high school should start later in the morning.

- Children need to be more physically active in the classroom.

- If sensory neural connections are not repeatedly stimulated in the first few months of life when the brain is still in its formative period, they atrophy and die.

- Females seem to have stronger connections between the two halves of their brain than do men.

This is quite a list; but remember this is only a fraction of the ideas emerging from the claims that invoke brain research. Some of the claims are far more wide-ranging than the few that appear above.

Complicating any attempts at an analysis of the research at Levels II and III is the variety of claims being made in the name of brain research. On many of the very specific claims, research at Level II has not been able to catch up with all the various findings and possible implications for education. At this point, however, there are too few objective, well-designed studies identifying specific educational purposes and methodologies based on brain research to provide an acceptable and reliable base in support of such claims. Moreover, the topic becomes confusing because so many innovators are now claiming brain research as a reason to do this or that. For example, learning styles advocates often point to brain research in support of their claims, but the applied research that does exist is often of poor quality. Similarly, brain-based teaching advocates such as Caine and Caine (1994) call for brain-based educational methodologies that include the integrated curriculum, thematic teaching, and cooperative learning. So the Level II research in these areas may well point to the efficacy of specific methodologies, but to do so may or may not necessarily be an accurate inference flowing from the brain research findings to date.

Medical and psychological research will continue and, of course, educators will undoubtedly continue to draw inferences for teaching and learning from it. But we are too close to the frontiers of knowledge in this area to legitimately cite research that promises improved test scores, or very much of anything else for that matter. Not surprisingly then, we could find no evidence of Level III program evaluation studies that demonstrate that either school or district adoption, or teacher training or workshop participation in brain-based programs result in better school practice, however one might choose to define it. Many of the school restructuring efforts seem to coincide with what certain educators are saying the brain research points to; that is, cooperative learning, smaller groups, search for deeper meaning, and so on, but those ideas have been touted on grounds independent of brain research as well. Possibly, however, future research in brain function will lend support to these efforts.

CONCLUSION

It is probably useful for educators to be informed of the research in brain function. The problem is, however, that it tends to be highly technical research from another field, that of medical research. The extent to which medical research will trickle down to the point that it yields real educational implications remains to be seen. Much of what is touted by brain-based teaching advocates resembles good sense teaching, so in that way it may be harmless at worst and useful at best. We, however, may be a number of years away from any major revelations that are directly applicable to life in classrooms or that provide a coherent set of principles for teaching and learning.

Our recommendation is that you attempt to keep informed of developments in this field. The research base at Level I will continue to grow exponentially. Our knowledge right now is quite primitive, but it won't stay that way. Look for a host of new insights down the road. We also recommend caution in investing your time in inservice activities in which methodologies are founded primarily on "brain research" because they will tend to be faddish and probably premature. The fact that the direct classroom applications are not presently there should not blind us from the realities that will emerge in the future. This area will in time come to have more to offer to teaching and learning than we can presently imagine.

REFERENCES

Caine, R.N., and Caine, G. (1990). Understanding a brain-based approach to learning and teaching. *Educational Leadership, 48*(2), 66–70.

Caine, R.N., and Caine, G. (1994). *Making connections: teaching and the human brain.* Menlo Park, CA: Addison-Wesley.

Carnine, D. (1990). New research on the brain: implications for instruction. *Phi Delta Kappan, 71*(5), 372–277.

Crick, F. (1994). *The astonishing hypothesis: the scientific search for the soul.* New York: Scribner.

Edelman, G.M. (1992). *Bright air, brilliant fire: on the matter of the mind.* New York: Basic Books.

Garger, S. (1990). Is there a link between learning style and neurophysiology? *Educational Leadership, 48*(2), 63–65.

Goleman, D. (1995). *Emotional intelligence.* New York: Bantam.

Hand, J. (1989). Split-brain theory and recent results in brain research: implications for the design of instruction. In Bass, R.K., and Dills, C.R. (Eds.), *Instructional development: the state of the art, II.* Dubuque, IA: Kendall/Hunt.

Kimura, D. (1992, September). Sex differences in the brain. *Scientific American, 267*(3), 118–125.

Kolb, D.A. (1985). *The learning style inventory.* Boston, MA: McBer & Co.

Levy, J. (1983). Research synthesis on the right and left hemisphere: We think with both sides of the brain. *Educational Leadership, 40*(2), 4, 66–71.

McCarthy, B. (1987). *The 4MAT system: teaching to learning styles with right/left mode techniques.* Barrington, IL: Excel, Inc.

Peterson, R.W. (1994). School readiness considered from a neuro-cognitive perspective. *Early Education and Development, 5*(2), 120–140.

Reiff, J.C. (1992). *What research says to the teacher: learning styles.* Washington, DC: National Education Association Professional Library.

Restak, R.M. (1984). *The brain.* Toronto: Bantam.

Springer, S., and Deutsch, G. (1989). *Left brain right brain* (3rd ed.). New York: W.H. Freeman.

Sylwester, R. (1990). An educator's guide to books on the brain. *Educational Leadership, 48*(2), 79–80.

Sylwester, R. (1994). What the biology of the brain tells us about learning. *Educational Leadership, 51*(4), 46–51.

Sylwester, R. (1995). *A celebration of neurons: an educators guide to the human brain.* Alexandria, VA: Association for Supervision and Curriculum Development.

Wittrock, M.C. (1981). Educational implications of recent brain research. *Educational Leadership, 37*(1), 12–15.

Zalewski, L.J., Sink, C., and Yachimowicz, D.J. (1992). Using cerebral dominance for education programs. *The Journal of General Psychology, 119*(1), 45–57.

6

TEACHING FOR INTELLIGENCE

Intelligence, in a word, reflects a micro-culture of praxis: the reference books one uses, the notes one habitually takes, the computer programs and databases one relies upon, and perhaps most important of all, the network of friends, colleagues, or mentors on whom one leans for feedback, help, advice, even just for company.

Jerome Bruner

Although we cannot turn mentally retarded individuals into intellectual geniuses, we can achieve meaningful increases in intellectual abilities. Any conclusions to the contrary can result only from failing to cite or take seriously the full range of the relevant data.

Robert Sternberg

This chapter and the one that follows examine the research base for two closely related topics, teaching for intelligence and thinking skills. We recognize that our decision to separate them into two parts is to some degree arbitrary. We hope you will agree with us that, while there is overlap, teaching thinking skills seems to have manifested itself in the tactical form of specific concrete programs, often commercial ones, and that teaching for intelligence represents a more strategic, generic set of ideas about teaching and learning. In this chapter, we examine several views of the broad construct of intelligence and how educators are bringing some of these ideas to the classroom. In the next chapter, we look at the more specific efforts that are being made to teach those very elusive mental processes called thinking skills.

WHAT IS INTELLIGENCE?

The debate over what constitutes intelligence is quite involved, and of long duration. At the heart of the matter is the perception that some people seem to be more mentally astute than others do, seem to learn more readily and thoroughly than others do, and seem to be able to solve certain problems more effectively than others do. But the "smart/dumb" dichotomy is much too simplistic to describe what is meant by intelligence, at least as psychologists and researchers in the field use it.

A number of unresolved issues complicate the discussion. Is intelligence a unified construct, or are there multiple types of intelligence? What roles do environment and heredity play in determining an individual's intelligence? Is intelligence specific to the culture in which one lives? Can intelligence be taught? And how can intelligence or the forms of intelligence, best be measured? Perhaps in the coming years answers to these questions will become more definitive as research on brain function moves forward.

Different individuals have answered each of these questions in a variety of ways over the years. Charles Spearman (1927) maintained that there is something called *general intelligence,* which is a basic capacity affecting all mental tasks. Proponents of this view note that those who do well on one type of mental task tend to do well on most others. Evidence of this is the fact that math and reading scores correlate quite highly, suggesting that there must be a general factor present to explain this. Spearman was able to document statistically that it is possible to derive a single quotient from the results of various tests of mental ability. He called this quotient "g" for general intelligence.

L.L. Thurstone (1938), however, maintained that there are several—more than 200—distinct mental abilities, including numerical ability, spatial ability, and verbal ability. He reached this conclusion in spite of the fact that tests of these presumably separate entities showed high intercorrelations. Thurstone's point was that a distribution of scores from different tests of mental ability could also be analyzed in ways that showed that they gathered around a number of distinct centers with each center measuring a particular cognitive ability (Singham, 1995). Thurstone's view is probably closer than Spearman's to that subscribed to by most professionals today.

Hernstein and Murray's (1995) controversial book, *The Bell Curve: Intelligence and Class Structure in American Life*, caused considerable debate, when, in the minds of many people, they attributed intelligence mainly to heredity. Their interpretation of already existing data seemed to shift the center of gravity toward nature in the long-standing nature or nurture debate. In essence, Hernstein and Murray appeared to conclude that there is a unitary construct called intelligence that can be measured by IQ tests, and that Spearman's thesis was essentially correct. Critics have attacked everything from the implied social and political agenda they attribute to Hernstein and Murray to their "overly simplistic" analysis of the data. Those interested in pursuing the issues outlined here would do well to read Mano Singham's (1995) thoughtful analysis of the problems associated with this type of research on intelligence.

While the layperson may continue to think of and talk about intelligence as if it were a single entity, certain professionals have been moving in another direction. Howard Gardner (1983) has proposed what has become a very popular model that he calls "multiple intelligences," and as we shall see, school districts from around the country have jumped at the chance to put his ideas into action. Gardner's work has been especially attractive to those educators who have become discouraged with the traditional idea that intelligence is based nearly exclusively on genetically endowed abstract reasoning abilities. They see students who show great "aptitude" or "talent" for this or that and wonder why, as Gardner has, the concept should not be expanded. We return to Gardner's work later in this chapter.

One of the more recent developments in the field is the work of Daniel Goleman (1995) who maintains that there is an entity that he calls emotional intelligence. Citing research on the brain and emotion, Goleman's thesis is that individual success can be better predicted by emotional health than by standardized IQ tests. He writes, "In a very real sense we have two minds, one that thinks and one that feels." Whether or not attention to this concept of intelligence will prove useful for educators and beneficial for children remains unknown. However, we offer this prediction: within the next few years this new theoretical model will be used to develop innovative educational programs much as Howard Gardner's theory has been used. The idea will simply prove too attractive to some program developers for this not too happen.

From the potentially wide range of issues and topics one could reasonably connect to the idea of teaching for intelligence, we have selected three of the most significant innovations. Each of the three is drawn from theoretical study and research in the general area of intelligence. While there is some overlap among the three, they represent distinctly different approaches both to the study of intelligence and to the educational implications that might be drawn from such study. The common thread found among them is the long gestation period of theorizing and problem solving out of which they each emerge.

We look first at the theory of Reuven Feuerstein and his educational program *Instrumental Enrichment*. It relates intelligence to the teaching of thinking and problem-solving skills in much the same way as do certain of the thinking skills programs examined in the Chapter 7. In this sense, Feuerstein's work emerges from the classic definitions of intelligence as the construct has been measured by IQ tests. The notable idea is that intelligence, according to Feuerstein, can be enhanced through appropriate teaching strategies.

Next, we examine Howard Gardner's theory of Multiple Intelligences and its rapidly expanding use in the schools. Gardner is concerned with the *content* of intelligence; that is, the different abilities behind intelligent behavior. Gardner points to recent advances in cognitive studies that he is convinced show best how to conceptualize intelligence. In brief, he thinks of intelligence basically as a person's biopsychological potential.

Finally, we turn our attention to the theory building of Robert Sternberg and the resulting programs based on his Triarchic Theory of Intelligence. Sternberg's work is an example of the focus on cognitive *processes* used by people in thinking operations His research is based primarily in a field of psychology known as information processing.

REUVEN FEUERSTEIN'S INSTRUMENTAL ENRICHMENT

The work of Israeli clinical psychologist Reuven Feuerstein, is based on a theory that intelligence is dynamic and not static, meaning that it can be altered with appropriate interventions. One of Feuerstein's more notable contributions to the field was his development of the *Learning Potential Assessment Device* (Feuerstein, 1979), an instrument that measures not merely the product of someone's thinking but the process itself. The student is presented with different problem-solving tasks, and, when needed, the test examiner *teaches* the student how to solve such problems in order to assess the extent to which the student has learned from the teaching. Thus, what emerges from the test-taking situation is a more dynamic assessment, one that predicts the student's potential. According to Feuerstein, cognitive development is dependent on direct intervention over time that teaches the mental processes necessary for learning how to learn. These interventions are sometimes called mediated learning experiences. In this sense, Feuerstein's work builds on Lev Vygotsky's idea of the Zone of Proximal Development, which is the range between which a learner can solve problems independently and the learner's ability to benefit from expert guidance.

Feuerstein's theorizing has led to the development of an elaborate curriculum called *Instrumental Enrichment,* which provides the kinds of needed mediated learning experiences (Feuerstein & Jensen, 1980, May; Feuerstein, Rand, Hoffman, & Miller, 1980). Frances Link (1991) describes the program as:

> . . . a direct and focused attack on those mental processes, which, through absence, fragility, or inefficiency, are to blame for poor intellectual or academic per-

formance. . . .In terms of behavior, *Instrumental En-richment*'s ultimate aim is to transform retarded per-formers, to alter their characteristically passive and dependent cognitive style to that of active, self-motivated, independent thinkers (p. 9).

The program consists of a 3-year series of content-free les-sons, called "instruments," which are grouped in 14 areas of cognitive abilities (see Fig. 6.1). It is intended for upper ele-mentary, middle, and secondary level students. Students do "instruments" with paper and pencil for about 2–3 hours a week. The teacher serves as the mediating agent and the in-struments are supposed to parallel the subject matter being taught by the teacher. In this sense, the program integrates with the existing course of study while "enriching" it with in-telligence-enhancing exercises. The program is sufficiently so-phisticated to make it crucial that teachers have a considerable amount of teacher training in its use.

FIGURE 6.1. FEUERSTEIN'S FOURTEEN INSTRUMENTS

Organization of Dots

Orientation in Space I

Comparison

Analytic Perception

Categorization

Instructions

Temporal Relations

Numerical Progressions

Family Relations

Illustrations

Transitive Relations

Syllogisms

Representational Stencil Design

Orientation in Space II

DOES IT WORK? THE RESEARCH

Advocates of the program say it does. Frances Link (1991) states: "Empirical data exist to document improvement in cognitive functions; improvement in self-concept [see our Chapter 4 on self-esteem], improvement in reading, writing, and mathematics subjects after two years of implementation" (p. 11). The claims imbedded in this statement are wide ranging, and perhaps not all are capable of being substantiated to the extent that one might hope.

A point of fundamental distinction between Feuerstein's program and many of the thinking skills programs detailed in Chapter 7, is that there is a Level II research base for *Instrumental Enrichment*. Within a few years of its development, a number of studies had been conducted on its effects. Savell, Twohig, and Rachford (1986) reviewed the initial body of research conducted in Israel, Venezuela, Canada, and the United States. They concluded that the evidence to that point showed positive effects for nonverbal measures of intelligence in all four countries, "in middle and low social class groups, in groups considered normal, as well as groups considered culturally or educationally disadvantaged," as well as in the hearing impaired. The effects, however, on other outcomes such as self-esteem, impulsivity, classroom behavior, and achievement were either "absent, inconsistent, or difficult to interpret." The positive results, however, were tied to those studies in which teachers had at least 1 week of training and students were involved with *Instrumental Enrichment* for at least 80 hours over a 2-year period.

Sternberg and Bhana (1986) conducted a second review of the research. They expressed concern about "teaching to the test," particularly the IQ-type tests, on which Savell et al. found positive gains. Nevertheless, Sternberg and Bhana were mildly supportive of the program. They stated, "we believe that when the full program is administered by carefully trained, intelligent, motivated, and conscientious instructors, gains can be attained on standard kinds of IQ and aptitude measures" (p. 63). If they are right, the results seem promising.

Whether this will translate into higher achievement remains to be determined.

Since that time there have been a few studies in the literature of Level II and Level III research on *Instrumental Enrichment*. For example, studies by Hoon (1990), Offenberg (1992), Kaniel and Reichenberg (1992), and Mulcahy (1993) generally report positive results, suggesting that *Instrumental Enrichment* can improve children's thinking (and therefore intelligence) when implemented over a long period of time and with well-trained teachers. The quality of these studies could be questioned with regard to elements of design and control of variables, but, as reviewers have noted, this is a very difficult area in which to conduct research. The indications from the research to date are that there may well be something here worth pursuing.

HOWARD GARDNER AND THE THEORY OF MULTIPLE INTELLIGENCES

Howard Gardner's book, *Frames of Mind*, was published in 1983 and was intended primarily for a limited audience of psychologists and other workers in the field of intelligence. Gardner was critical of the then prevailing views of intelligence, especially the idea of intelligence as a single construct. His work as an investigator in Harvard's Project Zero had convinced him, much as Thurstone had been convinced before him, that intelligence is composed of a number of factors distinctly different from one another. Where Thurstone had thought that the number of different kinds of intelligence might be in the range of 200, Gardner more modestly settled on seven. He does speculate that there may be more, but he has been able to document seven. Gardner noted that brain research had shown that stroke victims, for example, who might show considerable language loss, still maintained other capabilities. This was proof to him that certain functions are separate enough to make the case for different intelligences. Studying individuals of great ability in one area but who might not excel at all in other areas also shaped Gardner's thinking about separate intelligences.

Gardner questioned the value of the *general intelligence* construct, along with the more traditional views of intelligence that defined it operationally by tests focused primarily on logic, verbal, and quantitative abilities. Instead, he states that his interest is on those intellectual processes that are not covered by the *general intelligence* concept. Gardner rejects "the distinction between talent and intelligence; in my view, what we call 'intelligence' in the vernacular is simply a certain set of 'talents' in the linguistic and/or logical-mathematical spheres." Gardner has now identified eight intelligences and is looking for more (see Fig. 6.2). He writes that,

> . . . as a species, human beings have evolved over the millennia to carry out at least these seven forms of thinking. . . . Although all humans exhibit the range of intelligences, individuals differ—presumably for both hereditary and environmental reasons—in their current profile of intelligences. Moreover, there is no necessary correlation between any two intelligences, and they may indeed entail quite distinct forms of perception, memory, and other psychological processes (Gardner & Hatch, 1989, p. 5).

Gardner has cautioned that "MI theory is in no way an educational prescription," and that "the theory does not incorporate a 'position' on tracking, gifted education, interdisciplinary curricula, the layout of the school day, the length of the school year, or many other 'hot button' educational issues" (1995, p. 206). Gardner believes that many of the current uses of the theory are misdirected, and states simply that the theory implies that we need to broaden our definition of intelligence to include those other areas of mental abilities, to cultivate them in children, to approach learning in a variety of ways, and to personalize education. One change flowing at least in part from Gardner's work is the broadening of means of assessing learning. He thinks this trend will continue and that it will bring about corresponding changes in the creation of environments more conducive to alternative and fair assessment practices. Gardner (1993) further mused that,

Figure 6.2. Howard Gardner's Multiple Intelligences

1. **Linguistic intelligence** which involves sensitivity to the meaning of words, their order and syntax, the sounds, rhythms, and inflections of language, and the uses of languages.
2. **Musical intelligence** which consists of sensitivities to rhythm, pitch, and timbre. It also has an emotional component. Gardner relates musicians' descriptions of their abilities that emphasize an individual's natural feel for music and not the reasoning or linguistic components of musical ability.
3. **Logical-mathematical intelligence** that emerges from interaction with objects. By a sequence of stages the person is more able to perform actions on objects, understand the relations among actions, make statements about actions, and eventually see the relations among those statements.
4. **Spatial intelligence**, which is the capacity to perceive the physical world, accurately, to perform transformations and modifications on these perceptions, and to produce or recreate forms.
5. **Bodily-kinesthetic intelligence** which involves a person's ability to use the body in highly specific and skilled ways, both for expressive (the dancer) and goal-directed (the athlete) purposes.

Personal intelligence which takes two forms:

6. **Intrapersonal intelligence** is the ability to access one's own feelings and to label, discriminate, and symbolically represent one's range of emotions in order to understand behavior.
7. **Interpersonal intelligence** involves the ability to notice and make distinctions about others' moods, temperaments, motivations, and intentions.
8. **Naturalist intelligence** is the ability to draw on features of the natural world to solve problems (the chef, gardner, florist).

I hope that in the next twenty years, a number of efforts will be made to craft an education that takes
multiple intelligences seriously. . . .Perhaps, if careful
studies are done, we will even know *why* some educational approaches work and why some do not. (p. 250)

RESEARCH ON MULTIPLE INTELLIGENCES: A BRIDGE TOO FAR?

At Level I Gardner claims that "MI theory is based wholly on
empirical evidence and can be revised on the basis of new empirical findings" (1995, p. 203). *Frames of Mind* includes a survey
of a wide range of literature and psychological research on intelligence that serves as the basis for MI theory. It is actually quite
extensive, and work has been done to develop assessment instruments in an attempt to measure the intelligences (see
Gardner & Hatch, 1989). Considerable work has been done
through Harvard Project Zero to measure the intelligences and to
implement some ideas in school settings. But to this point, from a
technical measurement viewpoint, the results have been mixed at
best.

As Gardner himself has said, educators have interpreted this
theory in literally hundreds of ways. For example, at one school
it was concluded that

We have found that multiple intelligences is more than
a theory of intelligence; it is, for us, a philosophy
about education with implications for how kids learn,
how teachers should teach, and how schools should
operate. . . .For example, teachers can help a child
whose strength is bodily-kinesthetic use that talent to
learn multiplication facts or spelling words; capitalize
on children's interpersonal intelligences by using the
study of personalities as a pathway to the study of
history; or use graphs and tables to record the similarities and differences among Native American tribes
to help students with strong logical-mathematical intelligence. (Hoerr, 1994, p. 30)

Other far reaches include having kids singing (musical intelligence) the multiplication facts or dancing to the four basic food groups. Unquestionably, there is little hard evidence that these uses of the theory actually lead students to learn more. Whether Gardner has liberated or highjacked a term that has been used with consistent meaning for 100 years is an open question.

The questions for researchers are whether school-based implementations of this theory lead to higher academic achievement (dependent variable) or to increases in the eight intelligences (independent variable). The jury is out on academic achievement, but the possibilities for enhancing forms of intelligence seem promising.

ROBERT STERNBERG AND THE TRIARCHIC THEORY OF INTELLIGENCE

While Gardner is representative of psychologists who have focused on the *content* of human intelligence, Robert Sternberg of Yale University has emerged as a leader among those interested in intelligence as a *process*. Sternberg is widely known as a leading *information processing* (IP) theorist. He has synthesized his research-based construct into a theory of intelligence that quantifies IP abilities. By Sternberg's definition, to think productively is to be able to process information effectively. His theory identifies a three-part (triarchic) description of mental abilities: contextual intelligence, experiential intelligence, and componential intelligence. He has also identified six factors basic to successful information processing (see Fig. 6.3).

Sternberg's pioneering efforts in information processing and a resultant theory of intelligence (1990a) emphasize thinking processes common to everyone. New perceptions of what intelligence, and therefore thinking skills, means have begun to emerge from his work. Sternberg has developed what he calls a "triarchic theory of intelligence," one that breaks down cognitive behavior into thinking, adapting, and problem solving. Thinking, which he calls "componential intelligence," includes planning, performance, and knowledge acquisition.

FIGURE 6.3. ROBERT STERNBERG'S SIX FACTORS

---

1. **Spatial ability**, or the ability to visualize a problem spatially, skills one would associate with geometry, geography, architecture, mechanical drawing, art, map making and interpreting, and so on.
2. **Perceptual speed**, or the ability to grasp a new visual field quickly, something that brings to mind the playing of Nintendo video games, and so on.
3. **Inductive reasoning**, or the ability to reach conclusions and generalize from evidence or other information.
4. **Verbal comprehension ability**, or the ability to comprehend text either quickly or at deeper levels.
5. **Memory**, or the ability to store and retrieve information, ideas, etc.
6. **Number ability**, or the ability to manipulate numerical ideas and to learn algorithms.

Adapting, which he calls "contextual intelligence," is composed of selecting, reshaping, and maximizing ideas. And problem solving, which he calls, "experiential intelligence," involves insight, automaticity, creativity, and efficiency.

It should be noted that Sternberg is doubtful that cognitive theories such as his own can necessarily improve teaching. A theory of intelligence is one thing; implementing such a theory in a classroom is quite another. He also addresses the idea of whether thinking skills can be applied generically or whether they are domain-specific, a matter of great importance to those who teach subjects in school settings. He suggests that people, rather than the skills themselves, are the issue. He suggests that some pupils (as well as teachers) are domain specific while others are domain general. Yet, he does maintain that we can "achieve meaningful increases in intellectual abilities" (1996, p. 51).

In seeming contradiction to his statement of skepticism about school-based applications, Sternberg, focusing specifically on the aspects of intelligence related to creativity, has identified a number of strategies "that teachers and administrators may use to make students, staff—and themselves—more creative" (1995/1996, p. 81). Among those "strategies" e creative" (1995/1996, p. 81). Among those "strategies" are encouraging the questioning of assumptions, modeling creativity, allowing mistakes, encouraging risk taking, and letting students define problems.

RESEARCH ON THE TRIARCHIC MODEL

The Level I research base carried out by Sternberg and his colleagues in the development of the triarchic theory is substantial. He built his work on the already extensive development of theories of information processing. The logical next step appears to be the development of instruments or measuring devices of some kind designed specifically to test intelligence as a process, as he suggests it is. His work has been put into practice on a limited scale through the Yale Practical Intelligence for School Curriculum, and an evaluation study that shows these skills can be taught (Sternberg, Okagaki, & Jackson, 1990). The relative newness of Sternberg's theory means that it has not been put into practice to the extent that the other two models have been. Time will tell whether the theory remains credible, and, in the likely event that it will, to what extent it can be used successfully in school settings.

CONCLUSION

The pioneering works of Feuerstein, Gardner, and Sternberg suggest that intelligence can be taught and enhanced. This idea runs counter to traditional assumptions that intelligence is something you are endowed with only. There is much evidence to suggest that intelligence can be raised, including the well-known illustration of recent generational gains in intelligence test scores by Japanese school children. That they and other Asian countries have witnessed a considerable rise in the average height of the population in the space of a generation is also well documented. The thinking that better diet, health care, and so forth, have brought this about in a relatively short time span encourages those who advocate intervention strategies.

The work we cite in this chapter is both more foundational and theoretical than the examples we cite in the closely related chapter which follows. In a sense, this chapter serves as potential Level I research for the teaching of thinking skills, our next topic, in school settings. Whether developers take full and thoughtful advantage of the profound ideas of Feuerstein, Gardner, and Sternberg is yet another matter.

REFERENCES

Ben-Hur, M. (Ed.) (1994). *On Feuerstein's instrumental enrichment: a collection.*

Bruner, J. (1996). *The culture of education.* Cambridge, MA: Harvard University Press.

Feuerstein, R. (1979). *The dynamic assessment of retarded performers: the learning potential assessment device, theory, instruments, and techniques.* Baltimore: University Park Press.

Feuerstein, R., and Hoffman, M.B. (1985). The importance of mediated learning for the child. *Human Intelligence International Newsletter, 6*(2), 1–2.

Feuerstein, R., and Jensen, M.R. (1980, May). Instrumental enrichment: theoretical basis, goals, and instruments. *The Educational Forum,* 401–423.

Feuerstein, R., Rand, Y. Hoffman, M.B., and Miller, R. (1980). *Instrumental enrichment: an intervention program for cognitive modifiability.* Baltimore: University Park Press.

Gardner, H. (1983). *Frames of mind.* New York: Basic Books.

Gardner, H. (1993). *Multiple intelligences: theory in practice.* New York: Basic Books.

Gardner, H. (1995). Reflections on multiple intelligences: myths and messages. *Phi Delta Kappan, 77*(3), 206–209.

Gardner, H., and Hatch, T. (1989). Multiple intelligences go to school: educational implications of the theory of multiple intelligences. *Educational Researcher, 18*(8), 4–9.

Goleman, D. (1995). *Emotional intelligence.* New York: Bantam.

Hernstein, R.J., and Murray, C. (1995). *The bell curve: intelligence and class structure in American life.* New York: Free Press.

Hoerr, T.R. (1994). How the New City School applies the multiple intelligences. *Educational Leadership, 52*(3), 29–33.

Hoon, S.S. (1990). Feuerstein's instrumental enrichment: an exploratory study for activating intellectual potential in slow learners. ERIC Document Reproduction Service No. ED329813.

Kaniel, S., and Reichenberg, R. (1992). Instrumental enrichment—effects of generalization and durability with talented adolescents. *Gifted Education International, 8*(3), 128–135.

Link, F. (1991). *Instrumental enrichment*. In Costa, A.L. (Ed.) (1991). *Developing minds: programs for teaching thinking*. Alexandria, VA: Association for Supervision and Curriculum Development, 9–11.

Mulcahy, R. (1993). *Cognitive education project. Summary project.* ERIC Document Reproduction Service No. ED367682.

Offenberg, R.M. (1992). *A study of the effects of instrumental enrichment on middle-grade, minority students*. Report No. 9225. ERIC Document Reproduction Service No. ED361462.

Savell, J.M., Twohig, P.T., and Rachford, D.L. (1986). Empirical status of Feuerstein's "Instrumental Enrichment" (FIE) technique as a method of teaching thinking skills. *Review of Educational Research, 56*(4), 381–409.

Singham, M. (1995). Race and intelligence: what are the issues. *Phi Delta Kappan, 77*(4), 271–278.

Spearman, C. (1927). *The abilities of man: their nature and measurement*. New York: Macmillan.

Sternberg, R. (1990a). Practical intelligence for success in school. *Educational Leadership, 48*(1), 35–39.

Sternberg, R. (1990b). *Metaphors of mind: conceptions of the nature of intelligence*. New York: Cambridge University Press.

Sternberg, R. (1995/1996) Investing in creativity: many happy returns. *Educational Leadership 53*(4), 80–84.

Sternberg, R. (1996). The school bell and the bell curve: why they don't mix. *NASSP Bulletin, 80*(577), 46–56.

Sternberg, R.J., and Bhana, K. (1986). Synthesis of research on the effectiveness of intellectual skills programs: snake-oil remedy or miracle cures? *Educational Leadership, 44*(2), 60–67.

Sternberg, R.J., Okagaki, L., and Jackson, A.S. (1990). Practical intelligence for success in school. *Educational Leadership, 48*(1), 35–39.

Thurstone, L.L. (1938). Primary mental abilities. *Psychometric Monographs, No. 1.*

Yekovich, F.R. (1994). *ERIC/AE Digest. Current issues in research on intelligence.* Washington, DC: Office of Educational Research and Improvement.

7

THINKING SKILLS PROGRAMS

We have a lot of evidence that teaching content alone, and hoping it will cause students to learn to think, doesn't work. The teaching of content alone is not enough.

Arthur Costa

There is a danger that the teaching of "thinking skills"—if it survives to become part of mainstream educational practice—may one day become to thinking what diagramming sentences and memorizing rules of grammar too often have become to writing.

John Baer

Most teachers do not know what intellectual standards are nor why they are essential to quality thinking.

Linda Elder & Richard Paul

Almost all national, state, district, and school lists of goals include something from the grab bag called thinking skills. Thousands of people have attended the international conferences on critical thinking held annually at Sonoma State University in California and sponsored by the Foundation for Critical Thinking. In addition, the Association for Supervision and Curriculum Development (ASCD) has published a guide describing 27 commercial programs designed for teaching thinking–problem solving–critical thinking skills (Costa, 1991). A number of these programs claim widespread usage and success. The developers of the *Higher Order Thinking Skills (HOTS)* program, for example, claim that it has been used by 2,000 schools in 49 states (Pogrow, 1995).

Thinking skills is a general term that tends to incorporate problem solving, critical thinking, "higher order" thinking, divergent thinking, and creative thinking, and, as we mentioned in the previous chapter, thinking skills are also tied into various views on intelligence. Even for a profession that often seems to have little respect for the meaning of words, the terminology is rather loose. The various goals lists one finds in the literature tend to be skills-focused, typically employing such terms as critical thinking skills, higher order thinking skills, problem solving skills, strategic reasoning skills, productive thinking skills, and so on, all used more or less interchangeably. The common ground seems to encompass the kinds of school experiences that purport to transcend memory work, textbook usage, drill and practice, and patterned, repetitive assignments.

The implication of all this is that these "skills" are located at a higher place on some taxonomic register and, therefore, ought not to be confused with lower level thinking skills such as remembering or explaining—skills for which, if one can believe the rhetoric, there will be less and less demand as we enter the 21st century. Before we look at programs and their effectiveness, let us give you two pieces of advice: (1) be wary of programs that promise to deliver decontextualized "skills" of any kind, and (2) be wary of programs that purport to get students ready for an unknown and infinitely complex future.

THOUGHTS ABOUT THINKING

One would be hard-pressed to find someone who thinks that thinking skills are unimportant. This may well be even more the case nowadays as it becomes increasingly obvious to everyone that the knowledge explosion makes it ever more difficult to "master" content. There are, however, several problems that seem to be endemic to the entire area labeled "thinking skills."

For starters, there is little agreement about what thinking skills are. Virtually every program has a list of skills to be developed, but the concepts are quite abstract in many cases with a range of definitions applied to any given thinking skill. For example, "classification" is often identified as an important thinking skill because it is so associated with scientific thought and expression. But what is meant by the term "classification"? Putting things in groups? Organizing whole taxonomies? Recognizing that different attributes lead one to assign something to a particular category? This is very vexing because "classification" is a rather concrete skill compared to, say, "evaluation."

Another problem is that of measuring thinking skills. It is a rather difficult challenge compared to measuring certain physical skills, such as one's ability to run 100 meters in so many seconds. We know of no outstanding thinking skills test, particularly one with a performance base, to which we could refer you. Selected portions of standard IQ tests are about as good as anything we have. And the several tests specifically designed to measure thinking skills that are available have no agreed-on validity if for no other reason than they define the various constructs differentially.

A third issue is whether thinking skills can be taught successfully to students independent of content. This remains a matter of some debate. Most experts have concluded that they probably cannot. So, the issue of transfer is problematic. Can someone who has been taught how to analyze (a typical skill) use "analysis" as a generic skill applicable to chemistry, literature, geography, personal problems, and so forth? It doesn't seem likely, although there may be something to it. And how does one teach others to analyze in a generic sense? Analysis, after all, can be based on evidence, experience, intuition, or on other factors Here, in our opinion, is the essence of the argument: the better one's knowledge is of something, the better one's position is to do meaningful analysis. Having knowledge, even in considerable store, does not guarantee one's ability to analyze; an absence of knowledge, however, of a given field precludes any ability to perform meaningful analysis in that field.

Apparently, not everyone agrees. Edward de Bono (1991) suggested that thinking can be directly taught as a skill or set of skills. His thinking skills program, called CoRT, an acronym for Cognitive Research Trust, emphasizes content-free thinking strategies. An example is the "Plus, Minus, Interesting" (PMI) strategy. Students are given a hypothetical situation and are asked to list as many "pluses," "minuses," or "interestings" as they can about the problem. One of the situations is the question, "What if all cars were painted yellow?" According to de Bono, activities like these enable students to use effective thinking strategies that have transfer value to unknown future situations. This attractive assertion, however, has little empirical support.

Another issue is that of a huge assumption which may, in fact, not be warranted. That assumption is that teachers themselves possess these various thinking skills. If they do not, how could they possibly teach them? In his book, *A Place Called School*, curriculum researcher John Goodlad writes, "The emphasis on facts and recall of facts in quizzes demonstrates not just the difficulty of teaching and testing for more fundamental understanding but the probability, supported by our data, that most teachers simply do not know how to teach for higher levels of thinking. . . " (Goodlad, 1984, p. 237). The extent to which teachers possess these abilities, or could themselves be taught to model or teach them, is largely unknown. This could well be the stuff of a fruitful research agenda.

Lastly, we know very little about how people think. We know much more about the products of people's thoughts than we know about how they arrive at those products. Vast philosophical and scientific arguments are waged over the brain versus mind issue, just to name one example. There is some considerable debate about whether thinking is a conscious or an unconscious process (Baer, 1988). So, if we are not sure how people think, how can we proceed with the business of teaching them how to think in such a way that is compatible with given individuals' styles or approaches to situations that demand thinking? Perhaps *apropos* of that, the current model of practice that one can readily deduce from extensive classroom observation is that thinking skill is something students already possess in varying degrees, and like "citizenship," it is something you bring to your work, not something that is directly taught by teachers.

All of this notwithstanding, there seems to be no shortage of would-be innovators willing to jump into the breach. Programs abound, and the thinking skills movement is going full-force across the country.

A useful perspective for considering these matters is offered by Brandt (1984, 1988). He describes teaching **for** thinking as the engagement of content and learning activities and the development of language and conceptual abilities through teacher questioning, student-to-student interaction, group discussions, and so on. Brandt identifies teaching **about** thinking as encouraging students to be aware of their thinking, reflecting on it, and learning to control it, what is often referred to as metacognition. Students are asked to monitor their own thinking and to make deliberate use of various thinking frames, perhaps as found in such programs as Talents Unlimited, CoRT, and Tactics (see "References"). And Brandt suggests that teaching **of** thinking represents the attempt to teach particular mental skills such as summarizing, paraphrasing, and decision making. This last concern is no doubt the weakest area, and the one we know least about.

The thinking skills movement is manifest in two forms: (1) the import and adoption of specific curricula or programs (see Fig. 7.1 for a sample listing), and (2) the development and implementation of a matrix of thinking skills throughout the curriculum by a school district or perhaps by a given school. The former often involves the implementation of one or more of the more popular commercial programs. The latter represents an "infusion" model where teachers agree to introduce and revisit thinking skills across a variety of subject areas. In either case, the efforts are intended to focus on the development in learners of thought processes in which they are perceived to be lacking or in need of greater proficiency. Invariably, one finds reference to such "skills" as analysis, synthesis, evaluation, decision making, creativity, information processing, problem solving, organization, communication, and reasoning.

FIGURE 7.1. SAMPLE THINKING SKILLS PROGRAMS FOR SCHOOLS

Instrumental Enrichment
Cognitive Research Trust (CoRT)
Talents Unlimited
Philosophy for Children
Higher Order Thinking Skills (HOTS)
Project Impact
Tactics for Thinking
Structure of the Intellect (SOI)
Odyssey
Strategic Reasoning
Thinking to Write

Whether these are in fact skills in the same sense as those needed by an expert carpenter or golfer is not always clear. The more tangible an operation (for example, skillfully using bow and arrow, or needle and thread), the more readily we can agree that it is a skill, or set of skills, and something that can be taught as well. But even in such concrete situations, a truly skilled person is someone who can coordinate, articulate, and make seamless a number of subskills which come together into a whole which, to quote the oft-cited Gestalt expression, is greater than the sum of its parts. Figure 7.2 provides an example of a typical set of thinking skills and accompanying strategies.

Most thinking skills programs are sufficiently complex to require a considerable amount of faculty inservice training if they are to succeed. Teachers are acquainted through training sessions with detailed descriptions of the skills to be taught, sample lesson plans, activities, ways to evaluate, and more. Usually, emphasis is placed upon strategies whereby teachers can incorporate thinking skills into different subject areas and apply them to various age levels. Some of the programs are designed to stand alone as curriculums in and of themselves. These are often used in so-called gifted and talented classes.

FIGURE 7.2. A TAXONOMY OF THINKING SKILLS

I. Thinking Strategies

Problem Solving

1. Recognize a problem
2. Represent the problem
3. Devise/choose solution plan
4. Execute the plan
5. Evaluate the solution

Decision Making

1. Define the goal
2. Identify alternatives
3. Analyze alternatives
4. Rank alternatives
5. Judge highest-ranked alternatives
6. Choose "best" alternative

Conceptualizing

1. Identify examples
2. Identify common attributes
3. Classify attributes
4. Interrelate categories of attributes
5. Identify additional examples/nonexamples
6. Modify concept attributes/structure

II. Critical Thinking Skills

1. Distinguishing between verifiable facts and value claims
2. Distinguishing relevant from irrelevant information, claims or reasons
3. Determining the factual accuracy of a statement
4. Determining the credibility of a source
5. Identifying ambiguous claims or arguments
6. Identifying unstated assumptions
7. Detecting bias
8. Identifying logical fallacies
9. Recognizing logical inconsistencies in a line of reasoning
10. Determining the strength of an argument or a claim

Figure 7.2 continues on the next page

III. Information-Processing Skills
  1. Recall
  2. Translation
  3. Interpretation
  4. Extrapolation
  5. Application
  6. Analysis (compare, contrast, classify, seriate, etc.)
  7. Synthesis
  8. Evaluation
  9. Reasoning (inferencing): inductive, deductive, analogical

Source: Adapted from Beyer, B.K. (1988a). Developing a scope and sequence for thinking skills instruction. *Educational Leadership*, 45(7), 27.

PROGRAM IMPLEMENTATION

To give you a clearer picture of what these programs are like, we selected one commercial example and one locally developed example. They are reasonably representative of the range of programs available.

TALENTS UNLIMITED

Talents Unlimited was developed in the early 1970s and has been adopted by more than 1500 school districts in 49 states. It is or has been in use in seven different countries. With more than 80 trainers nationwide, Talents Unlimited claims to be one of the most widely disseminated thinking skills programs in the country. It is currently disseminated through the U.S. Government's National Diffusion Network.

Talents Unlimited is based on these assumptions:

" 1. People have talents (strengths or preferences) for different thinking processes.

2. Training in the use of these thinking processes can enhance one's potential in various areas of talent and at the same time foster positive feelings about oneself [see Chapter 4, "Self-Esteem Programs"].

3. Training in particular thinking processes can be integrated with knowledge or content in any subject area and can enhance academic achievement.

4. The various thinking processes are also linked to success in the world of work." (Schlichter et al., 1988, p. 36)

Instruction is focused on 19 thinking skills to be applied to academic content in five "talent" areas. A detailed staff development program is required prior to and concurrent with implementation. The staff development inservice emphasizes understanding of the thinking skills and strategies to help the teacher integrate the 19 key skills into the academic curriculum. In addition, the inservice acquaints teachers with lesson materials. Figure 7.3 illustrates the talent areas and corresponding sample teaching strategies.

WRITING AS A THINKING AND LEARNING TOOL

At a local, noncommercial level, the faculty at Bernards High School, Bernardsville, New Jersey, initiated a staff development program called Writing as a Thinking and Learning Tool (Fig. 7.4). "With no additional expenditure for materials and no burden of added content for teachers, we designed this program to tackle head-on the task of improving students' critical and creative thinking through writing" (Bland & Koppel, 1988, p. 58).

Training for teachers focused on techniques for creating a "thinking environment" in the classroom, the process approach to writing, and strategies for implementing each of the three program components in all subject areas. According to their own evaluation, the project produced the following results:

+ Improved student problem solving and clarity of thinking.

+ Increased and immediate feedback to students about their thinking.

+ Increased participation in sharing ideas and opinions by students.

FIGURE 7.3. TALENTS UNLIMITED'S SIX TALENT AREAS AND SAMPLE ACTIVITIES

Talent Area	Sample Activity
1. **Productive Thinking**—to generate many, varied and unusual ideas and then to add onto those ideas to improve them.	Students working in a math unit on surveying and graphing are asked to think of a variety of unusual topics for a survey they will conduct and graph.
2. **Communication**—to convey needs, feelings, and ideas effectively to others. The related skills of communication are description, comparison, empathy, nonverbal communication, and the networking of ideas.	In an attempt to describe the emotions of different groups of colonists, 5th graders studying the American Revolution role-play both Loyalists and Rebels as they hear a reading of the Declaration of Independence.
3. **Forecasting**—to look into the future to predict things that might happen or looking into the past to consider what might have happened. Forecasting involves predicting both cause and effect relationships.	Students who are conducting a parent poll on their school's dress code are encouraged to generate predictions about the possible causes for low returns on the survey.
4. **Decision Making**—to outline, weight, make final judgments, and defend a decision on the many alternatives to a problem.	Students who are preparing to order materials through the Scholastic Books campaign make final selections by considering such criteria as cost, interest, and reading level.
5. **Planning**—to design a means for implementing an idea by describing what is to be done, identifying the resources needed, outlining a sequence of steps to take, and pinpointing possible problems.	Students who are studying the unusual characteristics of slime mold are asked to design experiments to answer questions they have generated about the behavior of the mold.

6. **Academic**—To develop a base of knowledge and/or skill about a topic or issue through acquisition of information and concepts.

Students read from a variety of resources to gain information about the Impressionist period and then share the information in a discussion of a painting by Monet.

Source: Adapted from Hobbs, D.E., and Schlichter, C.L. (1991). Talents Unlimited. In Costa, A.L. (Ed.) (1991). Developing minds: programs for teaching thinking. Alexandria, VA: Association for Supervision and Curriculum Development, pp. 73–78.

FIGURE 7.4. BERNARDS HIGH SCHOOL'S DO-IT-YOURSELF CRITICAL THINKING PROGRAM

Purposes:

1. To train any interested teacher of any subject area, grades 7–12, in strategies to improve thinking through the use of writing;

2. To assist the trained teachers in implementing and refining the strategies through peer coaching and inservice workshops;

3. To conduct formal and informal evaluation activities to determine the effect of these strategies on the quality of student thinking, both oral and written.

Program Components:

1. Producing ideas—brainstorming, classifying, prioritizing, inferring, predicting and evaluating. Sample teaching strategies—free association, cubing, mind maps, and clustering.

2. Expressing ideas—prioritize, classify, elaborate, and connect ideas. Sample teaching strategies—think writing, practice essays, serial writing, oral composing, group essays, conferring and questioning.

3. Refining expression—the development of a finished product. Sample teaching strategies—checklists, peer conferences, oral reading.

Source: Bland, C., and Koppel, I. (1988). Writing as a thinking tool. *Educational Leadership*, 45(7), 58–60.

    ◆   Growing student ability to transfer thinking
skills from one subject to another.

Most of us would be delighted with such outcomes. We are,
however, unsure of exactly how the people at Bernards were
able to document their findings. Just imagine, for starters, the
list of variables at stake. How was thinking ability measured?
Were comparison groups used? To what extent was this already happening as a result of traditional teaching or pupil
maturation? How was evidence of student ability to transfer
thinking skills from subject to subject documented? These nag-
ging questions are seldom addressed with sufficient rigor. They
get lost in the enthusiasm that accompanies innovation. Nevertheless, we commend them for an attempt at program
evaluation, something that rarely happens in any systematic
way.

THE RESEARCH BASE FOR THINKING SKILLS PROGRAMS

CAN WE GET THERE FROM HERE?

Certain problems seem to be inherent in the research on
thinking skills. Any evaluation of the research base must be
done with the following things in mind:

    ◆   It is difficult to conduct research in an area for
which there exists no generally agreed-on set of
definitions of terms. Mathematics achievement,
by way of contrast, can be operationally defined
by a set of constructs, although even this isn't
easy to reach total agreement on. Mathematics is
largely defined by the various textbooks in use,
by the goal structure of the National Council of
Teachers of Mathematics (NCTM), and by the
various standardized tests that are available.
One can make no such parallel claims about
thinking skills. Remember the Supreme Court
justice who said that while he couldn't define
pornography, he knew it when he saw it? Let us

suppose we could say we know good thinking when we see it. It would be at least a place to start, but even if we could say that, it's a pretty shaky foundation on which to build.

♦ We are not particularly adept at measuring thinking skills. A few such tests exist, for example, the Cornell Critical Thinking Test. Some IQ and abilities tests contain scales that may be somewhat appropriate to this area, but the "skills" are diverse (see Fig. 7.2) and difficult to measure and evaluate. We may be years away from valid, reliable, agreed-on instruments of assessment.

♦ Given the first two problems, it follows that the means to achieve curriculum alignment seem presently insurmountable. What we are left with, are measurement instruments specific to a given curriculum or local program. These instruments, while often interesting, are plagued by problems of reliability, validity, and subjectivity.

♦ Thinking skills no doubt develop over a long period of time, and they routinely defy attempts to trace their realization to a specific unit or curriculum experience. In addition, it has been suggested by more than one observer that school environments in general may not be particularly supportive of the very thinking skills that advocates tend to promote. And as Arthur Costa has noted, "the change in student behavior is bound to be diverse and elusive" (Brandt, 1988, p. 11).

♦ The idea that thinking skills are content-specific and cannot be taught generically must be seriously entertained until such time as it is discredited. We don't think that idea will be discredited. And if this is so, how does one

construct content-free tests to measure thinking
skills?

Mostly, we are left with observations, impressions, and anecdotal records to document increases in student thinking
skills. Any teacher who has ever had to fill out that part of a
report card knows what shaky grounds we are on when we
give a "+" to Mary for her ability to "solve problems independently." And how many teachers would take either the
credit or the blame for the pluses and minuses we marked in
the category for the 30 kids in that class?

BASIC RESEARCH ON THINKING

At Level I, one finds a surprisingly small amount of information claimed by thinking skills advocates about basic or
pure research in this area. However, it occurs to us that the basic research can be traced mainly to two areas: brain research
and cognitive science. It is certainly reasonable to assume that
the work of such researchers as Gardner, Feuerstein, and
Sternberg, which we cited in the Chapter 6, forms much of the
theoretical basis of some, but not all, thinking skills programs.

No doubt we are on the threshold of important knowledge
of human brain function. The research referred to in Chapter 5
on brain-based learning is the best we can do for now to give
you any insights into this area. Much is at stake here including
heredity, nutrition, and experience.

The work in cognitive science includes such stage theories
as those advanced by Piaget (1970) and Kohlberg (1987), research in information processing such as that done by Robert
Sternberg (1990), and research in constructivist thought such as
that conducted by Driver (1983). The work of Lev Vygotsky
(1987) in the area of the codevelopment of language and
thought is extremely important A book well worth reading to
acquaint you with these areas is *Cognitive Development Today* by
Peter Sutherland (1992).

Of course, we would be remiss if we were to neglect to
mention the work of Benjamin Bloom, whose *Taxonomy of Educational Objectives for the Cognitive Domain* (1956) has influenced

the development of more than one lesson plan or district guide over the years. Bloom suggested that a hierarchy of thought exists. At the lower cognitive register are found, in ascending order, knowledge, comprehension, and application; at the higher cognitive register are found, in ascending order, analysis, synthesis, and evaluation. These six levels of cognition have been accepted by millions as gospel, and have been used as a template for teacher questions, lesson plan objectives, and anything else related to student thinking. Actually, Bloom's *Taxonomy* is an imaginative theoretical construct with little empirical foundation. Is it really true, for example, that synthesis requires greater intellectual endeavor than does comprehension? It is probably the case that to synthesize something, comprehension is required, just as it may well be the case that to comprehend something, synthesis of some kind is required. And is a simple evaluation a "higher" intellectual function than a penetrating analysis? The proof simply isn't there. Bloom's overly simplistic use of the very terms that are the essence of his taxonomy is disquieting. To equate "knowledge," for example, with lower registers of cognition when it ought to be abundantly clear that knowledge of something can be profound as well as trivial is to visit semantic confusion on us.

IS THERE ANY EVIDENCE? LEVELS II AND III RESEARCH

Given the ambiguities of research at Level I, it is predictable that the research at Level II is rather weak. We found a number of studies that investigated the development of higher order thinking skills (a construct which has not really been established) as educational outcomes, but they are scattered throughout the literature on mastery learning, cooperative learning, outcome-based education, and peer coaching, among other topics, and are not research studies on the kinds of programs we describe in this chapter. For example, Hembree (1992) examined problem-solving attainment primarily in mathematics instruction and concluded that heuristics training provided the largest gains in problem-solving performance, but with a number of limitations. This tells us, however, little about thinking skills programs per se, either commercially or teacher-developed.

We have found a number of claims in popular education journals such as *Educational Leadership*, that describe the benefits of these programs, but we have not found even a modest number of published empirical studies to support most of the supposed benefits. For certain advocates of thinking skills programs (as with many other innovations mentioned in this book) this lack of research seems to be no obstacle. Stanley Pogrow (1995) seems to have discovered a new type of research, called "pattern sense making," that overrides traditional cause-and-effect studies. For schools using his Higher Order Thinking Skills (HOTS) program he states: "It seemed natural to form a network to exchange information and ideas. The network makes possible a more realistic type of research than is possible in the highly controlled (contrived) settings of limited scope and limited duration in which most educational research takes places." Such an arrangement allows for information flow and spontaneous feedback. This research, Pogrow writes,

> . . . has generated fundamental new knowledge about the nature of the learning needs of educationally disadvantaged students. In addition, this approach to research has generated very different conclusions from those of conventional research—conclusions that I believe are more valid and valuable for making national and school policy than those generated from either the prevalent quantitative or qualitative research techniques. (p. 20)

Thus Pogrow furnishes us with an original theoretical paradigm, he develops a specific program, and he conducts the research himself. Not only are the results efficacious, by his own admission, but his theoretical work has made possible conclusions that are "more valid and valuable" than those derived using other techniques.

The difficulties and ambiguities of thinking skills assessment have not gone unnoticed by those who have reviewed the research. Norris' (1985) review focused more on the general nature of critical thinking than on any cause-and-effect relationships. It is, however, a useful review for anyone contemplating curriculum changes in this area. He concluded that we really don't know much about critical thinking and quite sensibly offered only a few tentative conclusions, among them that critical thinking is not a generic tool and that it is sensitive to context.

Both the Norris review and a review by Sternberg and Bhana (1986) highlighted the problems associated with the research on thinking skills, and those problems remain over a decade later. Sternberg and Bhana's review sought to determine whether thinking skills programs are "snake-oil remedies or miracle cures." They evaluated five programs that had been cited in the annals of program evaluation and found most of the research to be very weak in design and possibly biased. Even setting aside these serious problems, they found the results to be inconclusive and none of the evaluations useful for determining which portions of the programs worked and which did not. They concluded, "Some thinking skills training programs are probably not a whole lot better than snake oil, but the good ones, although not miracle cures, may improve thinking skills" (p. 67).

Cotton (1992) is more sanguine about the research base at Level II and Level III. She examined 33 "key documents, [of which] 22 are research studies or evaluations." The other 11 were reviews or syntheses of research. In these studies, thinking skills were defined in a wide variety of ways, including analysis, synthesis, evaluation, making predictions, making inferences, metacognitive activities and a host of other things. She reached these conclusions (pp. 4–6):

+ Thinking skills instruction enhances academic achievement.

+ Research supports instruction in many specific skills and techniques, including study skills, creative and critical thinking skills, metacognition, and inquiry training.

- ◆ Various instructional approaches enhance thinking skills.

- ◆ Computer-assisted instruction helps to develop thinking skills.

- ◆ Research supports the use of several specific thinking skills programs, including a number of those listed in Figure 7.1.

- ◆ Training teachers to teach thinking skills leads to student achievement gains.

In spite of Cotton's optimism, we are not comfortable with either the amount or quality of the research used to support such broad conclusions as these. Of course, we invite you to examine the studies that Cotton reviewed. But short of that, reread any one of the foregoing six conclusions. We think you can quickly imagine conditions that would make the claim subject to a number of qualifiers. The claims are somewhat reminiscent of the effective schools claims in that they may confuse cause and effect, are not weighted in helpful proportion, and raise the specter of untoward variables and rival hypotheses. The claims may point in basically the right direction, but the evidence is not sufficient at this point to meet our standards. We would prefer to think of them as promising hypotheses in need of further testing.

The professional literature, especially that chronicled in policy journals such as *Educational Leadership*, not to mention the many teacher magazines, is replete with success stories, but few penetrating analyses. The advocates and enthusiasts are certainly out there in profusion. Thinking skills has become one of the very lucrative inservice and materials areas, and at its worst it preys on the vulnerability of professionals of good will who so much would like to improve the quality of students' thinking. At its best it may well offer some help when strategies are integrated with good content in an atmosphere that is genuinely conducive to the engagement of reflective thought.

CONCLUSION

We make no claim that these programs fail to provide students with thinking skills. We have simply not found strong evidence that they do. The research in this area is muddled to say the least. We cannot, for example, even define or document the separate existence of thinking skills. Attempts to organize them into hierarchies may bear little resemblance to reality. Most of the evidence in favor of these programs is anecdotal. On the other hand, when one examines the activities and teaching strategies found in most of the programs, they seem to have some potential.

At this time, we believe that the decision to purchase and implement one of these programs and to invest teachers' time in inservice training cannot be reasonably based on the research evidence. Ironically, the pure research base is quite good and is improving almost daily, but the connections between pure research and the work of program builders are primitive. However, if in your professional judgment a particular thinking skills program looks good to you because of the interesting activities and strategies, that may be a logical basis on which to give it a closer look, in which case we hope you will just as carefully consider the content and ideas you are trying to teach as well as the environmental conditions in which you want learning to take place.

REFERENCES

Baer, J. (1988). Let's not handicap able thinkers. *Educational Leadership*, 45(7) 66–72.

Beyer, B.K. (1987). *Practical strategies for the teaching of thinking.* Boston: Allyn and Bacon.

Beyer, B.K. (1988a). Developing a scope and sequence for thinking skills instruction. *Educational Leadership, 45*(7), 26–30.

Beyer, B.K. (1988b). *Developing a thinking skills program.* Boston: Allyn and Bacon.

Bland, C., and Koppel, I. (1988). Writing as thinking tool. *Educational Leadership, 45*(7), 58–60.

Bloom, B. (Ed.) (1956). *Taxonomy of educational objectives.* New York: Longman.

Brandt, R. (1984). Teaching of thinking, for thinking about thinking. *Educational Leadership, 42,* 3.

Brandt, R. (1988). On teaching thinking: a conversation with Art Costa. *Educational Leadership, 45*(7), 10–13.

Costa, A.L. (Ed.) (1985). *Developing minds: a resource book for teaching thinking.* Alexandria, VA: Association for Supervision and Curriculum Development.

Costa, A.L. (Ed.) (1991). *Developing minds: programs for teaching thinking.* Alexandria, VA: Association for Supervision and Curriculum Development.

Cotton, K. (1992). *Teaching thinking skills.* School Improvement Research Series, Close-up #11. Portland, OR: Northwest Regional Educational Laboratory.

de Bono, E. (1983). The direct teaching of thinking as a skill. *Phi Delta Kappan, 64*(10), 703–708.

de Bono, E. (1991). The CoRT Thinking Program. In Costa, A.L. (Ed.) (1991). *Developing minds: programs for teaching thinking.* Alexandria, VA: Association for Supervision and Curriculum Development, pp. 27–32.

Driver, R. (1983). *Pupil as scientist?* London: Open University Press, Milton Keynes.

Elder, L., and Paul, R. (1995). Critical thinking: why teach students intellectual standards, I & II. *Journal of Developmental Education, 18*(3), 36–37; *19*(1), 34–35.

Gardner, H. (1983). *Frames of mind.* New York: Basic Books.

Goodlad, J. (1984). *A place called school.* New York: McGraw-Hill.

Hembree, R. (1992). Experiments and relational studies in problem-solving: a meta-analysis. *Journal for Research in Mathematics Education, 23*(3), 242–273.

Hobbs, D.E., and Schlichter, C.L. (1991). Talents Unlimited. In Costa, A.L. (Ed.) (1991). *Developing minds: programs for teaching thinking.* Alexandria, VA: Association for Supervision and Curriculum Development, pp. 73–78.

Kohlberg, L. (1987). Child psychology and childhood education: a cognitive-developmental point of view. New York: Longman.

Nickerson, R.S., Perkins, D.N., and Smith, E.E. (1985). *The teaching of thinking.* Hillsdale, NJ: Lawrence Erlbaum.

Norris, S.P. (1985). Synthesis of research on critical thinking. *Educational Leadership, 42*(8), 40–45.

Paul, R. (1993). *Critical thinking: what every person needs to survive in a rapidly changing world* (3rd ed.). Santa Rosa, CA: Foundation for Critical Thinking.

Piaget, J. (1970). *Science of education and the psychology of the child.* New York: Viking Press.

Pogrow, S. (1995). Making reform work for the educationally disadvantaged. *Educational Leadership, 52*(5), 20–24.

Resnick, L.B. (1987). *Education and learning to think.* Washington, D.C: Academy Press.

Schlichter, C.L. (1986) Talents Unlimited: an inservice education model for teaching thinking skills. *Gifted Child Quarterly, 30*(3), 119–123.

Schlichter, C.L., Hobbs, D., and Crump, W.D. (1988). Extending Talents Unlimited to secondary schools. *Educational Leadership, 45*(7), p. 36–40.

Sternberg, R.J., and Bhana, K. (1986). Synthesis of research on the effectiveness of intellectual skills programs: snake-oil remedy or miracle cures? *Educational Leadership, 44*(2), 60–67.

Worsham, A.M., and Stockton, A.J. (1986). A model for teaching thinking skills: the inclusion process (*Phi Delta Kappa Fastback, 236*). Bloomington, IN: Phi Delta Kappa.

Sutherland, P. (1992). *Cognitive development today.* London: Paul Chapman Publishing Limited.

Vygotsky, L.S. (1986). *Thought and language*. Cambridge, MA: MIT Press.

8

WHOLE LANGUAGE LEARNING

Whole Language—two words that have become a label for an exciting grass-roots teacher movement that is changing curricula around the world. . . .Never in the history of literacy education has there been such genuine excitement on the part of educators.

Dorothy Watson

A Whole Language approach that does not incorporate sufficient attention to decoding skills leaves in its wake countless numbers of youngsters who, in the words of one teacher, are surrounded by "beautiful pieces of literature that [they] can't read."

American Educator

Whole language has emerged as a complete pedagogy, rich, diverse, and complex.

Ken Goodman

Whole language is a philosophy of how literacy best develops in learners. It represents a perspective on language and learning which is founded primarily on the use of literature programs, big books, predictable books, book discussion groups, authentic stories rather than basal readers, acceptance of developmental spelling, and emphasis on the writing process. It is based on the premise that human beings "acquire language through actually using it for a purpose, not through practicing its separate parts until some later date when the parts are assembled and the totality is finally used" (Altwerger, Edelsky, & Flores, 1987, p. 145).

Whole language has emerged as a force in the school curriculum for at least two reasons. One reason is a reaction to the skills-based language programs with their heavy emphasis on the technical (phonics, grammar, correct spelling, etc.) rather than the conceptual aspects of learning. The other reason is that new theories of learning have emerged in recent years, and whole language advocates have been encouraged by these developments.

Whole language is rooted in part in a learning theory called *constructivism*. Constructivism is based on the premise that the learner constructs all knowledge, personally, socially, or in combination, and therefore, learning is a more subjective affair than one might imagine. No two people can or should construct the same knowledge (although it might be quite similar) because each of us has our own unique experiences, our own schema or knowledge structure, our own learning styles, and our own particular motivation to learn.

Because this is so, the thinking goes, it is more appropriate to expose learners to broad ideas than to particularistic skills. The former permits individual accommodation, while the latter assumes that everyone (at least within a group) needs the same thing. And that same thing is a reductionist approach to learning as opposed to a holistic approach to learning. Of course, this is somewhat of an oversimplification since whole language advocates have rarely said that the teaching of basic reading and grammar skills is always inappropriate; what we are talking about here are points of emphasis.

Some observers have noted the similarities between whole language and an approach that was popular a generation ago called *language experience*. Language experience was based on the premise that reading and writing should come primarily from the child's own experience rather than from predetermined, one-size-fits-all sources such as basal readers. For example, a teacher takes the class for a walk around the environs of the school, and afterward, using large pages of newsprint and felt pen, writes a story that the children tell based on the experience. The children would then practice reading and illustrating their own story. Often, children in language experience classes would write and illustrate their own "books" which they would share with others or give to their parents or others. The premise was twofold: that reading and writing go together like hand and glove, and that personal experience is

the key to becoming a reader or a writer. The idea of "ownership" as a motivating force has been claimed by more than one
group over the years. The idea can be traced back at least to
Francis Bacon, who said the key to learning is found in experience, one's own and not someone else's.

GRABBING HOLD OF A "SLIPPERY QUARRY"

One of the major problems with the whole language
movement is its variety of definitions. It has been described as
a "slippery quarry" and as "something hard to measure"
(McKenna, Robinson, & Miller, 1990a). Even whole language
advocates openly admit that the concept is difficult to define
and that it defies "a dictionary-type definition." Basically,
whole language is a philosophy of teaching and learning that
proposes that all language concepts are closely interconnected,
that to separate them is artificial, and that they are best learned
in a natural or "whole" manner. This description contrasts with
the traditional reductionist, skill-focused approach to language
where children begin with letters, sounds, blends, and pho-
nemes, or what more than one proponent of whole language
has called, "barking at text." Instead, whole language flows
from the child's personal, natural language patterns and with
the reading and writing of stories and other forms of literature
that draw upon the child's experience. The oft-cited analogy is
the natural untaught process of learning to walk. Readers of
this book who wish to pursue this issue of definition more
deeply are encouraged to read "The Rhetoric of Whole Language," by Moorman, Blanton, and McLaughlin, and "Deconstructing the Rhetoric of Moorman, Blanton, and McLaughlin:
A Response," by Goodman. Both articles appear in the October–December, 1994, issue of *Reading Research Quarterly.*

Several key terms are closely associated with whole language learning. One of those terms is "meaning-centered." A
meaning-centered approach seeks relevance and personal
meaning and avoids isolated skills as the road to literacy. Another term found in the repertoire of whole language advocates
is "integration." Since language is the root of much of our

learning, whole language classrooms provide integrated language experiences which touch variously on all parts of the curriculum—art, music, science, social studies, and so forth. And a third term is "natural learning." We don't directly teach people to walk or even to talk. It happens along the way in a supportive environment. Therefore, the argument goes, so should learning to read and write be made as natural as possible. Figure 8.1 illustrates the set of common assumptions and beliefs held by many whole language advocates.

An integral component of whole language philosophy is the nurturing of the natural process by which a child comes to think about language as a result of his or her prior knowledge and life experiences. In this respect, the social and affective components of learning are highly valued and attended to by whole language teachers. Social experiences tend to be holistic and often highly charged effectively, for better or worse. They lend themselves to particularistic analysis only in retrospect. Perhaps in the most fundamental sense of learning, the difference between whole language and traditional language programs is that whole language emphasizes whole-to-part learning while traditional forms emphasize part-to-whole learning. In other words, they are diametrically opposing points of view.

WHOLE LANGUAGE IN THE CLASSROOM

In whole language, phonics and word drills are downplayed. Instead, students are encouraged to learn to read and write much as they learned to speak—naturally. Emphasis is placed on encouragement with a focus on success in a natural setting rather than on errors, corrections of mistakes, and "word attack" skills. It is believed by whole language advocates that not only will children more readily learn in a creatively rich literary environment that "nurtures" and "celebrates" reading and writing, but that they will **want** to read and write as a result. Intrinsic motivation and relevance are stressed as the teacher facilitates, rather than directs, the learning process.

FIGURE 8.1. COMMON BELIEFS OF WHOLE LANGUAGE ADVOCATES

According to whole language theory, teachers should:

- **Focus on meaning, not the component parts of language.** Children learn language from whole to part. Therefore, instruction in reading and writing should begin by presenting whole texts—engaging poems and stories—rather than zeroing in on the "bits and pieces" that make up language.

- **Teach skills in context, not in isolation.** Children learn the sub-skills of language most readily when these skills are taught in the context of reading and writing activities. Teachers should coach children in skills as the need for the skills arises, rather than marching children in lockstep through a sequenced skills curriculum.

- **Get children writing, early and often.** Reading and writing develop best in tandem. When children write, they master phonics relationships because they must constantly match letters with sounds to write what they want to say.

- **Accept invented spelling.** Whole language teachers do not expect perfect spelling from the beginning. Instead, they encourage children to make their best efforts. "Invented spelling" reveals to what degree the young writers have cracked the phonetic code and over time will improve.

- **Allow pupils to make choices.** When children have some control over their learning, they are more motivated and retain what they learn longer.

What Whole language is not:

- **Breaking language into its component parts.**
- **Teaching skills in isolation or in a strict sequence.**
- **Relying on basal readers with controlled vocabulary.**
- **Using worksheets and drill.**
- **Testing subskills.**

Source: Adapted from the Association for Supervision and Curriculum Development. Whole language: finding the surest way to literacy. *Curriculum Update* (Fall, 1995).

Teachers who consider themselves to be users of the whole language approach fall into vaguely defined, often overlapping categories. Purists tend to eschew basic skills approaches altogether, while eclecticists try to accommodate a blend of whole language and traditional reading and writing instruction. A more all-encompassing position tends to take whole language to the limits, making it an entire curriculum as the classroom takes on the trappings of open education or interdisciplinary studies. But most users of whole language focus its use on the more conventional areas of the language arts curriculum.

School districts that adopt whole language programs often require experienced teachers to take some training designed to move them from the traditional approach to language arts to the whole language approach. Prospective teachers in such districts are often screened based on their knowledge of and willingness to use whole language. This phenomenon has become somewhat problematic in the wake of the decision by the California State Board of Education to seriously rethink its previously uncritical acceptance of whole language reading instruction.

Figure 8.2 illustrates some of the differences between traditional and whole language views of the curriculum. A review of the elements of curriculum and instruction found in Figure 8.2 reveal that a fundamental difference is found between the two approaches with respect to learning goals, teacher role, student activities, materials used, methods of assessment, and the very structure of the classroom. Needless to say, any teacher, administrator, or district contemplating such a basic change should be well aware of the implications, and should be able to defend such a change to parents and other interested parties.

FIGURE 8.2. CLASSROOM IMPLICATIONS FOR CONTRASTING VIEWS OF EDUCATION

	Traditional	*Whole Language*
Learning Goals	Specific objectives in each subject area, usually identified by the school, district, or state. The objectives are hierarchical and tied to textbooks or teacher guides. The focus is on the product, with particular emphasis given to a student's deficits.	Teachers work with students to create a curriculum based on the interests and strengths of the individual student. Learning focuses on the process and learning in a functional context.
Teacher Role	A transmitter of information with major responsibility for determining what and how students should learn.	A facilitator of learning helping the student with the process of learning, sharing responsibility for learning with the student.
Materials	Basal readers, skill books and worksheets, social studies, math, language, science textbooks.	Student-selected reading materials, meaningful projects involving a variety of integrated materials from the various disciplines.
Class Structure and Activities	Students in traditional rows, with direct instruction predominant. Students may be grouped by achievement level. Minimal use of group learning activities. Teaching of skills in isolation from other parts of the curriculum with separate periods of the day for the various subjects.	Variable seating arrangements with considerable flexibility. Subjects integrated with language and reading, with considerable group and cooperative learning activities. Limited direct instruction, or only when the need arises within the context of the learning activities at a meaningful time.
Evaluation	Standardized tests, workbooks, worksheets, teacher-made tests that	Teacher observations of the learning process, writing samples, student

evaluate isolated skills mastery. The frame of reference for evaluation is an external standard or group norm.	self-evaluation, and port-folios. Students are evaluated against them-selves to identify growth in various areas.

POLITICS AND WHOLE LANGUAGE

There is another aspect of the whole language movement, which some whole language enthusiasts are possibly unaware. At the deepest philosophical level, whole language represents something more than another way to teach kids how to read and write. Its source is found in a strong desire for education to play the role of change agent in the social and political fabric not only of schools, but society as a whole. This is hardly a new idea. George Counts, who probably would have approved wholeheartedly of the politics of whole language, wrote a book, *Dare the Schools Build a New Social Order?* on this very theme in the 1930s. It is this social and political agenda that has fueled much of the debate about whole language. A number of reading researchers and professionals have commented on this phenomenon, but one of the more penetrating analyses is provided by McKenna, Stahl, and Reinking (1994).

They have identified the social-political aspect of the whole language agenda as spelled out by certain leaders in the movement. They note that some whole language advocates see "education as a vehicle for individual liberation and the class-room as a model for an egalitarian society" (p. 213). They interpret Kenneth Goodman, a prominent exponent of whole language teaching, as someone who "appears to see whole language, not as method of teaching reading, but an aspect of an approach to creating a more just world. From this analysis, whole-language advocates do not see the goal of education as improving test scores. Their critique of test scores . . . is based on . . . a questioning of the imposition of a standard or norm on an individual child" (p. 214).

Indeed, a number of whole language advocates are very open about these beliefs. Edelsky, Altwerger, and Flores (1991), write that whole language "has a unique potential to be a liberatory pedagogy. . . ." It is also, they continue, ideally suited for helping "subvert the school's role in maintaining a stratified society." Whole language "devalues the major language-based devices for stratifying people," and "huge chunks of time usually devoted to exercises are freed for projects in which students can analyze social issues like the systemic injustice and inequality that affects all our lives" (pp. 53–54).

The battle lines are sharply drawn. As McKenna et al. noted in their analysis, "to compromise whole language would be to compromise that [political] goal." Critics point out that whole language is built on a theory that may be less about learning to read and write, except as tools of liberation, than about social change and "reorganizing power relationships in schools."

THE RESEARCH BASE FOR WHOLE LANGUAGE

Whole language advocates claim that "the research base for whole language philosophy is broad and multidisciplinary. It includes research in linguistics, psycholinguistics, sociology, anthropology, philosophy, child development, curriculum, composition, literary theory, semiotics, and other fields of study" (Newman & Church, 1989, p. 20). Movement leader Kenneth Goodman, who cites such luminaries as Jean Piaget, Lev Vygotsky, Noam Chomsky, and the linguist Michael Halliday as influencing his thinking, has proclaimed that, "Whole language has emerged as a complete pedagogy, rich, diverse and complex" (1996, p. 135). These claims are daunting, and it might lead one to conclude that such a deeply structured Level I foundation augurs well for the results of this approach. The proof, however, is ultimately found in how or to what extent theoretical contributions are brought together to form a coherent teaching-learning construct or, in more grades terms, a "complete pedagogy."

Other examples of the claims are found in books such as *The Administrator's Guide to Whole Language* (Heald-Taylor, 1989), in which an entire chapter is devoted to whole language research. Allusions are made to some 50 studies which cover a range of related topics that include writing, oral language, reading, and developmental studies. Prominent among the researchers cited are Kenneth Goodman, Donald Graves, Delores Durkin, Marie Clay, and Frank Smith. This book was published at a time of largely uncritical enthusiasm and unbridled expansion of the whole language movement.

More recently, Adams and Bruck (1995) reviewed the whole language research base, concluding that to the extent to which whole language proponents equate learning to read with learning to talk (i.e., that it is a "natural" process much like learning to walk), they are wrong. They concluded further that to the extent to which whole language procedures minimize the role of skilled decoding in reading comprehension, they are wrong. And they conclude that the resulting pedagogical practices of whole language teaching and learning are wrong. Adams and Bruck base their rather strong conclusions on a systematic examination in which they compare whole language claims with empirical results.

Further, Keith and Paula Stanovich (1995) add that, "[empirical] research has consistently supported the view that reading is not acquired naturally in the same way as speech" (p. 93). Keith Stanovich maintains, "That direct instruction in alphabetic coding facilitates early reading instruction is one of the most well-established conclusions in all of behavioral science. Conversely, the idea that learning to read is just like learning to speak is accepted by no responsible linguist, psychologist, or cognitive scientist in the research community" (*American Educator*, 1995, p. 4).

Thus the conclusion that whole language has indeed a credible pure or basic (Level I) research foundation is certainly debatable, to say the least. Furthermore, that the philosophical basis of whole language is one of a clearly thought-out theory of learning rests on its claim and is clearly challenged by Stanovich when he writes that, "these [theoretical] ideas have unfortunately come into education half baked and twice distorted. Legitimate philosophy of science was picked up and reworked by scholars in a variety of humanities disciplines who were not philosophers by training and who used the work for their own—often political—agendas" (1993, p. 288). The basic research and the theoretical model of whole language is its primary line of support. It rests, its critics say, on shaky foundations. The theoretical construct has been used to give both inspiration and direction to whole language teaching and learning practices at the classroom level. It is to this level, that of implementation, that we now turn.

The practical questions are: What do students learn in whole language classrooms? Do students attain higher levels of literacy? Is the learning qualitatively improved in whole language classrooms? This is the domain of applied research (Level II). Our answer to those questions is that evidence is lacking. Let us see why this is so.

How Do We Do It?

Empirical researchers have observed that investigating the effects of whole language instruction is difficult because of the lack of an agreed upon definition of whole language. As we suggested previously, people mean different things when they use the term. It should also be noted that a number of whole language advocates claim that "traditional" methods of assessment are inappropriate when it comes to evaluating this approach to teaching and learning (McKenna, Robinson, & Miller, 1990a, p. 4).

McKenna, Robinson, and Miller (1990a) have suggested a cooperative research agenda designed to treat these problems. They propose that these eight steps be taken:

+ The concept must be defined to enable researchers to know whether a program represents whole language or not, or at least how to categorize a given program;

+ Both experimental and quasi-experimental research is needed;

+ Qualitative studies should also be employed;

- The effects on student attitudes should be studied;

- Longitudinal studies should be undertaken;

- Learner characteristics as they interact with traditional and whole language instruction should be identified;

- Studies should identify the role of teacher variables in instruction;

- Collaborative research partnerships between researchers and whole language advocates should be developed.

Of course, this very reasonable agenda is needed not merely for whole language program assessment but for program assessment in general.

Some whole language advocates, however, take strong exception to the idea of an imposed research agenda. In an article titled, "Whose Agenda Is This, Anyway?" Carole Edelsky (1990) wrote that traditional research forms have little relevance to whole language because "two competing views are more than different 'takes' on language arts instruction; they are conflicting educational paradigms. Each uses different discourse; maintains different values; and emanates from a different educational community" (p. 7). In a response to her response, McKenna et al. wrote, "in essence, people share a system of beliefs and they claim they have evidence to support their beliefs. But, when you look up what [whole language advocates] cite as evidence, it is often just someone else's published beliefs" (McKenna, Robinson, & Miller, 1990b, p. 12). This has all the earmarks of a stalemate.

The debate about research methodology in the reading profession has obviously been quite rancorous, and suggestions have been made to resolve this dispute that "invoke a spirit of charity" (Stanovich & Stanovich, 1995). The strident nature of the debate is a reflection of how strongly these beliefs are held. As McKenna et al. (1994) have noted, "To compromise whole language would be to compromise that [political] goal." When people have such fundamentally different worldviews, it would be naive at best and probably closer to folly to think that they might readily agree to a research agenda.

In fairness, it should be stated that many whole language advocates are not necessarily opposed to any form of evaluation research. Rather they question the appropriateness of the measures used, which are, typically, standardized tests. Such tests, whole language proponents claim, isolate learning in bits and pieces and ask children to show their knowledge in unnatural settings.

What kinds of program evaluation do whole language proponents advocate? First of all, they would propose that qualitative research, rather than quantitative, be emphasized. They suggest that writing samples that could be judged as process rather than product would be a place to start. Also, they are very interested in determining students' attitudes toward learning to read and write. To get a sense of students' attitudes, it would be necessary to conduct personal interviews and to employ other, similar qualitative data-gathering procedures. Basically, whole language advocates feel that placing the assessment marbles in the quantitative-product bag is a mistake that leads to irrelevant conclusions about student learning. This leaves the potential consumer in a quandary because we can all appreciate the sensitivity toward attitude development and the employment of more "natural" measures of achievement. On the other hand, it is much easier to compare quantitative achievement results between this reading program and that one when districts are faced with the expensive decisions associated with program adoption and implementation.

Goodman (1996) has argued that, "Reductionist research in reading has inevitably focused on recognition of bits and pieces of language rather than on comprehension of real texts. But we can't assume that perception of letters and words in the process of making sense of real meaningful texts is the same as recognizing letters and words in isolation or in highly reduced contexts. And we can't assume that comprehension follows successive recognition of words" (p. 5). This statement suggests rather strongly that, from Goodman's perspective, what we have are two completely different goal structures and agendas, one empirical-reductionist and the other global-expansionist. To compare them, it would seem to follow, is not merely difficult but less than a good use of one's time. As Goodman writes, "Whole language teachers have taken control of the body of knowledge about how reading and writing work and have built their own pedagogy on that knowledge—their teaching theory and practice" (p. 117). Such phrases as "have taken control" and "have built their own pedagogy" speak for themselves.

WHAT WE DO KNOW

In spite of all this, what does the research we **do** have say about the effectiveness of whole language programs? The most comprehensive review of the research on whole language effectiveness was conducted by Steven A. Stahl and Patricia D. Miller in 1989, and updated in 1994 by Stahl, Michael McKenna, and Joan Pagnucco. The reviews included both quantitative and naturalistic or qualitative studies. In 1989, Stahl and Miller wrote, "Our review . . . concludes that we have no evidence showing that whole language programs produce effects that are stronger than existing basal programs, and potentially may produce lower effects. The alternative, that whole language programs are too new to evaluate, also suggests a lack of evidence of their efficacy. In short both views foster doubt as to the prudence of a widespread adoption of such an approach, pending evidence of its effectiveness" (Stahl, 1990, p. 143).

This review of whole language research outcomes is not without its critics. Many whole language advocates reject its definitions of whole language and the methodologies of the research itself (Schickendanz, 1990; McGee & Lomax, 1990). The 1994 Stahl et al. review concluded once again that whole language did not produce advantages in achievement, and that eclectic programs seemed to produce the most positive effects. They concluded that the evidence suggested that the strongest type of program "might include a great deal of attention to decoding, especially in the early grades, but would give a greater emphasis to the reading of interesting and motivating texts. . . . [S]uch a program would incorporate much from whole language but include more teacher-directed instruction, especially in terms of decoding and comprehension strategies." They also noted, however, that this is not likely to sit well with whole language people because many of them are convinced that, "one cannot have a little whole language and a little of something else. Partial moves toward whole language are acceptable only as a way station to becoming a true whole language teacher" (p. 182).

Its staunchest critics have called whole language a "disaster," and it is true that the empirical evidence in support of whole language learning is tenuous to deficient at best. Increasing numbers of professionals and laypersons have concluded that there are major problems and that many children, particularly young children from homes where little reading takes place as a matter of course, and who need to learn the fundamentals, simply do not learn to read well when whole language is the principal philosophy guiding instruction. The notion put forth by whole language advocates that learning to read is a naturalistic process much like learning to walk or talk (a notion that is disputed by a large number of linguists and psychologists) breaks down in the absence of home-based role models either of learning to talk using proper grammar or learning to read when little evidence of reading is found in the home.

Reacting to the drumbeat of parent criticism and declining student achievement, the California has modified its earlier embrace of whole language and is currently advocating a more balanced approach with an increased phonics-based emphasis (California Department of Education, 1996). It should, however, be kept in mind that states and districts embraced whole language in the first place because of the perception that more traditional forms of literacy instruction were not meeting children's needs. So, we have another example of the pendulum swing so recognizable to those who have been in the profession for considerable time. Figure 8.3 presents the highlights of California's new emphasis on phonetic awareness, correct spelling, systematic, explicit phonics approaches, and so on. Especially worth noting is the advocacy of early intervention programs for children at risk of reading failure. The *Report of the California Reading Task Force* contains much of the familiar rhetoric, including the insight that "there is a crisis. . . " (California Department of Education, 1995, p. 1). Among other things, the California Task Force concluded that "many language arts programs have shifted too far away from direct skills instruction" (p. 1). Statutes instituted in 1995 require that the State Board of Education "adopt materials in grades one through eight that include systematic, explicit phonics, spelling, and basic computational skills" (1996, p. 1).

FIGURE 8.3. CALIFORNIA'S BALANCED APPROACH TO READING

Program components:

A strong literature, language, and comprehension program that includes a balance of oral and written language;

An organized, explicit skills program that includes phonemic awareness (sounds in words), phonics and decoding skills to address the needs of the emergent reader;

Ongoing diagnosis that informs teaching and assessment that ensures accountability;

A powerful early intervention program that provides individual tutoring for children at risk of reading failure

Instructional Components

Phonemic awareness
Letter names and shapes
Systematic, explicit phonics
Programmatic instruction in correct spelling
Vocabulary development
Comprehension and higher order thinking
Appropriate instructional materials

Source: California State Department of Education (1996). *Teaching Reading: A Balanced, Comprehensive Approach to Teaching Reading in Prekindergarten Through Grade Three.* Sacramento: Author.

SO WHERE DOES THIS LEAVE US?

Whole language advocates continue to tout their approach primarily on the basis of theory, enthusiasm, and testimonials. While these are significant factors which should not be cynically cast aside, they simply are not be enough to go on when it comes to spending big money on new programs and teacher retraining. The fact of the matter is that we simply lack the empirical evidence necessary to state that schools that wish to improve student reading ability and test scores in the areas of the language arts should adopt the whole language approach. But here's the rub: raising standardized test scores conflicts with the goals and objectives held by whole language advocates. Their agenda, they state, is more complex than one whose learning outcomes can be captured by the reductionist mentality so pervasive in standard measures. So those who choose to adopt a whole language approach to language arts must do so for reasons they find compelling, and those reasons will have to be sought in sources beyond the empirical record as it exists to date.

We want our children to learn to read, to use it as a knowledge-seeking tool, and to enjoy reading, three different but closely related outcomes. Some evidence exists to suggest that both teacher-directed, phonics-based instruction and some student-centered, literature-based learning are needed. What we need is a research agenda that will get us closer to the answers of sequence, balance, and the best use of children's learning time.

REFERENCES

Adams, M. J. and Bruck, M. (1995). Resolving the "Great Debate." *American Educator, 19*(2) 7–20.

Altwerger, B., Edelsky, C. and Flores, B. (1987). Whole language: what's new? *The Reading Teacher, 41*(2), 144–154.

American Educator (1995). Learning to read: schooling's first mission. *19*(2) 3–6.

Association for Supervision and Curriculum Development. Whole language: finding the surest way to literacy. *Curriculum Update* (Fall, 1995).

California Department of Education (1995). *Every child a reader: the Report of the California Reading Task Force*. Sacramento: Author.

California Department of Education (1996). *Teaching reading: a balanced, comprehensive approach to teaching reading in prekindergarten through grade three*. Sacramento: Author.

Cambourne, B. (1988). *The whole story*. Auckland, New Zealand: Ashton Scholastic.

Edelsky, C. (1990) Whose agenda is this anyway? a response to McKenna, Robinson, and Miller. *Educational Researcher*, 19(8), 7–11.

Edelsky, C., Altwerger, B., and Flores, B. (1991). *Whole language: what's the difference*. Portsmouth, NH: Heinemann.

Goodman, K.S. (1989). Whole-language research: foundations and development. *The Elementary School Journal*, 90(2), 207–221.

Goodman, K.S. (1994). Deconstructing the rhetoric of Moorman, Blanton, and McLaughlin: a response. *Reading Research Quarterly*, October–December, 340–346.

Goodman, K.S. (1996). *Ken Goodman on reading: a commonsense look at the nature of language and the science of reading*. Portsmouth, NH: Heinemann.

Goodman, Y.M. (1989). Roots of the whole language movement. *The Elementary School Journal*, 90(2), 113–127.

Heald-Taylor, G. (1989). *The administrator's guide to whole language*. Rich C. Owen Publisher.

Manning, G., Manning, M., and Long R. (1990). *Reading and writing in the middle grades: a whole-language view*. Washington, DC: National Education Association.

McGee, L.M., and Lomax R.S. (1990). On combining apples and oranges: a response to Stahl and Miller. *Review of Educational Research*, 60(1), 133–140.

McKenna, M.C., Robinson, R.D., and Miller J.W. (1990a). Whole language: a research agenda for the nineties. *Educational Researcher, 19*(8), 3–6.

McKenna, M.C., Robinson, R.D., and Miller J.W. (1990b). Whole language and the need for open inquiry: a rejoinder to Edelsky. *Educational Researcher, 19*(8), 12–13

McKenna, M.C., Stahl S.A., and Reinking D. (1994). A critical commentary on research, politics and whole language. *Journal of Reading Behavior, 26*(2), 211–233.

Moorman, G., Blanton, W., and McLaughlin, T. (1994). The rhetoric of whole language. *Reading Research Quarterly,* October–December, 309–329.

Morrow, L.M. (1992). The impact of a literature-based program on literacy achievement, use of literature and attitudes of children from minority backgrounds. *Reading Research Quarterly, 27*(3), 251–275.

Newman, J.M. and Church S.M. (1989). Myths of whole language. *The Reading Teacher, 44*(1), 20–26.

Pressly, M. (1994). State-of-the-science primary-grades reading instruction or whole language? *Educational Psychologist, 29*(4), 211–216.

Schickendanz, J.A. (1990). The jury is still out on the effects of whole language and language experience approaches for beginning reading: a critique of Stahl and Miller's study. *Review of Educational Research, 60*(1), 127–131.

Stahl, S. (1990). Riding the pendulum: a rejoinder to Schickendanz and McGee and Lomax. *Review of Educational Research, 60*(1), 141–151.

Stahl, S.A. and Miller P.D. (1989). Whole language and language experience approaches for beginning reading: a quantitative research synthesis. *Review of Educational Research, 59*(1), 87–116.

Stahl, S.A., McKenna, M.C., and Pagnucco, J.R. (1994). The Effects of whole-language instruction: an update and a reappraisal." *Educational Psychologist, 29*(4), 175–186.

Stanovich, K.E. (1993). Romance and reality. *The Reading Teacher*, *47*(4), 280–291.

Stanovich, K.E., and Stanovich, P.J. (1995). How research might inform debate about early reading acquisition. *Journal of Research in Reading*, *18*(2), 87–105.

Watson, D. (1990). Defining and describing whole language. *The Elementary School Journal*, *90*(2), 129–141.

9

LEARNING STYLES

Students are not failing because of the curriculum. Students can learn almost any subject matter when they are taught with methods and approaches responsive to their learning style strengths.

Rita Dunn

Like the blind men in the fable about the elephant, learning styles researchers tend to investigate only a part of the whole and thus have yet to provide a definitive picture of the matter before them.

Lynn Curry

The idea of learning styles is appealing, but a critical examination of this approach should cause educators to be skeptical.

Vicki E. Snider

We sometimes pretend something is true not because there's evidence for it but because we want it to be true

Carl Sagan

The thesis of learning styles is that individuals vary considerably in how they learn. This is to say that any given person has what are called modality strengths that are, one supposes, determined by a combination of hereditary and environmental influences. These modality strengths, which translate into preferences to learn and communicate visually, orally, spatially, tactilely, and so on, are one's learning style. Beyond that there are some further considerations, for example, whether one learns better in a quiet or busy setting, a formal or relaxed environment, or together or alone.

All of this is quite intriguing, and it has led to the development of a range of models some of which are quite elaborate. Dunn, Dunn, and Price have noted that learning style is predicated on "the manner in which at least eighteen different elements from four basic stimuli affect a person's ability to absorb and retain" (1979). Other equally complex learning styles models have been developed by Gregorc, McCarthy, and Hunt.

It has been suggested that learning styles are not merely a phenomenon of individual differences but that differences are also found among and between cultures. Bennett (1990) has noted that Native American students "approach tasks visually, seem to prefer to learn by careful observation which precedes performance, and seem to learn in their natural settings experientially." Bennett suggests further that African American students tend to be field-dependent learners, which means that they tend to take their cues from the social environment and that much of their motivation comes from factors external to the material to be learned itself. More recently, the term field-dependent appears to have been replaced by the term "field-sensitive" (Swanson, 1995). Added to the cultural dimension is that of social class as a factor in determining how one learns. Given the relatively fluid social and economic mobility one finds in the United States, one wonders whether a person's learning style might change with a corresponding change in class.

If this is all true, what we have is compound interest because the suggestion is that to find a given individual in the vast matrix of teaching and learning, we must determine not merely the person's individual style, but that person's cultural and social context as well. This could lead teachers quickly into a labyrinthine world of diagnosis in the search for style. But it doesn't have to be that complicated, say the purveyors of learning styles.

The National Task Force on Learning Styles and Brain Behavior gives us the following definition of *learning style*:

> Learning style is that consistent pattern of behavior and performance by which an individual approaches educational experiences. It is the composite of characteristic cognitive, affective, and physiological behaviors that serve as relatively stable indicators of how a learner perceives, interacts with, and responds to the learning environment. It is formed in the deep structure of neural organization and personality [that] molds and is molded by human development and the

cultural experiences of home, school, and society. (Bennett, 1990, p. 158)

This definition is quite broad and all encompassing, to say the least. Cornett (1983) offers a similar, simplified definition: "[E]ssentially, learning style can be defined as a consistent pattern of behavior but with a certain range of individual variability. . . ." Guild and Garger (1985) point out that the idea of learning style includes cognitive style, teaching style, leadership style, and psychological type. Dunn et al. (1995) write that "learning style is the way in which individuals begin to concentrate on, process, internalize, and retain new and difficult academic information." Figure 9.1, which is found on the next page, illustrates three areas of style characteristics including cognition, conceptualization, and affect. A review of Figure 6.1 will give you a sense of the characteristics of these broad categories and the researchers who have developed ideas related to them.

It is common to categorize learning styles into some type of taxonomy of human characteristics of learning behavior. The various taxonomies include cognitive, affective, and physiological considerations. Thus, with respect to cognition, a person might exhibit concrete, abstract, sequential, and random learning characteristics. With respect to affect, a person might find quite different sources for their motivation to learn or they might experience different feelings about how they are responded to as they learn. And with respect to physiological considerations, a person might have preferences for different seating, light, temperature, and room arrangement.

LEARNING STYLES AND INTELLIGENCE

Learning styles advocates stress the idea that each of us receives and processes information differently, and because this is so, teachers should make every attempt to know how students learn best. The logic of this thought dictates to us that all styles are different but equal, and that intelligence and ability are equally but differentially distributed among human beings. Typical school assignments tend to discriminate in favor or against certain learners. But the issue may not be one of ability if

FIGURE 9.1. THREE AREAS OF STYLE CHARACTERISTICS

Category	Characteristics	Researchers
1. *Cognition* — perceiving, finding out, getting information	sensing/ intuition	Jung, Myers-Briggs, Mok, Keirsey and Bates
	field dependent/field independent abstract/ concrete	Witkin, Gregorc, Kolb and McCarthy
	visual, auditory, kinesthetic, tactile	Barbe and Swassing, Dunn and Dunn
2. *Conceptualization* — thinking, forming ideas, processing, memory	extrovert/ introvert	Jung, Myers-Briggs, Keirsey and Bates
	reflective observation/ active experimentation	Kolb and McCarthy
	random/ sequential	Gregorc
3. *Affect* — feelings, emotional response, motivation, values, judgments	feeler/thinker	Jung, Myers-Briggs, Mok, Keirsey and Bates
	effect of temperature, light, food, time of day, sound, design	Dunn and Dunn

Adapted from Guild, P.B., and Garger, S. (1985), *Marching to Different Drummers*, Alexandria, Virginia: Association for Supervision and Curriculum Development, p. 9.

one person learns much and another little from, say, a particular lecture. It may be that the lecture format was more suited to one person's learning style than to another's. What this says is that otherwise capable people are left behind in many cases simply because the approach to learning was inappropriate, not because they were incapable of learning the idea.

The relationship between various learning styles and ability to learn subject matter is not well established. It tends to remain, in our opinion, within the realm of speculation. Witkin (1977), a pioneer researcher in this field, maintained that any given style is not superior to another, a proposition that immediately intersects with ideas of the definition of intelligence. But the problem with this is that the very definition of intelligence is being thoughtfully reexamined by such researchers as Howard Gardner (1983, 1993), and the chances are that what we presently mean by intelligence as measured by IQ tests and what we will mean by intelligence in the future are two different things. At present, analytical abilities are considered basic to one's intelligence as measured by IQ tests. Global, intuitive learners tend to score much lower on tests of analytical abilities. Are they therefore less intelligent than analytical thinkers who obviously score higher? Well, it depends on one's definition of intelligence.

IMPLICATIONS FOR THE CLASSROOM

Learning styles advocates point to two major areas of concern for the focus of teachers' energies. Those areas are style assessment and style matching. In other words, what we need to do is discover a learner's style and match how we teach the learner accordingly.

A variety of learning styles assessment instruments exist for children as well as for adults. They cover all the areas noted in Figure 9.1. The best known instruments are the *Myers-Briggs Type Indicator*, the *Learning Styles Inventory*, and the *Embedded Figures Test*. Because they are tools for assessing an individual's learning style, the outcome, or test result, is positive no matter what it is. This seems in some ways a rather curious thing. For example, in the *Embedded Figures Test*, if one is unable to identify certain figures against the background in which they are embedded, it is considered not an inability but rather a global, or "field-sensitive" way of looking at things. On the other hand, the ability to identify the various figures merely means that one has an analytical, or field-independent, approach to learning. This may be one of the first instances in the annals of testing where failure to solve a problem merely puts one in a different but equal category.

In addition to the diagnostic instruments themselves, there are learning styles workbooks that show learners how to identify their styles. Based on the results, the books offer suggestions for how to approach classes and topics, how to study and prepare for exams, and how to deal with teachers whose own teaching styles vary. Thus, the effort on the part of a learner to adapt their style to that of a teacher, or teacher to learner, represents a kind of coping strategy.

The other major issue, *matching* teachers and students with respect to style, becomes crucial once people have been properly diagnosed. This brings to mind images created by the old insight that somewhere out there is the ideal learning environment. Maybe for some it brings to mind thoughts of Abraham Lincoln studying by firelight in a crude log cabin. Or one can imagine Aristotle walking through the shaded groves of ancient Athens speaking for the centuries while eager disciples follow in his wake taking in his every word. Or imagine a little child sitting in his or her mother's lap being told, for the nth time, a certain story. Then there is the kid who is simply great at arcade games but who has little interest in or seemingly little ability to do paper and pencil work.

We could go on, but you get the idea. Each of us probably has some sense of the optimum conditions that make learning more appealing and meaningful for us.

The challenge for the teacher is to use different modalities, such as stories, explanations, projects, and activities, to reach all the different learners in the class effectively, and to use special techniques to meet different styles, such as overviews for global learners and linear explanations for analytical learners.

Advocates propose a number of teaching strategies that encompass the variety of learning styles. One might say that this is the essence of good teaching anyway. Here is a list of some of the ways to reach different styles:

- Using questions at a variety of levels of thinking;
- Providing an overview of material before proceeding to specifics;
- Allowing sufficient time for information to be processed adequately;
- Using examples and activities directed to both left and right hemispheres of the brain;
- Providing set induction and closure activities;
- Setting clear purposes before any listening, viewing, or reading experience;
- Using spaced practice;
- Using multisensory means to convey ideas to be learned.

These strategies would probably benefit most learners in most learning situations, and would, according to learning style theory, reach, differentially, all types of learners.

On more narrow grounds, specific strategies are thought to work better with certain styles. Figure 9.2 is an example of instructional strategies designed to meet the needs of field-dependent (global-intuitive) learners. Schools have long been thought to discriminate against field-dependent learners, for example. Textbooks, workbooks, lectures, and verbal explanations tend traditionally to be quite linear and analytical in their approaches to knowledge. To overcome this, teachers are urged to use the strategies illustrated in Figure 9.2 because they are particularly appropriate and helpful to global thinkers. Supposedly, lists could be generated appropriate for each style.

THE RESEARCH BASE FOR LEARNING STYLES

The learning styles literature is related to the literature of brain research, but the two movements are not synonymous.

FIGURE 9.2. INSTRUCTIONAL STRATEGIES FOR
FIELD-DEPENDENT LEARNERS

---

1. Present learning in a global way: focus on the "big picture"; give an overview and the concept.

2. Make connections among content, integrate learning, and identify relationships among subjects.

3. Provide a context for learning and a sense of the purpose of the learning.

4. Provide structure, clear expectations, direction, and organization.

5. Personalize content. Give frequent illustrations relating to students' and teachers' experiences.

6. Emphasize a positive class climate and helpful relationships with others.

Source: Guild, P. (1990). *Using learning styles to help students be successful.* Seattle, WA: Seattle Public Schools.

The brain research investigators tend to focus on medical research and research in such areas as cognitive science as the source of their learning theories. Learning styles advocates allude to brain research, but tend to base their position more on psychological research such as the work done by Witkin of *Embedded Figures Test* fame. They cite brain research because it is obviously related more and more to psychological research, but for these people, brain function research is not the primary focus.

There are two types of Level I research on which learning styles is supposedly based. The first is brain research that includes research conducted by Reuven Feuerstein (a theory of intelligence), Herman Epstein (brain growth spurts, sex differences in hemisphere specialization), and Fox and Wittrock (split brain research, selective attention).

The second type of basic research is the psychological research on individual differences conducted throughout the 20th century. Because of his work on personality types, Carl Jung is cited as one of the pioneers in this area. Witkin's work in the development of the *Embedded Figures Test*, and I.B. Myers and Leslie Briggs' work in the development of their types indicator, have served to operationalize the definition of differences in learning found among human beings.

A host of instruments that purport to diagnose learning styles has been derived from the work of Jung, Witkin, and Myers and Briggs. In most cases, developers cite the seminal work of these figures as providing the foundation of a specific learning styles instrument. A problem with these assessment inventories, however, is that they are plagued by troubles of validity and reliability. In other words, do they really measure what they claim to measure (validity) and are they stable measures of someone's style over time (reliability)? A significant and troubling issue with the research at this level can be traced to the ambiguities of the meaning of learning style. For example, a factor analysis of four such instruments showed that each instrument was measuring distinctly different characteristics (Ferrell, 1983).

In our opinion, Level II research on learning styles is quite weak. We noted this in the first edition of this book, and we stand by the comment in this edition. Proponents of learning styles maintain that style-based instruction increases learning (Dunn et al., 1995). The most far-reaching claims appear to be made by Rita Dunn and Marie Carbo, both of whom do research and teach workshops for teachers around the country on the topic of learning styles, and both of whom have materials for teachers and school districts to purchase. Thus, they each play the triple role of theorist-researcher, developer, and purveyor of learning styles ideas, instruments, and materials, something that if it were done in the medical profession would raise the proverbial red flag. But this is, of course, not the medical profession.

Both Dunn (1995) and Carbo (1992) tout the importance of the social–physical–emotional–intellectual learning environment, claiming that such variables as temperature, light, body position, and so on, should be accommodated to the individual's style. They make further claims about the necessity of matching instructional techniques between teacher and learner.

They cite various research studies and sources to support these claims while buttressing their positions with anecdotal accounts of great teachers, breakthrough classrooms and leading-edge-school success.

Many outside the movement are critical of the research used to support learning styles (Kavale, Hirshoren, & Forness, 1997; Adams and Englmann, 1996; Curry, 1990). The criticisms include these points:

- The validity and reliability of the instruments are questionable; many learning styles theorists have not distinguished learning styles constructs from intelligence (Curry, 1990).

- The experimental designs employed in classroom-based learning styles research are weak to nonexistent and have inadequate controls. Robert Slavin states: "What has never been studied, to my knowledge, is the question of whether teachers who adapt to students' styles get better results than those who don't" (O'Neil, 1990).

- Bias on the part of the researchers, possibly due to "mercenary" interests (Kavale & Forness, 1990; Kavale, Hirshoren, & Forness, 1997) in learning styles results.

- The Hawthorne Effect generated by the enthusiasm of doing something new may explain some of the results (Kavale, Hirshoren, & Forness, 1997).

- Many studies in the learning styles literature have been conducted by graduate students preparing their dissertations under the direction of faculty members who have a vested interest in substantiating a particular learning styles conceptualization (Curry, 1990; Kavale, Hirshoren, & Forness, 1997).

With respect to these concerns, we turn to a recent meta-analysis (Dunn et al., 1995) of the most ubiquitous learning styles model, that of Dunn and Dunn. The authors note efficacious outcomes favoring styles-based teaching as reported in 10 published (and one unpublished) research articles representing investigations that range from elementary to college levels. They also note positive results for special education and learning-disabled students. Further, their meta-analysis included 36 different studies with a database of 3,181 participants. They conclude that "students whose learning styles are accommodated would be expected to achieve 75% of a standard deviation higher than students who have not had their learning styles accommodated" (p. 353). This would represent an Effect Size of .75, considered to be rather high and impressive.

A closer look, however, at Dunn et al.'s meta-analysis raises several questions. The 11 studies alluded to in the previous paragraph were, with two or three exceptions, reported in journals that have little or no reputation for publishing carefully refereed, empirical studies—*Teaching K-8, Principal, Educational Leadership, Journal of College Student Development*. Further, of the 36 studies included in the meta-analysis itself, only one was to be found in a published journal. We stated at the beginning of this book our concern that unpublished research is basically evidence that has not been evaluated by expert jurors. The 35 unpublished studies were doctoral dissertations, a source known to be notoriously deficient and uneven in quality. Twenty-four of the cited dissertation studies were done at St. John's University under the direction of Dunn and her colleagues, raising serious issues of conflict of interest, but also raising the question of why the studies are unpublished, uncritiqued, and difficult to access. The *Annotated Bibliography of Research* (1992, 1995) cited by Dunn et al. is also unpublished. The St. John's University Center for the Study of Teaching and Learning issues it.

Kavale et al. (1997) cite numerous methodological and interpretive problems with the Dunn et al. meta-analysis. They raise serious questions about the procedures used to derive the large effect size. Also, even if one was to accept the questionable effect size that Dunn et al. claim, there is the relative ease of introducing other teaching procedures (e.g., reinforcement, homework) that have large, well-established effect sizes. They conclude that

The Dunn et al. (1995) meta-analysis has all the hall-
marks of a desperate attempt to rescue a failed methodology. The weak rationale, curious procedures, significant omissions, and circumscribed interpretation
should all serve as cautions to the educational community before accepting the findings as truth when, in
reality, they remain far removed from the truth. (p. 23)

Thus, although there is new reporting on the effects of
learning styles on academic achievement, we stand by our
original position that the entire construct has a dubious theoretical base, that it suffers greatly from lack of definition, and that
for teachers and administrators to invest time and effort in its
pursuit is not a good use of their time.

At Level III, we have seen no published account to indicate
that any large-scale program evaluation has ever been conducted to determine whether an inservice program or a districtwide intervention in learning styles changes anything. In
spite of this disquieting finding, learning styles inservice training and preservice training continues apace as though there
were compelling evidence of its positive contribution to school
life.

CONCLUSION

The concept of learning styles is appealing. Who wouldn't
want to think that everyone has equal ability and that it is
merely given to each of us in different ways? Howard Gardner's
pioneering work in the development of a theory of multiple intelligences offers great hope for education because it gives us a
reality base for considering a wide range of behaviors and abilities within the scope of that elusive word, "intelligence." But his
work could be translated into learning styles applications only
tangentially. Who wouldn't want to try to find the best way for a
child to learn? We all recognize the bias inherent in a school
system where so much of the learning reward structure is devoted to reading print and writing answers. Many of the strategies identified for teaching and learning by learning styles advocates make perfect sense, not because of the validity of the

learning styles construct, but because they contain elements of strategies for which there is empirical support. However, at this point in time, we feel that the burden is still on the learning styles advocates to provide a clearer sense of the beneficial outcomes of a styles-based approach, something we feel they have not done. Certainly, a decision to change methodologies or to do wholesale retraining of teachers based on the research in this area would be a mistake because neither the quantity nor the quality of the evidence is there.

REFERENCES

Adams, G.L., and Engelmann, S. (1996). *Research on direct instruction: 25 years beyond DISTAR*. Seattle, WA: Educational Achievement Systems.

Barbe, W.B., and Swassing, R.H. (1979). *Teaching through modality strengths*. Columbus, OH: Zaner-Bloser, Inc.

Bennett, C.I. (1990). *Comprehensive multicultural education: theory and practice* (2nd ed.). Boston, MA: Allyn and Bacon.

Carbo, M. (1992). Giving unequal learners an equal chance: a reply to a biased critique of learning styles. *Remedial and Special Education 13*(1), 19–29.

Cornett, C.E. (1983). *What you should know about teaching and learning styles*. Bloomington, IN: Phi Delta Kappa Educational Foundation.

Curry, L. (1990). A critique of the research on learning styles. *Educational Leadership 48*(2), 50–56.

Dunn, R. (1990). Rita Dunn answers questions on learning styles. *Educational Leadership 48*(2), 15–21.

Dunn, R., Beaudry, J., and Klavas, A. (1989). Survey of research on learning styles. *Educational Leadership 46*(6), 50–58.

Dunn, R.S., Dunn, K.J., and Price, G. (1979). Learning styles/teaching styles: should they...can they...be matched. *Educational Leadership 36*(4), 238–244.

Dunn, R., Griggs, S., Olson, J., Beasley, M., and Gorman, B. (1995). A meta-analytic validation of the Dunn and Dunn model of learning-style preferences. *Journal of Educational Research 88*(6), 353–362.

Ferrell, B.G. (1983). A factor analytic comparison of four learning styles instruments. *Journal of Educational Psychology 75*(1), 33–39.

Gardner, H. (1983). *Frames of mind: a theory of multiple intelligences.* New York: Basic Books.

Gardner, H. (1993). *Multiple intelligences: the theory in practice.* New York: Basic Books.

Guild, P. (1994) The culture/learning style connection. *Educational Leadership 51*(8), 16–21.

Guild, P.B., and Garger, S. (1985). *Marching to different drummers.* Alexandria, VA: Association for Supervision and Curriculum Development.

Gregorc, A.F. (1982). *An adult's guide to style.* Maynard, MA: Gabriel Systems, Inc.

Kavale, K.A., and Forness, S.R. (1987). Substance over style: assessing the efficacy of modality testing and teaching. *Exceptional Children 54*(4), 228–239.

Kavale, K.A., and Forness, S.R. (1990). Substance over style: a rejoinder to Dunn's animadversions. *Exceptional Children 56*(4), 357–361.

Kavale, K., Hirshoren, A., and Forness, S. (1997). *Meta-analytic validation of the Dunn and Dunn model of learning-style preferences: a critique of what was Dunn.* Unpublished manuscript. Department of Special Education, University of Iowa.

Keefe, J. (1986). *Profiling and utilizing learning style.* Reston, VA: National Association of Secondary School Principles.

Kolb, D.A. (1985). *The learning style inventory.* Boston, MA: McBer & Co.

McCarthy, B. (1987). *The 4MAT system: teaching to learning styles with right/left mode techniques.* Barrington, IL: Excel.

McCarthy, B., and Morris, S. (1995). *4MAT in action: sample units for grades K–6.* (3rd ed.). Barrington, IL: Excel.

McCarthy, B., and Morris, S. (1995). *4MAT in action: sample units for grades K–12*. (3rd ed.). Barrington, IL: Excel

Myers, I.B. (1962). *Introduction to type*. Palo Alto, CA: Consulting Psychologists Press, Inc.

O'Neil, J. (1990a). Findings of styles research murky at best. *Educational Leadership 48*(2), 7.

O'Neil, J. (1990b). Making sense of style. *Educational Leadership 48*(2), 4–9.

Snider, V.E. (1990). What we know about learning styles from research in special education. *Educational Leadership 48*(2), 53.

Snider, V.E. (1992). Learning styles and learning to read: a critique. *Remedial and Special Education, 13*(1), 6–18.

Swanson, L.J. (1995). *Learning styles: a review of the literature*. (ERIC Document Reproduction Service No. ED387067).

Witkin, H., and Goodenough, D. (1981). *Cognitive styles: essence and origins*. New York: International Universities Press.

10

INTERDISCIPLINARY CURRICULUM

Many adults today do not understand interdisciplinary curriculum with its child-centered approach to teaching and learning. This doesn't look like "school" to them. They are unaware of 80 years of research, done in the twentieth century, on how children learn.

Marianne Everett

Herein lies one of the problems with the notion of integrated curriculum: Do theory and practice converge to produce more thorough or comprehensive learning experiences for students, or do teachers run the risk of leaving wide gaps in students' understanding of important concepts and subject matter?

Terrence Mason

All things are connected.

Chief Seattle

The nationwide restructuring movement has led schools in a multitude of cases to consider the implementation of interdisciplinary curriculums. The main arguments for interdisciplinary curriculums, or integrated studies as they are sometimes called, are twofold: (1) the knowledge explosion is very real and there is simply too much information to be covered in the curriculum; and (2) most school subjects are taught to students in isolation from other, potentially related, subjects.

One idea behind interdisciplinary teaching and learning is that by combining subjects around themes or projects, a certain economy is achieved because much of the repetitious material that occurs from subject to subject is eliminated. And flowing from the first idea is a second, which posits that when subjects are connected, students begin to see meaningful relationships because the subject matter serves as a vehicle for learning

145

rather than as an end in itself. These are among the primary claims of the advocates of interdisciplinary curriculum. A summary of the rationale for the integration of the curriculum, along with some of the problems with doing so is presented in Figure 10.1.

FIGURE 10.1. ARGUMENTS FOR AND AGAINST INTEGRATING THE CURRICULUM

Arguments for integrating the curriculum

+ **Psychological/developmental**—Research in developmental and cognitive psychology suggests that individuals learn best when encountering ideas connected to one another.

+ **Sociocultural**—The current curriculum, especially in the secondary school, is fundamentally obsolete and does not address the needs, interests, and capacities of today's students.

+ **Motivational**—The integrated curriculum deemphasizes rote learning and content coverage, and because it is often organized around student-selected themes and provides for choice, it will enhance student interest and motivation.

+ **Pedagogical**—The traditional curriculum is so vast and intractable that educators cannot hope to cover all the so-called essentials for productive living, and therefore they should focus their efforts on providing experiences leading toward internalization of positive attitudes toward learning.

Obstacles to successful curriculum integration

+ **The trivialization problem**—It is sometimes appropriate for teachers to address ideas within a single content area, and that some ideas are best understood without introducing confusing or inconsequential subject matter.

+ **The "skills" problem**—A number of educators maintain that students can attempt interdisciplinary work only after they have mastered some elements of disciplinary knowledge, and if integration activities dominate the curriculum, there will be inadequate time to teach these skills.

♦ **The teacher knowledge problem**—If teachers lack knowledge and skills within multiple disciplines, their ability to integrate those disciplines is highly problematic.

♦ **The school structure problem**—Many teachers have never experienced subject integration themselves, being products of discipline-based schooling throughout their lives, which means that vast retraining and reconceptualizing must take place.

♦ **The assessment problem**—The mode of assessment in most school systems is not able to effectively assess students' attainment of deep understanding, the stated goal of integrated learning.

Source: Adapted from Mason, T.C. (1996). Integrated curricula: potential and problems. *Journal of Teacher Education*, 47(4), 263–270.

Heightened teacher collaboration, greater student involvement, higher level thinking, better content mastery, real-world applications, and fewer fragmented learning experiences are among the improvements that supposedly follow suit when a change to interdisciplinary curriculum is made. Most teachers and administrators dream of these outcomes, so the claims tend to be rather attractive.

Integrating the curriculum is not a new idea. The learning done in most "natural" situations including apprenticeships, for example, tends to be interdisciplinary. But in school settings, the idea of interdisciplinary learning and teaching came to the fore as part of the progressive educational movement of the early 20th century. In ways that modern educators may not even realize, the progressive movement achieved much in this regard. Language arts and social studies, "subjects" taken for granted in today's elementary curriculum, are themselves interdisciplinary versions of several former separate subjects. And at the secondary level, many districts have for several years integrated their mathematics programs, shucking off the old algebra–geometry–advanced algebra sequence. There are many other examples of progressive influence, including the growing tendency to do "real world" investigations, which by definition are problem-focused rather than being on a single academic discipline.

The current trend, however, goes somewhat further than the prior attempts to coalesce, say, history, geography, and civics into something called social studies. Today, the movement is dedicated to crossing new frontiers between and among school subjects. It should be noted, however, that the philosophical premise remains the same as that advanced during the original progressive movement. Let's take a moment to examine that premise.

ALL THINGS ARE CONNECTED

"Traditional" school programs tend to be subject-centered. That is, the organizing focus in teaching and learning is on separate school subjects, or academic disciplines. In most cases, those subjects are offered separately, even in elementary classrooms. At the secondary level, the distinction is even clearer, as signaled by the organization of the school faculty into departments based on academic disciplines. Each subject has a sequence to it, one that generally becomes more technical and abstract through the succeeding years. Each subject also has a scope within a given grade level. The scope of a subject has to do with how broad or wide-ranging the treatment is. The scope and the sequence tend to represent the boundaries of a given subject. But the point is that the focus is always on the subject and its domain of knowledge and skills. The best way to understand the traditional curriculum is to think of its dominant form, the textbook. This is so because most textbooks are written for a particular subject at a particular level, for example, fourth grade mathematics.

Interdisciplinary curriculum, on the other hand, takes a quite different approach to teaching and learning. It is far more than a mere blending of separate subjects. It represents a philosophy of student-centered, often socially relevant learning. By placing the learner rather than the subject matter at the center of gravity, projects and activities take precedence over academic disciplines. This is so because this seems to be the way children and adolescents learn when given a choice. In other words, it is closer to the "natural" way that people learn. The academic disciplines, from such a perspective, are regarded as tools for learning rather than as ends in themselves. If they are tools, so the argument goes, why not blend them wherever it makes sense to do so?

Interdisciplinary programs typically eschew textbook treatments. Thus, the curriculum is changed in more ways than one. Most curriculums in American schools are textbook-driven. Textbooks tend to configure and control both scope and sequence. But interdisciplinary curriculums focus on group activities and projects; textbooks, if they are used at all, are relegated to the status of a resource. The curriculum still has to come from somewhere, and if it is not to come from textbooks, what are its sources?

The curriculum in interdisciplinary settings tends to be site-based. This is disconcerting to commercial publishers because generic textbooks published for use everywhere are simply not applicable. Interdisciplinary curriculums are often tied to local issues, especially when those local issues have global connections. Examples include studies of local water supplies, wetlands, and pollution. Or, equally often, interdisciplinary units will be constructed around a compelling theme such as architecture, patterns in nature, or cultural heritage.

Teachers and students are generally involved together in the planning and development of the theme or issue chosen for study. Often, a study begins with a brainstorming session where the teacher leads students through the construction of a "webbing" similar to that shown in Figure 10.2. The webbing, or map, gives focus and structure to the unit, project, or investigation while allowing many avenues of individual or group work. This stage is considered to be very crucial, apparently, because the sense of "ownership" or investiture in the curriculum is thought by advocates to be a motivating force throughout the study. See Figure 10.3 for a step-by-step approach to developing an interdisciplinary unit.

FIGURE 10.2. AN EXAMPLE OF WEBBING

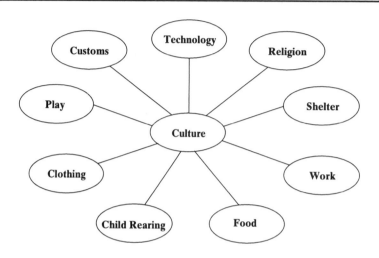

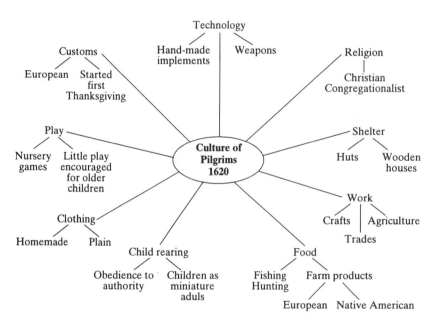

Source: Ellis, A.K. (1991). *Teaching and learning elementary social studies* (4th ed.). Boston: Allyn and Bacon, p. 108.

FIGURE 10.3. A PROCEDURE FOR DEVELOPING INTEGRATED UNITS OF STUDY

Step 1—**Selecting an organizing center.** The "organizing center" is the focus of the curriculum development (i.e., theme, topic of study, concept). Once parameters are explored, the topic must be broadened to provide a base for investigation from various points of view in preparation for the next developmental step.

Step 2—**Brainstorming associations.** A graphic device (i.e., planning wheel) is useful as teachers and students begin to explore the theme from the perspectives of various discipline fields. The organizing center for the theme is the hub of the wheel; each spoke is a discipline area. The open-ended technique of brainstorming is used to generate spontaneous ideas that will be recorded on the wheel.

Step 3—**Establishing guiding questions to serve as a scope and sequence.** This step takes the array of brainstormed associations from the wheel and organizes them. Now the course of study begins to take shape. A framework for the unit of study will develop naturally as scope and sequence-guiding questions are developed.

Step 4—**Writing activities for implementation.** Guiding inquiry questions have been formulated, now the means for exploring them must be developed. Activity design is crucial because it tells what students will be doing. Bloom's taxonomy is a good guideline for activity design, as it will help ensure the cultivation of higher-level thought processes.

Source: Jacobs, H.H. (Ed.) (1989). *Interdisciplinary curriculum: design and implementation.* Alexandria, VA: ASCD, pp. 63–56.

A criticism of interdisciplinary curriculums is one that is obvious to any essentialist. Because the units are teacher-student developed, they tend to have a seemingly random flavor. The essentialist's need for an orderly scope and sequence of knowledge and skills is often not met, to say the least. To interdisciplinary advocates, who mostly tend to be progressives, this is the beauty of such a curriculum. It is fair to say, however, that interdisciplinary curriculums often tend to favor social studies, language arts, and the arts, though not necessarily in any systematic way, while slighting mathematics, and this is a serious problem. It is not insoluble, but it is difficult to overcome.

There is also a phenomenon known as "the tyranny of integration." Sometimes teachers become so committed to integrated studies that they find themselves trying to integrate everything they teach. This can quickly lead to a different kind of artificiality. The fact of the matter is that not everything probably can or should be integrated. Matters of discretion become paramount when such factors are weighed. The simple idea that is too easily lost sight of is that integration is a *means* to an end and not an end in itself.

THE RESEARCH BASE FOR THE INTERDISCIPLINARY CURRICULUM

REMEMBER JOHN DEWEY?

The primary theoretical basis of interdisciplinary curriculum is found in progressive educational philosophy. The progressive movement, which included such luminaries as John Dewey, William Kilpatrick, George Counts, and Harold Rugg, reached its zenith earlier in this century. It is a child-centered approach to learning that places great emphasis on creativity, activities, "naturalistic" learning, real-world outcomes, and, above all, experience.

Progressive education came to be known for what it opposed as much as what it advocated. This was a matter of great concern to Dewey and others. Progressives were opposed to the factory-like efficiency model on which schools depended (and still do). They decried the artificial instruction and learning driven by textbooks and written exams. They said that school learning was so unlike the real world that it has little or no meaning to the average child. Robert Hutchins, not a progressive, said it best: "Students resort to the extracurriculum because the curriculum is so stupid."

In his classic work, *Interest and Effort in Education,* Dewey wrote eloquently, establishing the thesis of progressivism and therefore of interdisciplinary studies:

> Our whole policy of compulsory education rises or falls with our ability to make school life an interesting and absorbing experience to the child. In one sense, there is no such thing as compulsory education. We can have compulsory physical attendance at school; but education comes only through willing attention to and participation in school activities. It follows that the teacher must select these activities with reference to the child's interests, powers, and capacities. In no other way can she guarantee that the child will be present. (Dewey, 1913, p. ix)

Such theorizing about the nature of education is foundational to interdisciplinary curricular efforts.

The other, more recent theoretical basis for interdisciplinary curriculum is found in constructivist theory. As we noted in an earlier chapter, constructivism is a theory of learning that states that each person must construct his or her own reality. The constructivity principle states that "construction should always precede analysis" (Post et al., 1992, p. 10). Put another way, this means that experience is the key to meaningful learning; not someone else's experience abstracted and condensed into textbook form, but one's own direct experience. The current interest in the contributions to thought and language made by the Russian psychologist Lev Vygotsky (1962; see also Moll, 1993) has especially bolstered the argument for the social interactionist aspects so readily prevalent in the group projects associated with interdisciplinary teaching and learning. So, in this sense, the traditional curriculum of learning alone and doing mainly seatwork is not merely turned around, it is stood on its head. Although the work done in constructivist thought is quite recent, it is essentially in harmony with the earlier thinking of the progressives.

Advocates of integrating the curriculum also cite Level I research in the area of brain function (see Chapter 5). They point to research that indicates that the brain seeks patterns and that this is a basic process. They believe that the brain actually resists learning that is fragmented, personally meaningless, and presented in isolation. Contrariwise, they note that knowledge is learned more quickly and remembered longer when constructed in a meaningful context in which connections between and among ideas are made.

But not everyone agrees. The author Thomas Sowell is particularly critical of interdisciplinary teaching and learning, calling it "another popular buzzword." He notes that much of what passes for interdisciplinary is in fact *"nondisciplinary,* in that it simply ignores boundaries between disciplines." He states further that, "academic disciplines exist precisely because the human mind is inadequate to grasp things whole and spontaneously, or to judge 'the whole person.' Thus mathematics must be separated out for special study, even though it is an ingredient in a vast spectrum of other activities" (Sowell, 1995, p. 205). Sowell's point of view is shared by many who feel that depth of subject matter, crucial coverage, the sequencing of important skills, and other related concerns are inevitably shortchanged in interdisciplinary efforts. Further, this point of view holds that there are indeed many opportunities to relate any single discipline to other spheres of knowledge, and that good teachers have always done that while preserving the integrity of their discipline.

BOLD CLAIMS—LITTLE EVIDENCE

Research at Levels II and III is somewhat dependent on investigations of highly related topics such as block scheduling, team teaching, and self-contained programs, where, by inference, one might conclude that these approaches at least lend themselves to interdisciplinary efforts. This may be explained by the observation that interdisciplinary curriculum is itself a large holding company of educational variables that, put together, defies classic research methods. There would simply be too many variables to control if one set out to do traditional controlled studies of the topic as a whole. Often the interdisciplinary curriculum is integrated into other reform efforts, for example, block scheduling, which make the task of isolating the curriculum as treatment difficult, to say the least. Additionally, assessment of the outcomes most sought after by advocates of this type of curriculum arrangement is problematic because of the tendency of advocates to challenge the validity of traditional paper and pencil testing.

Kathy Lake (1994) has examined the available research and has concluded that there are "no detrimental effects on learning when students are involved in an integrated curriculum" (p. 7). How one can conclude that there are no detrimental effects is not clear, but perhaps Lake means that there have been no documented or discernible detrimental effects. She was able to locate a few studies dating back as far as 1965 to show that some students actually learned more in the integrated curriculum, and she noted some educational advantages such as teacher cooperation. However, she was cautious about reaching conclusions about the benefits of integrated studies because of the limited amount of research.

Since Lake's summary of the research, at least one Level II study of note has been reported. Morrow, Pressley, and Smith (1995) report the interesting results of a well-crafted study of the effects of integrating literacy and science programs. Their results indicate "clear support for integrating literacy and science instruction at the third-grade level with respect to the development of language arts competencies," which "did not come at a cost to science content learning"(p. 25). If advocates of integrating the curriculum wish to substantiate their enthusiastic claims with empirical data, additional studies will have to be conducted. At this stage, the number of empirical studies remains so small that any kind of meaningful meta-analysis that might point to some generalized findings is precluded.

Vars (1996) notes that "more than 100 studies" have shown that students in interdisciplinary programs "do as well as, and often better than students in so-called conventional programs" (p. 148). His review of the research in interdisciplinary curriculum and instruction is actually more a summary and synthesis of findings than a critical, analytic examination of the quality of the research. In this light, we are reluctant to conclude that the research base is convincingly supportive of interdisciplinary efforts. Our assessment is that the number of confounding variables and rival hypotheses is sufficient to warrant caution. Still, his contribution is considerable, and we would urge interested readers to examine the many published studies he cites. Vars wisely concludes, "In short, research on the effects of interdisciplinary curriculum and instruction affirms the benefits of these approaches, but warns against raising unrealistic expectations in the minds of teachers, students, or parents" (p. 159).

The difficulties inherent in conducting good Level II research have not kept enthusiasts from making wide-ranging claims of the efficacious outcomes of interdisciplinary curriculums. The following six claims are presented in the name of "research" done in this area. While the claims are intriguing and possibly accurate, we feel that they go well beyond any sound empirical base at this time.

The first claim is that **interdisciplinary curriculum improves higher level thinking skills.** Here the term, "metacurriculum" is invoked. The term metacurriculum refers to the larger, more transcendent ideas that emerge when people focus on problems to be solved rather than on the reductionist, bits-and-pieces activities that occupy so much of school life. The suggestion is that students will become more skilled in flexible thinking as they are placed in learning situations that address connections rather than the kinds of computation, workbook, and seatwork skills of the traditional separate subjects curriculum. If evidence exists to substantiate this claim, we were unable to find it.

This leads to the second claim that **learning is less fragmented.** Students are provided with a more coherent set of learning experiences and, therefore, with a more unified sense of process and content. If, for example, a theme such as "patterns in the environment" is selected for study, then knowledge and skills from the various disciplines must "cohere" or integrate because they are merely means to a more relevant end, rather than being ends in themselves. This thought has considerable appeal. Who wants to argue against coherence? It is, however, based on a logical discontinuity which could lead one to conclude that a teacher who uses an interdisciplinary curriculum is more likely to present a more connected, coherent world view of learning than does a teacher assigned to teach a single subject. In fact, connections are what any good, well-informed teacher attempts to make, and it is just possible that teacher knowledge, both subject-specific and general, may have as much to do with the making of connections than anything else.

Claim number three is that **interdisciplinary curriculum provides real-world applications, hence heightening the opportunity for transfer of learning.** It is often the case that interdisciplinary units have real-world connections built into them. However, that could be said as well of units taught within the frame of a separate subject. However, the probability is greater that real-world applications will take place in interdisciplinary curriculum settings than in traditional school circumstances. There may well be something to the claim that interdisciplinary efforts with their real-world emphasis lead to learning transfer, but in light of the scant evidence it is more a matter of speculation than conclusion. It is, after all, possible that a real-world emphasis may get in the way of some of the reflective, long-term work necessary to fit people for careers in, for example, physics or the arts. Most skilled pianists, for example, had to spend many hours studying music theory and practicing piano, delaying "relevance" often for years.

The fourth claim is that **improved mastery of content results from interdisciplinary learning.** The case is made in the literature for better understanding, greater retention, and even academic gains as demonstrated by test scores. Perhaps so, but the evidence is not sufficiently in place. More often the case can be made that no evidence is present to lead us to conclude that interdisciplinary curriculum and instruction causes harm to student achievement when compared to other approaches.

Claim number five is that **interdisciplinary learning experiences positively shape a learner's overall approach to knowledge.** The idea is that students will develop a heightened sense of initiative and autonomy in their thinking conduct. Related to this is the idea that students improve their moral perspective by learning to adopt multiple points of view on issues. This is an interesting hypothesis, and we encourage the testing of it.

Claim six in the literature is that **motivation to learn is improved in interdisciplinary settings.** Students become engaged in "thoughtful confrontation" with subject matter. More students are reached because of the greater need for different perspectives and learning styles in solving broad-based problems. Teachers themselves become more motivated because teacher-to-teacher contact is enhanced as team efforts are called for in planning, teaching, and evaluating. We make no counterclaim that such an assertion is false, merely that the claim itself is unsupported by evidence.

We conclude that although these claims are at present largely unsupported, they should not be dismissed out of hand. Rather they should be treated as important hypotheses for some focused Level II research. If the claims are changed to hypotheses, we have before us an excellent research agenda that should keep investigators busy for several years, much as good Level II research has been successfully conducted for the cooperative learning agenda.

There appears to be a minimal amount of activity at Level III, with some notable exception. *Humanitas,* an interdisciplinary humanities program for secondary students, was evaluated in the Los Angeles Unified School District using what appears to be a very careful design (Aschbacher, 1991). The program evaluation, carried out by the Center for the Study of Evaluation at UCLA, could well serve as a model for this type of sorely needed research. Achievement comparisons of *Humanitas* students and other students from comparison groups showed that the program had very positive effects on students' writing and history content knowledge during the first year. The improvement continued as students stayed in the program, which they did in greater percentages than did their counterparts in four comparison schools. Other sophisticated aspects of the evaluation included surveys of students, teachers, and administrators, observations in classrooms, analyses of teachers' assignments and examinations, reviews of student portfolios, and an examination of such "educational indicators" as school attendance, discipline problems, and "college-oriented" behaviors by students. Classroom observation, for example, showed that *Humanitas* students spent more time per day in thoughtful discussions with a greater number of students contributing than did comparison groups. And even though *Humanitas* students received assignments judged to be harder than those given to comparison group students, the *Humanitas* students liked school better than did comparison students. We recommend a careful reading of the evaluation study (Aschbacher and Herman, 1989) by personnel in any district interested in doing serious program evaluation. It is a sophisticated, penetrating analysis that serves not only as a guide for meaningful program assessment but as a guide for planning and implementing programs.

Going back more than half a century, one encounters what is generally considered to be the most celebrated program evaluation study ever conducted. It was called "The Eight Year Study," sponsored by the Progressive Education Association, now defunct, but then still a force in education. The purpose of the Eight Year Study (begun in 1933 and reported in 1942) was to determine whether a curriculum designed to meet the "needs and interests" of students is as effective at preparing students for college as is a traditional, subject-centered program. The study involved 30 progressive or experimental high schools that were matched as closely as possible with traditional comparison schools. Much of the curricular experience in the progressive schools was interdisciplinary in nature. The results of the Eight Year Study indicated that students from the progressive schools were as well prepared for college as their traditional counterparts with regard to academics and were more involved in such social and extracurricular activities as yearbook, student government, and clubs. In spite of the evidence, the many pressing issues of World War II obscured the results, and as Decker Walker writes, "the reforms of this period survived only in isolated places and as the seeds of further reforms" (Walker, 1990, p. 72).

We realize that it is stretching things a bit to claim the Eight Year Study as a program evaluation of interdisciplinary curriculums. However, many of the curricular offerings in the progressive schools were what are called "core curriculum," which is a way of combining subjects like English and history, for example, into a single offering called "Social Living." In fact, much of middle school philosophy emerged from the progressive movement, and one of the middle school tenets is to coalesce subjects into integrated studies using block scheduling.

OTHER RESEARCH

Finally, there are some emergent research findings that offer tentative support to the use of an integrated curriculum. One source of such research is the updated effective schools findings. Effective schools research has been conducted for several decades, yielding a variety of lists of school characteristics that distinguish "more effective" schools from schools that are less so. These characteristics are thought by some to have a cause-and-effect relationship with respect to learning. However, we would caution you to recall that correlations derived by this type of research are not the same as cause-and-effect findings. Such attributions can really only be considered hypotheses, yet to be tested empirically. Still, these characteristics do point toward possibilities of why some schools may be better than others. The most recent effective schools research (Cotton, 1995) identified the following among a long list of classroom and school attributes:

- ♦ Teachers provide instruction that integrates traditional school subjects, as appropriate.
- ♦ Teachers integrate workplace readiness skills into content-area instruction.
- ♦ Administrators and teachers integrate the curriculum, as appropriate.

A second body of research is emerging from the many restructuring efforts currently under way across the nation. Lee

and Smith's study of 820 secondary schools led them to conclude that, "the consistent pattern of findings allows us to
make quite unequivocal statements about the organizational
structure of high schools: students learn more in schools which
are restructured" (Lee & Smith, 1994a, p. 23). About 25% of
these restructured schools were using "interdisciplinary
teaching teams" (Lee & Smith, 1994b).

We recognize the limitations inherent in any hard-and-fast
attempt to apply this research to interdisciplinary teaching and
learning. But the results reported in this chapter do give us a
place to begin, a kind of port of entry to this intriguing landscape. What is needed now is a systematic way in which to
enlarge both the quality and quantity of the findings derived
from carefully crafted qualitative and quantitative research
studies. Perhaps what it will take is the establishment of some
sort of center for the study of interdisciplinary curriculum.

CONCLUSION

The idea of approaching the school curriculum from an interdisciplinary perspective rather than that of separate subjects
is a compelling idea. We know that separating academic disciplines for scholarly purposes probably makes sense, but even
that premise can be questioned in light of the crossing of frontiers in, for example, biology and psychology or genetics and
linguistics. But for children and adolescents who are still in the
process of adapting, organizing, and otherwise constructing
their own schema, such an artificial separation seems to make
little sense. On the other hand, students can readily understand
the purpose of a project or an activity based on an interesting
theme or issue. However, such reasoning would be stronger if
it were more fully supported by empirical evidence.

We also know that schools are often a curious place where
large numbers of people, students and teachers, congregate but
are expected to work separately and only rarely to collaborate.
Obviously, interdisciplinary studies are a way of bringing people together. Teachers we have known who have become involved in interdisciplinary *teaching* have told us that they are
really getting to know some of their colleagues for the first

time even though they may have worked next door to them for years. Students, too, because of the project nature of interdisciplinary studies, are given greater opportunity to work with each other. Such experiences surely work to the greater benefit of teachers and students.

On the other hand, we feel that the claims made in the name of interdisciplinary curriculum are expansive and may only raise hopes beyond reasonable expectations. If you decide to approach the curriculum from an interdisciplinary perspective, we recommend that you do so for reasons of collegiality and real-world applications. But if you are expecting that such a move will result in higher test scores, we can only say that the evidence is tentative.

Perhaps this is the time and place to say that higher test scores, a very admirable goal, are not alone a sufficient reason for having schools. Both of us have spent a considerable amount of time in Russian schools. There is little doubt that the test scores of Russian students are superior to those of American students. But consider the system that they have lived in as a way of life. Higher test scores alone have not improved the quality of life in Russia and in the other former Communist countries of Eastern Europe. School is also about social intelligence, citizenship, participation, and decision making. Please don't misunderstand us—we are not making an argument for ignoring test scores. To do so would be folly. So, of course, the best answer is to raise test scores and to meet participatory needs as well. This is the spirit in which we urge you to consider interdisciplinary studies. Professional judgment, whether in education or in some other field, is always a difficult, complex enterprise.

REFERENCES

Altshuler, K. (1991). The interdisciplinary classroom. *The Physics Teacher, 29*(7), 428–429.

Anderson, K. (1991). Interdisciplinary inquiry. *School Arts, 91*(3), 4.

Aschbacher, P.R. (1991). Humanitas: a thematic curriculum. *Educational Leadership, 49*(2), 16–19.

Aschbacher, P.R., and Herman, J.L. (1989). *The Humanitas program evaluation final report, 1988–1989.* Los Angeles: UCLA Center for the Study of Evaluation.

Brophy, J., and Alleman, J. (1991). A caveat: curriculum integration isn't always a good idea. *Educational Researcher, 49*(2), 66.

Busshman, J.H. (1991). Reshaping the secondary curriculum. *The Clearing House, 65*(2), 83–85.

Cotton, K. (1995). *Effective schooling practices: a research synthesis 1995 update.* Portland, OR: Northwest Regional Educational Laboratory.

Dewey, J. (1913). *Interest and effort in education.* Boston: Houghton Mifflin.

Everett, M. (1992). Developmental interdisciplinary schools for the twenty-first century. *The Education Digest, 57*(7), 57–59.

Jacobs, H.H. (Ed.) (1989). *Interdisciplinary curriculum: design and implementation.* Alexandria, VA: ASCD.

Jacobs, H.H. (1991). Planning for curriculum integration. *Educational Leadership, 49*(2), 27–28.

Lake, K. (1994). *School improvement research series VIII: integrated curriculum.* Portland, OR: Northwest Regional Educational Laboratory.

Lee, V.E., and Smith, J.B. (1994a). *Effects of high school restructuring and size on gains in achievement and engagement for early secondary school students.* Madison, WI: Center on Organization and Restructuring of Schools.

Lee, V.E., and Smith, J.B. (1994b). High school restructuring and student achievement. *Issues in Restructuring Schools: Issue Report No. 7.* Madison, WI: Center on Organization and Restructuring of Schools.

Mason, T.C. (1996). Integrated curricula: potential and problems. *Journal of Teacher Education, 47*(4), 263–270.

Moll, L.C. (Ed.) (1993). *Vygotsky and education: instructional implications and applications of sociohistorical psychology.* New York: Cambridge University Press.

Morrow, L.M., Pressley, M., and Smith, J.K. (1995). *The effect of a literature-based program integrated into literacy and science instruction on achievement, use and attitudes toward literacy and science.* Reading Research Report No. 37. Athens, GA: National Reading Research Center.

Post, T.R., Ellis, A.K., Humphreys, A.H., and Buggey, L.J. (1997). *Interdisciplinary approaches to curriculum: themes for teaching.* Upper Saddle River, NJ: Merill/Prentice-Hall.

Sowell, T. (1995). *The vision of the anointed.* New York: Basic Books.

Spady, W.G., and Marshall, K.J. (1991). Beyond traditional outcome-based education. *Educational Leadership, 49*(2), 67–72.

Vars, G. (1991). Integrated curriculum in historical perspective. *Educational Leadership, 49*(2), 14–15.

Vars, G. (1996). The effects of interdisciplinary curriculum and instruction. In Hlebowish, P., and Wraga, W. (Eds.). *Annual review of research for school leaders.* New York: Scholastic.

Vygotsky, L.S. (1962). *Thought and language.* Cambridge, MA: MIT Press.

Walker, D. (1990). *Fundamentals of curriculum.* Orlando, FL: Harcourt Brace Jovanovich.

11

COOPERATIVE LEARNING

An essential instructional skill that all teachers need is knowing how and when to structure students' learning goals competitively, individualistically and cooperatively. Each goal structure has its place; an effective teacher will use all three appropriately.

David and Roger Johnson

The future of cooperative learning is difficult to predict. My hope is that even when cooperative learning is no longer the "hot new method," schools and teachers will continue to use it as a routine part of instruction. My fear is that cooperative learning will largely disappear as a result of the faddism so common in American Education.

Robert Slavin

Oh, they had cooperative learning when I was a kid; they just didn't call it that. They called it cheating.

former teacher Arlen King

I first heard of cooperative learning from Roger Johnson back in 1969. We had just finished a tennis match, a rather competitive one as I recall, and Roger told me about this idea he and his brother David had to change the social fabric of classrooms. If I were going to cite one educational innovation that really merits the term "innovation" it would be cooperative learning. It rests on a firm foundation.

Arthur K. Ellis

Cooperative learning is one of the biggest, if not the biggest, educational innovations of our time. It has permeated all levels of teacher training from preservice to inservice. It has been estimated that more that 30,000 teachers and would-be teachers have been trained at the Minneapolis-based Cooperative Learning Center alone. And cooperative learning is not a peculiarly American educational phenomenon. It is touted from Israel to New Zealand, from Sweden to Japan.

The research claims that detail the elements of cooperative learning are more elaborate and documented than those of any other movement in education today. Study after study finds its way into the scholarly journals. Literally hundreds of articles, from research to practice, appear annually on this topic. The major professional subject matter associations have all published special editions showing how cooperative learning can be used in mathematics, social studies, language arts, science, and other subject areas.

The claims made on behalf of cooperative learning are legendary. Seemingly, it can solve any educational problem. Researcher Robert Slavin (1989–90), himself a recognized authority in the field of cooperative learning, warns:

> Another danger inherent in the success of cooperative learning is that the methods will be oversold and under trained. It is being promoted as an alternative to tracking and within class grouping, as a means of mainstreaming academically handicapped students, as a means of improving race relations in desegregated schools, as a solution to the problems of students at risk, as a means of increasing prosocial behavior among children, as well as a method for simply increasing the achievement of all students. Cooperative learning can in fact accomplish this staggering array of objectives, but not as a result of a single three-hour inservice session. (p. 3)

Of course, Slavin is perfectly correct that a brief introduction to such a complex idea is hardly sufficient to accomplish anything more than a sense of what cooperative learning is. But note his agreement with the wide range of educational problems that cooperative learning can productively address! If it could do half these things, it would be the pedagogical equivalent of a cure for cancer.

What is this apparently wonderful thing called cooperative learning? How does it work? Can it really bring about fundamental changes for the better in classroom life? Let's take a closer look at it so that you can begin to decide for yourself.

COOPERATIVE LEARNING MODELS

Cooperative learning takes on many different forms in classrooms, but they all involve students working in groups or teams to achieve certain educational goals. Beyond the most basic premise of working together, students must also depend on each other, a concept called *positive interdependence*. From here cooperative learning takes on specific traits advocated differentially by different developers. In some cases, cooperative learning is conceived of as a generic strategy that one could use in practically any setting or in any course of study. In other cases, cooperative learning is conceived of as subject-matter–specific strategy.

Five or more major models of cooperative learning exist. They have much in common, but the differences among them provide useful distinctions. All five represent training programs for teachers who, having taken the training, should be equipped to implement the various attendant strategies in their classrooms.

David and Roger Johnson of the University of Minnesota are the authors of the Learning Together model. The model is based in a generic group process theory applicable to all disciplines and grade levels. Students are placed in formal or informal base groups which are charged with solving problems, discussing issues, carrying out projects, and other tasks.

The Johnson and Johnson model is built on the five elements, which trace back to the theories of Morton Deutsch, mentioned in Chapter 1. The first element is positive interdependence in which students must believe that they are linked with other students to the point that they cannot succeed unless the other students also succeed. The second element is that of face-to-face interaction in which students must converse with each other, helping one another with the learning tasks, problems, and novel ideas. The third element is individual accountability in which each student must be held accountable for his or her performance with the results given to both the individual and the group. The fourth element is social skills in which students are taught and must use appropriate group interaction skills as part of the learning process. The fifth element is group processing of goal achievement in which student groups must regularly monitor what they are accomplishing and how the group and individuals might function more effectively. Obviously, teachers must be trained in these elements, and they must be able to teach them to their students in turn.

Robert Slavin of Johns Hopkins University has developed a cooperative learning model called Student Team Learning. His model is less generic than that of the Johnsons. In fact, it has at least four permutations, each of which is specifically designed to address different concerns. For example, his Cooperative Integrated Reading and Composition (CIRC) model is specifically designed for learning reading and writing in grades 3 through 6. His Team Assisted Individualization (TAI) model is designed for mathematics learning in grades 3 through 6. Slavin's approach to cooperative learning represents a sophisticated set of strategies which, as he has stated, cannot be acquired in a three-hour workshop session.

Other notable models include that of Shlomo and Yael Sharan of Israel, which is a general plan for organizing a classroom using a variety of cooperative tactics for different disciplines; that of Spencer Kagan, whose Structural Approach includes such intriguing procedures as Roundrobin, Corners, Numbered Heads Together, Roundtable, and Match Mine; and Elliot Aronson's Jigsaw, composed of interdependent learning teams for academic content applicable to various age groups. Figure 11.1, on the next page, illustrates the several models which we have described.

Used properly, cooperative learning is designed to supplement and complement direct instruction and the other teaching and learning activities typical of classroom life. Its main function is to replace much of the individual, often competitive, seatwork that so dominates American classrooms. John Goodlad's (1984) research showed that students on average initiate talk only 7 minutes per day. In cooperative learning environments, that figure changes dramatically.

It should be noted, as well, that the advocates of cooperative learning are not necessarily opposed to individualistic and competitive learning. Their opposition is to its near-complete dominance. Most cooperative learning advocates will say that

FIGURE 11.1. COOPERATIVE LEARNING ADVOCATES AND THEIR MODELS

Researcher/ Educator	Model	Focus
David Johnson & Roger Johnson	*Learning Together* ♦ Formal, Informal, and Cooperative Base Groups	Generic group process theory and skills for the teacher for developing a cooperative classroom. Applicable to all levels and disciplines.
Robert Slavin	*Student Team Learning* ♦ Student Teams-Achievement Divisions (STAD) ♦ Teams-Games-Tournament (TGT) ♦ Team Assisted Individualization (TAI) ♦ Cooperative Integrated Reading and Composition (CIRC)	STAD & TGT—general techniques adaptable to most disciplines and grade levels. TAI—specifically for grades 3–6 mathematics. CIRC—specifically for grades 3–6 reading and writing.
Shlomo Sharan & Yael Sharan	*Group Investigation*	A general plan for organizing a classroom using a variety of cooperative strategies for several disciplines.
Spencer Kagan	*Structural Approach* ♦ Roundrobin ♦ Corners ♦ Numbered Heads Together ♦ Roundtable ♦ Match Mine	"Content-free" ways of organizing social interaction in the classroom and for a variety of grade levels.

Figure 11.1 continues on the next page.

Eliot Aronson	*Jigsaw*	Interdependent learning teams for academic material that can be broken down into sections; for varying age groups.

there is a time and a place for each type of learning, but that there must be considerably more cooperative learning in classrooms than is presently the case.

Slavin's perspective is typical of the movement when he states that "cooperative learning methods share the idea that students work together to learn and are responsible for one another's learning as well as their own" (Slavin, 1991, p. 73). Slavin's well-stated phrase sums up the essence of cooperative learning. Read it carefully.

THE RESEARCH BASE FOR COOPERATIVE LEARNING

The Level I research can be traced back to the theories of group dynamics and social interaction developed in the 1930s by pioneer researcher Kurt Lewin. As Slavin notes, "A long tradition of research in social psychology has established that group discussion, particularly when group members must publicly commit themselves, is far more effective at changing individuals' attitudes and behaviors than even the most persuasive lecture" (Slavin, 1986, p. 276).

Lewin's ideas were further refined by the social psychologist Morton Deutsch, who derived a theory of group process based on shared goals and rewards. Deutsch (1949) postulated that when a group is rewarded based on the behavior of its members, the group members would encourage one another to do whatever helps the group to be rewarded.

The work of Lewin, Deutsch, and others led to new perceptions about the power of truly integrated groups to get things done, to sanction and support members, and to create a different social fabric. It is, of course, in one form or another, an old idea, and to their credit, cooperative learning advocates admit this rather freely. Socrates, for example, used cooperative dialogue between teacher and pupil to advance learning. The Gestalt movement in psychology, which arose in Europe late in the 19th century, furnishes much of the original paradigm. Its famous epigram, that "the whole of something is greater than the sum of its individual parts," is fundamental to cooperative efforts. The pioneering work in perception and structural wholeness of such legendary psychologists as Max Wertheimer led to new insights regarding the strengths of collaboration in problem solving. What may have been felt or even known intuitively by some over the centuries (King Arthur's legendary Round Table comes to mind), now had a basis of well-grounded theoretical support. This set the stage for researchers to focus on the efficacy of cooperative group learning in school settings.

At Level II, the sheer amount of empirical evidence that has accumulated from research studies in cooperative learning is staggering. There are literally hundreds of published individual studies as well as numerous reviews, syntheses, and meta-analyses. There appears to be no review, synthesis, or meta-analysis that concludes that cooperative learning is deficient as a means to raise student achievement. In general, the conclusions are the same, and all tend to be mainly supportive.

Slavin's (1991) synthesis of the research on cooperative learning yields four main conclusions, each of which is consistent with the pure or basic research and theoretical model derived from Wertheimer, Lewin, Deutsch, and others. The conclusions are rather sweeping, but they certainly have a sound empirical foundation:

♦ For enhancing student achievement, the most successful approaches have incorporated two key elements: group goals and individual accountability; that is, groups are rewarded based on the individual learning of all group members.

♦ When group goals and individual accountability are clear, achievement effects of cooperative learning are consistently positive; 37 of 44 experimental/control comparisons of at least 4 weeks duration yielded significant positive effects, and none favored traditional methods.

- Positive achievement effects of cooperative learning have been found to about the same degree at all grade levels from 2–12, in all major subjects of the curriculum, and in urban, rural, and suburban schools. Effects are equally positive for high, average, and low achievers.

- Positive effects of cooperative learning have been documented consistently for such diverse outcomes as self-esteem, intergroup relations, acceptance of academically handicapped students, attitudes toward school, and ability to work with others.

A more recent meta-analysis was conducted by Z. Qin and David and Roger Johnson (1995) in which these researchers examined the effects of cooperative learning on problem solving. Having examined research studies done between 1929 and 1993, they concluded that cooperative learners outperformed their competitive counterparts in all four of the problem-solving areas examined: linguistic, nonlinguistic, well-defined, and ill-defined. These researchers concluded, "The practical implications of the finding that cooperation generally improves problem solving are obvious: On the job and in the classroom, cooperative groups will be better able to deal with complex problems than will competitors working alone" (p. 140).

At Level III, Stevens and Slavin (1995a; 1995b) conducted an impressive school evaluation study, the results of which indicated that cooperative learning could be effective in changing the school and classroom organization and instructional approach. Their research also shows that such large-scale implementation can be done effectively, and that learning can be enhanced for a variety of types of students when cooperative learning is used appropriately. They concluded their evaluation with this commentary:

> This study is the first and only evaluation of a cooperative elementary school. It is not merely another study of cooperative learning; it is the only study to

evaluate cooperative learning as the focus of school-wide change, the only study to evaluate cooperative learning in many subjects at once, and one of the few to show the effects of cooperative learning over a multiyear period. (p. 347)

To our knowledge, this remains the only such published Level III research. This level of research is greatly needed by the profession, and, unfortunately, it is seldom present in the annals of innovation. Our hope is that this will be the first of many such studies on not only cooperative learning, but on all of the innovations mentioned in this book.

CONCLUSION

Of all the educational innovations we have reviewed in this book, cooperative learning has the best and largest empirical base. It is not a perfect base, and as Slavin (1989/1990) has pointed out, more research is needed at senior high school levels as well as at college and university levels. It is also instructive to note that a good beginning has been made in the conduct of much-needed program evaluation or Level III research. Slavin also notes that the appropriateness of cooperative learning strategies for the advancement of higher-order conceptual learning is yet to be established firmly. However, the Qin, Johnson, and Johnson research mentioned earlier is certainly a start in that direction.

We conclude this chapter by saying that for the administrator or teacher who wishes to bring about positive change in a more or less traditional school environment, cooperative learning would seem to be well worth exploring. To do it well takes considerable training and motivation. And to convince some parents and other community members that it is more than kids sharing answers with each other will take some doing. These are comments one could make about any innovation, but in this case, the innovator will have little trouble finding supportive evidence.

REFERENCES

Aronson, E., Blaney, N., Stephan, C., Sikes, J., and Snapp, M. (1978). *The Jigsaw classroom.* Beverly Hills, CA: Sage.

Deutsch, M. (1949). A theory of cooperation and competition. *Human Relations, 2,* 129–152.

Goodlad, J. (1984). *A place called school.* New York: McGraw-Hill.

Johnson, D., and Johnson, R. (1989). *Cooperation and competition: theory and research.* Edina, MN: Interaction Book.

Johnson, D., and Johnson, R. (1989). *Leading the cooperative school.* Edina, MN: Interaction Book.

Johnson, D., and Johnson, R. (1994). *Learning together and alone. Cooperative, competitive, and individualistic learning.* Edina, MN: Interaction Book.

Johnson, D., and Johnson, R. (1994). *Cooperative learning in the classroom.* Alexandria, VA: Association for Supervision and Curriculum Development.

Johnson, D., Johnson, R., and Holubec, E. (1988). *Cooperation in the classroom.* Edina, MN: Interaction Book.

Kagan, S. (1989). *Cooperative learning resources for teachers.* San Juan Capistrano, CA: Resources for Teachers.

Kagan, S. (1989/90). The structural approach to cooperative learning. *Educational Leadership, 47*(4), 12–16.

Lewin, K. (1947). *Field theory in social sciences.* New York: Harper and Row.

Qin, Z., Johnson, D.W., and Johnson, R.T. (1995). Cooperative versus competitive efforts and problem solving. *Review of Educational Research, 65*(2), 129–143.

Sharan, S. (Ed.) (1990). *Cooperative learning: theory and research.* New York: Praeger.

Slavin, R., et al. (Eds.) (1985). *Learning to cooperate, cooperating to learn.* New York: Plenum Press.

Slavin, R. (1986). *Educational psychology: theory into practice.* Englewood Cliffs, N.J.: Prentice-Hall.

Slavin, R. (1989/90). Research on cooperative learning: consensus and controversy. *Educational Leadership, 47*(4), 52–54.

Slavin, R. (1991). Synthesis of research on cooperative learning. *Educational Leadership, 48*(5), 71–82.

Slavin, R. (1995). Synthesis of research on cooperative learning. In Page, J.A. (Ed.) *Beyond tracking: finding success in inclusive schools.* Bloomington, IN: Phi Delta Kappa Educational Foundation.

Stevens, R.J., and Slavin, R. (1995a). Effects of a cooperative learning approach in reading and writing on academically handicapped and nonhandicapped students. *The Elementary School Journal, 95*(3), 241–261.

Stevens, R.J., and Slavin, R. (1995b). The cooperative elementary school: effects on students' achievement, attitudes, and social relations. *American Educational Research Journal, 32*(2), 321–351.

12

MASTERY LEARNING

We believe this solution is relevant at all levels of education including elementary–secondary, college, and even at the graduate and professional school level.

Benjamin Bloom

Bloom's 1968 piece ["Learning for Mastery"] is indeed one of the most generative works to appear in the educational psychology literature in decades.

Glenn Hymel & Walter Dyck

In 1963, John Carroll wrote an article in the *Teachers College Record* entitled, "A Model for School Learning" (Carroll, 1963). It was in that article that Carroll laid the groundwork for mastery learning when he stated that time spent and time needed to learn are keys to achievement. Carroll's point is that given sufficient opportunity to learn (allocated equity instruction time), and time spent actually learning (engaged learning time), the vast majority of students can achieve some specified, expected level of performance.

Benjamin Bloom is credited with making the concept practicable when he developed an instructional system designed to eliminate connotations of failure by allowing students to successfully acquire basic skills before moving on, in sequential fashion, to increasingly difficult skills. Bloom outlined his premise in an important article (1968) titled, "Learning for Mastery." So, it is rather easy to trace the beginnings of this movement back to the work of Carroll and Bloom. Since those early days, mastery learning has found a niche, and, in fact, has been used in over 30 countries around the world (Hymel & Dyck, 1993).

Mastery learning is distinguished from other approaches by focusing attention on the organization of time and resources to ensure that students are able to master instructional objectives. The compelling argument made by advocates is that mastery learning, when properly implemented, results in increased student achievement.

The theoretical construct on which mastery learning is based is quite simple: all children can learn when they are provided with conditions that are appropriate for their learning. This means that no two persons will necessarily learn something at the same rate. We already know that, but, surprisingly, schools seldom take it into account. In subject areas where the sequential learning of skills and concepts is at stake, it is all too often the case that when a student falls behind, he or she is doomed to mediocrity of performance at best and failure at worst. This is indeed a tragedy if Bloom and Carroll are right, that the material itself is not too difficult for the student to learn and that, given an appropriate amount of time, the student in fact *would* learn it.

REDUCTIONISM AT WORK

Although the antecedent conditions of mastery learning have been traced back over the centuries, its basis for curricular application can be traced back to the work of Ralph Tyler of the University of Chicago, who argued that curriculum should be organized around clearly defined educational objectives, the achievement of which can be ascertained through measures that also reflect those objectives (Tyler, 1949). This position has a superficially appealing symmetry. It is a behaviorist position premised on the idea of reductionism. Reductionism states that most work can be reduced to smaller component parts, which can be clearly identified and sequenced. This premise is at odds with most progressive learning theories which tend to be "holistic" in nature. Progressives feel that by reducing ideas to component parts certain intangibles are lost in the process. So, we have the great philosophical divide over whether the whole is equal to or greater than the sum of its parts. Tyler's thinking represented a refinement of those of his own mentor, Franklin Bobbitt, who in turn had been greatly influenced by the work of the inventor and engineer, Frederick Winslow Taylor. Taylor is considered to be the father of scientific management, particularly as it has been applied for nearly a century to industrial settings. He wrote a number of published articles in the late 19th and early 20th centuries on such topics as "piece-rate systems," "notes on [conveyor] belting," and "shop management." The idea in each was that any form of factory work done by unskilled laborers could be broken down into constituent parts, sequenced, "mastered," and thereby made more efficient. The goal, of course, was increased production of goods. Taylor's ideas became so popular and in demand that, in time, he published them in a small, but highly influential book titled *Principles of Scientific Management* (1911). It was only a matter of time before his ideas on factory work were appropriated by Franklin Bobbitt and Ralph Tyler, and later by Bloom himself, as having potential for school learning.

At any rate, Tyler's so-called rationale based on clearly purposed, specified, and measured experiences is fundamental to such classroom applications as behavioral objectives, lesson plans, teacher monitoring and adjusting, criterion-based testing, and, therefore, mastery learning. So the process is linear beginning with purpose and ending with assessment, but it is also spiraled in that a successful assessment leads upward to the next level, and so on. In his classic work, *Basic Principles of Curriculum and Instruction* (1949), Tyler proposed four questions to be addressed by anyone who sets out to plan, develop, or implement a program of curriculum and instruction:

♦ What educational purposes should the school seek to attain?

♦ What educational experiences can be provided that are likely to attain these purposes?

♦ How can these educational experiences be effectively organized?

♦ How can we determine whether these purposes are being attained?

In these four basic questions, Tyler addresses purpose, experience, organization, and assessment. Put another way, the questions ask why, what, how, and whether. That's all straight-

forward enough, and it would appear to encompass the required conditions of teaching and learning. Tyler's is a rational,
logical, systematic, linear approach to curriculum and instruction. And this is the basis of mastery learning.

Mastery learning is also deeply invested in behaviorism.
All the protocols are there: reinforcement, contingency planning, monitoring, and feedback with correctives and adjust-
ments. It is safe to say that mastery learning is teacher-directed
in the sense that the teacher directs the flow of learning, typically using a combination of teacher explication and prepared
materials such as worksheets. The point is that students do not
simply choose what they will do, how and when they will do
it, and so on. Someone other than the student directs the
learning. So, an element of behaviorism, de facto programmed
learning, is either explicitly or implicitly present. The student is
expected to demonstrate in some overt or performance sense
that he or she has learned (mastered) the material to some acceptable level (typically, 80% correct) in order to move on to the
next piece. We have heard the argument that mastery learning
is method-neutral, a point which we address in Chapter 13 on
outcome-based education. But if it were, this would allow for
indirect methods, including discovery and inquiry as well as
self-realization activities. To carry out such activities using
mastery protocols would seem curious, to say the least. It
could well be said, however, that mastery learning is *content*-neutral simply because one could, we suppose, take anything deemed worth learning and break it down into constituent, sequenced parts.

IMPLEMENTATION OF MASTER LEARNING

There are two forms of mastery learning, but they share
common elements. One form is *individualized instruction* and
the other is *group-based* mastery learning. Individualized instruction is commonly based on the premise of continuous
progress (note the linear terminology) where a student works
entirely at the student's own rate. Individualized instruction
done within the frame of mastery learning involves the establishment of formative evaluation procedures along the way,

mastery criteria for unit tests, and corrective activities for those learners who fall short of a given criterion on the first or following attempts. An interesting example of this form is known as the Kellar Plan or Personalized System of Instruction (Simmons, 1974). It is used mainly at the postsecondary level with unit objectives established for a course of study. Tests accompany each unit. Students may take the tests in different but parallel forms as many times as they need to until they achieve mastery or a passing score.

Another example of individualized instruction–mastery learning is used in certain private Christian schools. It is called ACE, or Accelerated Christian Education, a complete K–12 curriculum. In this program students progress on their own through a series of workbooks for each subject in the curriculum. Each unit has a test which students may take as many times as needed until they reach the mastery criterion, which is 80% correct. The role of the teacher is to monitor progress and to lend assistance where it is required. In this program, students may complete the 13 years of education in more or less time, depending on their ability, motivation, rate of learning, and so forth.

The second form of mastery learning, group-based learning, is most closely associated with the work of Benjamin Bloom. Bloom has posed an intriguing learning concept that he calls the "Two Sigma Problem" (Bloom, 1984). He and his associates at the University of Chicago discovered that an average achiever could raise his or her score on criterion measures by two standard deviations (two sigma) if that student were to shift from group learning to tutorial learning. What we are talking about here is moving someone from the 50th percentile to about the 98th percentile, which is not a bad move. This felicitous outcome appeared to hold up across subject matter boundaries.

Critics quickly pointed out that, of course, you can raise students' achievement by giving them individual attention as opposed to what happens in a class of 30 or so. But the real question is what happens in a tutorial that brings about the dramatic difference in achievement? The answer to that question might shed some light on how classrooms could be reconfigured to take advantage of the elements of tutorial teaching and learning. One answer could be found in peer teaching. Another could be found in cooperative learning.

But mostly group-based mastery learning has been carried out using something along the lines of Madeline Hunter's procedures (see Chapter 2), which involve reducing the learning to manageable units and daily lesson objectives, teaching to those objectives, formative evaluation activities, reteaching when necessary, and summative assessment. Figure 12.1 illustrates the group-based mastery learning approach. The vast majority of studies point to beneficial outcomes. A few questions have, however, been raised about mastery learning's efficacy over time. We turn our attention now to the research literature.

FIGURE 12.1. PRINCIPLES AND COMPONENTS OF GROUP-BASED MASTERY LEARNING

Principles

- All Students are capable of learning.
- Learning can be broken down into its component parts.
- Learning must be sequential.

Components

- Planning—Content or skill to be learned is analyzed and divided into small units with related specific objectives and performance criteria. Preinstruction assessment identifies instructional starting point.
- Instruction—Teachers use appropriate strategies based on careful sequencing of the learning. In many instances, direct instruction is used involving modeling and practice.
- Formative Evaluation—Assessment is frequently used throughout the instructional process to determine if the learner is mastering the sequential prerequisite skills.
- Reteaching—Based on the formative evaluation results, the student is retaught material as needed with

new or alternative approaches or examples and with additional practice.

♦ Final Evaluation—Assessment to determine the degree to which the new content or skills have been mastered.

THE RESEARCH BASE FOR MASTERY LEARNING

The Level I foundation of mastery learning is confusing. Everyone from Pestalozzi to Skinner is claimed as a developer of the deep structure. The problem we see here is the confusion that results philosophically when educators think that what they are doing effectively crosses the lines from essentialist orientations to progressive orientations. We merely suggest that to try both is to obscure a sense of purpose.

The amount of Level II research on mastery learning is formidable. Among those programs we examined, only the cooperative learning research base compares favorably with it in quality and volume. The research base extends back over two decades. We now look at the major reviews, syntheses, and meta-analyses of mastery learning research.

The earliest synthesis of mastery learning research was conducted by Block and Burns (1976). They found consistently positive results for mastery learning. They also reported that mastery learning improved affective outcomes. Thus students were not merely learning more; they felt better about school and themselves as a result of their experience.

Kulik, Kulik, and Cohen (1979) conducted the next review. Their review covered 75 studies of Kellar's Personalized System of Instruction (PSI). They found consistently higher achievement, less variability of achievement, and higher student ratings in college classes where PSI was used.

The most celebrated mastery learning studies were those conducted by Bloom and his associates (1984). We mentioned these studies earlier in this chapter. Bloom's research consistently showed that group mastery learning produced an effect size of 1.0. This means that the student who is tutored and who raises his or her achievement 2.0 effect sizes, or two standard deviations, will raise his or her achievement one standard deviation above the mean in a group-based mastery learning situation. To raise one's achievement by an effect size of 1.0 represents an incredible outcome, so great that one researcher called group-based mastery learning the educational equivalent of penicillin.

The individual studies and reviews continued apace. Guskey and Gates (1986) found positive effect sizes for students at both elementary and secondary levels. The effect sizes were not as large as those found by Bloom, but were still considered to be educationally significant. And contrary to what one might hypothesize, the most efficacious outcomes were found in language arts and socials rather than where one might expect to find them, in science and mathematics.

Guskey and Pigott (1988) used a much larger database than those found in past reviews in search of the effects of mastery learning. Again, the results showed that mastery learning yielded consistently positive results with respect to both cognitive and affective outcomes. The findings were consistently positive across subject areas and types of measures used, whether criterion- or norm-referenced. Effect sizes were larger at elementary levels than at secondary or college levels.

Kulik and Kulik (1986–87) examined the research that focused on the effects of mastery testing—a single facet of mastery learning. Of the 49 studies they reviewed, 47 indicated positive effect sizes. They suggested that even though mastery testing is only one part of mastery learning, it could be the most important part in helping to raise student achievement. Stallings and Stipek (1986) and Walberg (1985) also give mastery learning generally positive reviews and suggest that the research supports its implementation into the school curriculum.

The only cautionary note is that sounded by Slavin (1987). He wrote:

> I required that the studies had to have taken place over at least four weeks. The studies that produced the big effects—the ones that Bloom talks about and that are cited in a lot of other mastery learning syntheses— were conducted in three days, one week, two weeks,

three weeks. Requiring that the treatment had to be in place for at least four weeks brings down the mastery learning studies to a very small number, and I think that even four weeks is really too short. (Brandt, 1988, p. 24)

Slavin goes on to point out that in the few mastery learning studies where a genuine control group was in place, the difference in achievement between experimental and control groups was virtually nonexistent. Essentially, he appears to be saying that the studies in mastery learning are lacking in factors affecting external and internal validity. This would seriously damage the exportability of these studies.

Block, Guskey, Bloom, and Walberg have all questioned Slavin's conclusions. Guskey writes, "The results of these best-evidence syntheses . . . are often potentially biased, highly subjective, and likely to be misleading" (1988, p. 26). Guskey goes on to say that Slavin used an "idiosyncratic approach" to reach his conclusions, and that a considerable body of research shows that mastery learning works regardless of the length of the study. Block, Bloom, and Walberg quite agree.

The Level III research, or that done at the program evaluation level, is very much intertwined with the outcome-based education (OBE) program evaluation research discussed in Chapter 13. This is so because all the OBE findings involved mastery learning at the core of the curriculum. As we said, it is mainly anecdotal, and the quality of the research is hardly a known entity.

CONCLUSION

The research literature in mastery learning is largely positive. Some of the best-known names in educational research circles have weighed in as supporters of this approach to teaching and learning. In spite of Slavin's well-founded concerns, the research in support of mastery learning is about as strong as one can find in the annals of educational investigation. Study after study indicates the superiority of mastery learning over traditional methods in raising test scores.

For those who favor an essentialist approach to education, that is, one that emphasizes direct instruction in basic skills, there appears to be much promise here. If one's goal is raising test scores, mastery learning would seem to be worth serious consideration. And, after all, raising test scores is hardly a trivial goal. On the other hand, those who favor a more experiential approach, such as that advocated in progressive literature, should probably look elsewhere.

REFERENCES

Block, J., and Burns, R. (1976). Mastery learning. In *Review of research in education, Vol. 4*, L.S. Shulman (Ed.). Itasca, IL: Peacock.

Block, J., Efthim, H., and Burns, R. (1988). *Building effective mastery learning schools*. New York: Longman.

Bloom, B.S. (1968). Learning for mastery. *Evaluation Comment*, 1(2) [unpaginated].

Bloom, B.S.(1981). *All our children learning: a primer for parents, teachers and other educators*. New York: McGraw-Hill.

Bloom, B.S. (1984). The search for methods of group instruction as effective as one-to-one tutoring. *Educational Leadership*. 41(8), 4–17.

Brandt, R. (1988). On research and school organization: a conversation with Bob Slavin. *Educational Leadership*, 46(2), 22–29.

Burns, R., and Squires, D. (1987). Curriculum organization in outcome-based education. *The OBE Bulletin*, 3. San Francisco: Far West Laboratory for Educational Research and Development (ERIC Document Reproduction Service No. ED294313).

Carroll, J.B. (1963). A model for school learning. *Teachers College Record*, 64, 723–733.

Guskey, T.R. (1987). Rethinking mastery learning reconsidered. *Review of Educational Research*, 57(2), 225–229.

Guskey, T.R. (1988). Response to Slavin: who defines best? *Educational Leadership*, 46(2), 26.

Guskey, T.R. (1994). Defining the difference between outcome-based education and mastery learning. *School Administrator, 51*(8), 34–37.

Guskey, T.R., and Gates, S.L. (1986). Synthesis of research on the effects of mastery learning in elementary and secondary classrooms. *Educational Leadership, 43*(8), 73–81.

Guskey, T.R., and Pigott, T.D. (1988). Research on group-based mastery learning programs: a meta-analysis. *Journal of Educational Research, 81*(4), 197–216.

Hymel, G.M., and Dyck, W.E. (1993). The internationalization of Bloom's learning for mastery: a 25-year retrospective–prospective view. Paper presented at the Annual Meeting of the American Educational Research Association (ERIC Document Reproduction Service No. ED360333).

Kulik, C.C., and Kulik, J. (1986–87). Mastery testing and student learning: a meta-analysis. *Journal of Educational Technology Systems, 15*(3), 325–341.

Kulik, C.C., Kulik, J., and Cohen, A. (1979). A meta-analysis of outcome studies of Keller's Personalized System of Instruction. *American Psychologist, 34*(4), 307–318.

Levine, D.U. (1985). *Improving student achievement through mastery learning programs.* San Francisco: Jossey-Bass, 1985.

Murphy, C. (Ed.) (1984). *Outcome-based instructional systems: primer and practice. Education brief.* San Francisco: Far West Laboratory for Educational Research and Development (ERIC Document Reproduction Service No. ED249265).

Simmons, F. (1974). *PSI, the Keller plan handbook: essays on a personalized system of instruction.* Menlo Park, CA: W.A. Benjamin.

Slavin, R.E. (1987). Mastery learning reconsidered. *Review of Educational Research, 57*(2), 175–213.

Stallings, J., and Stipek, D. (1986). Research on early childhood and elementary school teaching programs. In *Handbook of Research on Teaching* (3rd ed.), M.C. Witrock (Ed.). New York: Macmillan.

Tyler, R. (1949). *Basic principles of curriculum and instruction.* Chicago: The University of Chicago Press.

Walberg, H. J. (1984). Improving the productivity of America's schools. *Educational Leadership, 41*(8), 19–27.

Walberg, H. (1985). Examining the theory, practice, and outcomes of mastery learning. In *Improving student achievement through mastery learning programs,* D.U. Levine (Ed.). San Francisco: Jossey-Bass.

13

OUTCOME-BASED EDUCATION

America has all but abandoned outcomes-based education—and with it the growing impetus for a genuine paradigm shift in educational practice. For more than three years, conservative critics of progressive public school reforms have carried out an intense attack against anyone or anything purported to be "outcomes based."... The term "OBE" has taken on a life of its own and become the rallying slogan and the automatic justification for attacks on anything nontraditional.

William G. Spady

I would argue that models such as mastery learning or outcome-based education can function at the levels of training and instruction, but they contradict the idea of education as induction into knowledge.

James McKernan

Parents have discovered that the curriculum teaches globalism in the light of peace and environment. That is, there can be no peace until we have a one-world government, an international police force, army, political system and common currency. We used to call this international socialism, better known as international communism. When parents protest, they are called paranoid or radical. No one seems to care if that's true or not. This is why parents who oppose modern OBE have organized in districts all over America.

Robert L. Simonds

I don't see the problem with having clear outcomes for something like drivers training. Driving is based on legally-agreed on rules, and we don't want teenagers running over people. Maybe having prior outcomes for the study of great literature and art is another question.

Avril Fulsdai

In the first edition of this book, written several years ago, we made the following statement regarding outcome-based education (OBE): "We are unaware of any serious objections to OBE in the literature....After all, who could find fault with an attempt to clarify the outcomes we seek?" Little did we know! Interestingly, it was the content of the outcomes and not the process that seems to have struck a nerve. More than anything, the OBE movement has shown how deeply divided we are as a society when it comes to agreement on just what children should be learning at school. And it is, however, typical of popular educational innovations that rise up like mushrooms after a spring rain that it takes several years for sustained, serious criticism to set in. In 1993, Pennsylvania became the first state to make public its list of outcomes, about 500 in all. The ensuing battles were monumental, and in the words of one writer, "After the Pennsylvania fight, other states that were headed toward outcome-based reform began retreating faster than the Union Army at Bull Run" (Dykman, 1994).

The criticisms of OBE come from two completely different camps, a phenomenon that has caught the movement in a pincer. Progressives have criticized OBE for what they believe is its inherently simplistic, behaviorist, reductionist worldview of education. They find abhorrent the idea that educators can or should forecast outcomes for complex educational experiences. As James McKernan noted in his quote opening this chapter, one can certainly do that for training, but not for deeper learning. John Dewey once wrote, "An end established externally to the process of action is always rigid." The other critics in this unlikely coalition are to be found on the conservative side, and they count among their numbers home school advocates, syndicated newspaper columnists, antiestablishment educators, and certain political leaders. Their objections are rooted in a deep distrust of the motives of the public school establishment. They tend to view OBE as a mechanism by which certain political and social agendas, including the values and beliefs attendant to them, will be carried out.

In the 1990s, more educational battles have been fought over OBE issues than over any other issue. This is so, in part, because OBE unwittingly became a kind of catchall for a whole host of issues that have been festering for some time between liberals and conservatives. The vehemence of the partisans is as great as anything we can remember in modern times in education. Lawsuits, board recalls, fired administrators, and name-calling are the order of the day. What is it about this particular innovation that has stirred such deep and lasting controversy? We look first at what OBE was (or thought it was) when it was conceived, how it was actually implemented in a number of places, and what are the objections to it. We conclude with a look at the research base that supports (or doesn't support) it.

WHAT IS OUTCOME-BASED EDUCATION?

According to William Spady, the person most closely identified with the OBE movement from its inception in 1980, outcome-based education is a "culminating demonstration of learning." That is, OBE focuses on identifying and defining specified educational results and teaching toward them. Spady maintains that our current educational paradigm is backward. He cites custody and the calendar as the decision-making forces that drive our system. He writes that "school decision making, curriculum planning, instructional and administrative operations" are all determined by the calendar. School year, semesters, units, credits, class periods, and so forth are the driving forces. Blocks of time have become the way of assessing student success or failure in the system. One could go on: students must stay in school until they are 16 years old, state laws require a minimum number of days in the school year, a certain number of hours per week in reading and math, and so on. This is the stuff of bureaucracy, not the right stuff.

A PRESCRIPTION FOR SCHOOL MALADIES

Its advocates propose OBE as a cure for our schools' bureaucratic ills. Spady defines OBE this way: "Outcome-Based Education (OBE) means organizing for results: basing what we do instructionally on the outcomes we want to achieve, whether in specific parts of the curriculum or in the schooling process as a whole" (Spady, 1988, p. 5). The terms "organizing for results" and "success for all" have emerged as trademarks of the OBE movement, which, in 1980, founded a Network for Outcome-Based Schools.

Another definition, this one from the Far West Laboratory for Educational Research and Development, states that OBE is "a comprehensive approach to teaching and learning and to instructional management that has its roots in the Mastery Learning and Competency-Based Education movements of the early 1970s" (Murphy, 1984).

Several philosophical premises underlie OBE practice, but four themes are always present. The first theme is that almost all students are capable of achieving excellence in learning the essentials of formal schooling. Teachers and administrators must truly believe this premise in order to make OBE a reality. Even though this first theme seems compelling, in fact most teachers, administrators, and parents probably do not believe it. Therefore, if they were to embrace OBE, they would have to redirect their thinking away from the traditional idea that some are capable of excellence, many of mediocrity, and some of failure.

The second OBE theme is that success influences self-concept—self-concept influences learning and behavior. The implication of this theme is not only that academics and affect are related, but that there is a cause-and-effect relationship, with academic achievement being the cause and improved self-concept being the effect. And in time, they begin to support each other so that the relationship is reciprocal. We advise a careful reading of Chapter 4 on self-esteem in this regard.

The third theme is that the instructional process can be changed to improve learning. The perceived problem with the instructional process as it presently exists is that objectives and measured outcomes are often unrelated. Therefore, instruction continues apace and tests are given aplenty, but they are essentially unrelated processes that yield unreliable results. Students receive little or no corrective feedback and reinforcement along the way, so that they often have a poor idea of how they are doing in any kind of formative sense. This is a theme repeated in Mastery Learning, Direct Instruction, and other behaviorist approaches to teaching and learning.

And the fourth theme is that schools can maximize the learning conditions for all students by doing the following:

- Establishing a school climate which continually affirms the worth and diversity of all students;

- Specifying expected learning outcomes;

- Expecting that all students perform at high levels of learning;

- Ensuring that all students experience opportunities for personal success;

- Varying the time for learning according to the needs of each student and the complexity of the task;

- Having staff and students both take responsibility for successful learning outcomes;

- Determining instructional assignments directly through continuous [formative] assessment of student learning;

- Certifying educational progress whenever demonstrated mastery is assessed and validated.

REVERSING THE ORDER OF THINGS

The traditional school-practice paradigm is one of writing objectives for a curriculum which is already in place or which has undergone some degree of modification. OBE turns the paradigm on its head (Fig. 13.1). Note the near reverse order of things.

In OBE the curriculum and the resulting educational experiences flow from the outcomes that you and your colleagues have determined are crucial. OBE people call this the design-down principle. That is to say, one begins by thinking about the loftiest outcomes possible long before one specifies the tasks and tests of school life. How that is different from beginning with goal statements, as some people have done for years, we aren't sure. Advocates of outcome-based education would answer that although people claim to have begun with goal statements for years, the fact that they seldom questioned the given axioms of school life (time, subject matter, custody, etc.) speaks for itself.

FIGURE 13.1. TWO EDUCATIONAL SYSTEM PARADIGMS

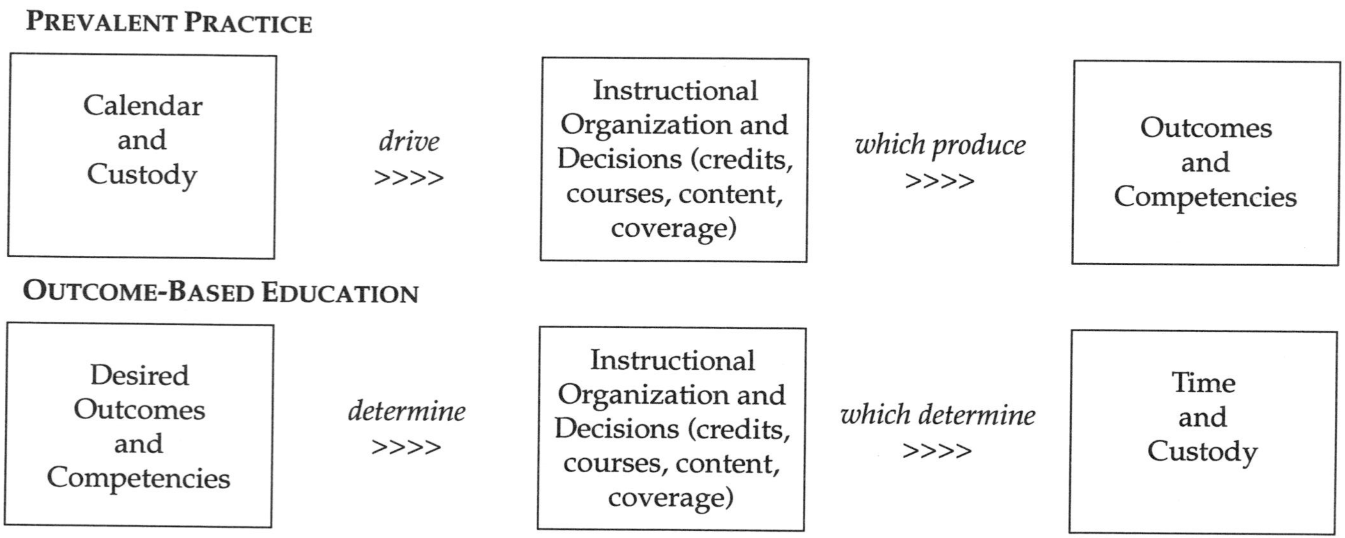

PREVALENT PRACTICE

Calendar and Custody

drive
>>>>

Instructional Organization and Decisions (credits, courses, content, coverage)

which produce
>>>>

Outcomes and Competencies

OUTCOME-BASED EDUCATION

Desired Outcomes and Competencies

determine
>>>>

Instructional Organization and Decisions (credits, courses, content, coverage)

which determine
>>>>

Time and Custody

Figure 13.2 illustrates the design-down principle in which one begins with clarity of focus on desired outcomes, which then become the controlling factor in curriculum and instruction decision making. If the outcomes are taken seriously, the thinking goes, then expanded opportunities and support for learning to truly happen must be put into place. This, as you might imagine, opens the door for mastery learning, generally a component of OBE.

FIGURE 13.2. OUTCOME-BASED DESIGN SEQUENCE AND GUIDING PRINCIPLES

Exit Outcomes >>> Program Outcomes >>> Course Outcomes >>> Unit Outcomes >>> Lesson Outcomes

1. **Clarity of focus on outcomes.** Curriculum, instruction, and evaluation should all be closely aligned with the desired educational outcomes. Students should always know what learning is expected of them and where they are in relation to the expected outcomes at all times.

2. **Design down from ultimate outcomes.** Curriculum and instructional decisions should be determined by the desired educational outcomes, rather than the other way around.

3. **Expanded opportunity and instructional support.** Content coverage is replaced by instructional coaching to ensure that the content is mastered, using formative evaluation, "second chance" instruction, and continual teacher encouragement and support.

4. **High expectations for learning success.** The teachers' underlying philosophy is that all students can learn and expect high quality work from students. Consequently, students may be expected to redo substandard work, take incomplete, and retake tests when necessary.

Source: Spady, W.G. (1988). Organizing for results: the basis of authentic restructuring and reform. *Educational Leadership*, 46(2), 7.

Built into the equation as an element of belief or philosophy of OBE is the success principle. The success principle implies that all students can learn and can produce work of good

quality, although it may take some students longer or more repeated efforts to do so than others.

An important point to note is that Spady makes it clear that
outcome-based education is concerned only with learning that
is cognitive and that can be demonstrated. Outcomes that are
affective in nature or value-laden do not fall under this curriculum model. The dichotomy between cognitive and affective, however, is not always so clear as the terms might imply,
and this has become a sticking point. Figure 13.3 gives his more
complete definition.

THE THREE FACES OF OUTCOME-BASED EDUCATION: TRADITIONAL, TRANSITIONAL, TRANSFORMATIONAL

Like all movements, OBE is differentially implemented in
real-world situations. At present, there appear to be three versions of what OBE means to school personnel. The purest form,
and the one touted by Spady, is Transformational OBE. As the
word "transformation" implies, this form of OBE calls for a
complete restructuring of the schools. Existing curriculum
models, instructional systems, and methods of assessment
would necessarily be replaced as dictated by the desired outcomes identified by school personnel. Anything less than this
represents compromise with the old ways of doing things, and
of course, in such circumstances one always risks the possibility of making great efforts merely to perfect a mistake.

Let us digress into what we hope will be a meaningful example. If a desired outcome of the school experience is that
students will think spatially, geometry comes quickly to mind.
The reason is that geometry is already in the curriculum, and it
always has been. But maybe (at least it is not out of the question) a course in architecture and design would get students to
the desired outcome more readily than would geometry. So in a
true transformation, all bets are off. The existing curriculum
must carry a burden of proof against the desired outcomes. It's
a rather refreshing idea in many ways, but it also has a tendency to destabilize the curriculum as we primarily know it.

FIGURE 13.3. WHAT IS AN OUTCOME?

Outcomes are high quality, culminating demonstrations of significant learning in context. Demonstration is the key word. An outcome is not a score or a grade, but the end product of a clearly defined process that students carry out. They are not values, attitudes, feelings, beliefs, activities, assignments, goals, scores, grades, or averages, as many people believe.

First, the demonstration must be high quality, which at a minimum, means thorough and complete, unlike conventional grading practices that accept and label student performances whether complete or not.

Second, the demonstration comes at the culminating point of the student's learning experiences. The term exit outcomes has emerged for those outcomes that occur at the close of a student's academic career.

Third, the demonstration must show significant learning; significant content is essential. Content alone, however, cannot be an outcome because it is inherently inert. Much like potential energy, it must be manifested through a demonstration process.

Fourth, all demonstrations of learning occur in some context or performance setting. We need only consider the difference between in-seat classroom demonstrations and public, on-stage performances to recognize how important this factor can be.

Source: Adapted from Spady, W. (1994a). Choosing out-comes of significance. *Educational Leadership, 51*(6), 18–22; and Spady, W., Marshall, K., and Rogers, S. (1994). Light, not heat, on OBE. *The American School Board Journal, 181*(11), 29–33.

At the other extreme is the form of OBE called Traditional. It is widely used today. The starting point for school districts using the Traditional form is the existing curriculum. Spady notes that this should more properly be called CBE, or Curriculum-Based Objectives, because the curriculum as it exists dictates the planning process. Here one would ask, "How can geometry help our students think spatially?" In one sense, this form serves the role of "straw man" which is beaten up by the

OBE purists as playing more of a confusing than a clarifying role in educational reform.

In between the two extreme forms, one finds Transitional OBE. Whether this form is analogous to the ill-fated attempt to "transition" Americans to the metric system of a few years ago (remember the highway signs that listed both mph and kph?), or whether it is a useful way to wean school systems away from the academic-discipline domination of traditional curriculum to clarifying outcomes in advance, is problematic.

IMPLEMENTING OUTCOME-BASED EDUCATION

The OBE implementation process begins with a commitment on the part of administrators, teachers, parents, and community to clarify educational outcomes for students. Here planners are encouraged to think as grandly as possible about the goal structure of education. This stage is crucial because it is here that planners have the opportunity to reinvent the purpose of the school. Subsequent decisions about materials, learning environments, grades, and so on, flow from the goal structure, for better or for worse.

Once the goal structure is secured, one enters the second stage of OBE, that of aligning the curriculum with a set of objectives. As basic and obvious as this seems, it isn't. This is so because the objectives are at least theoretically freed from the constraints of tradition. So now, having begun anew, we are able to close the gap between what we say will happen and, indeed, what does happen in classrooms.

Within actual classrooms, OBE is tolerant of a variety of teaching and learning strategies, but almost always mastery learning for each student is emphasized. Keep in mind that mastery learning is in fact method-neutral. Of course, it is far easier to "prove" mastery on the basis of text, worksheets, and so forth, than it is to document it where students are doing projects and activities; but that is an age-old problem. Student achievement, however, becomes the determining factor rather than time or schedule.

An evaluation plan, whatever forms evaluation takes, must be developed in such a way that evaluation is aligned with objectives and curriculum. In its extreme form, this involves teaching to the test. But given the alternative, teaching and testing as unrelated entities, it might not be such a bad idea. The point is that when teaching is aligned with testing, the latter becomes a natural outgrowth of the former. More than anything else, the OBE people have refocused our attention toward the concept of validity in assessment, and this itself is a major contribution.

OUTCOME-BASED EDUCATION
AND MASTERY LEARNING

Often mastery learning and outcome-based education (OBE) are thought of as synonymous. However, they really are not the same things. OBE is an overall planning and restructuring process at the macro level of school or district policy; often it involves mastery learning as a vital component. Mastery learning, as Benjamin Bloom defined it, is a micro level process. One implements it at the classroom level, and it is generally considered a part of the teaching and learning process.

Thomas Guskey (1994) has made an interesting analysis of this relationship. Guskey maintains that the guiding principles of OBE were set forth in Ralph Tyler's (1949) Basic Principles of Curriculum and Instruction, and that Tyler emphasized four fundamental questions:

- ♦ What educational purposes should the school seek to attain?
- ♦ What educational experiences can be provided that are likely to accomplish these purposes?
- ♦ How can these educational experiences be effectively organized?
- ♦ How can we determine whether these purposes are being attained?

"Tyler recognized, however, that 'in the final analysis, objectives are matters of choice and they must, therefore, be considered value judgments of those responsible for the school'" (p. 34). Guskey goes on to say that,

> Outcome-based education is principally a curriculum reform model with definite implications for assessing student learning. As such it directs the attention of educators to the first and fourth of Tyler's fundamental questions. . . .Mastery learning is, however, principally an instructional process designed to help teachers enhance their teaching procedures. . . .As such it focuses on the second and third of Tyler's fundamental questions. . . .The finest list of outcomes in the world, even if accompanied by valid assessment tools, represents at best a wish list. It will have little impact on student learning in the absence of effective instructional practices. . . .At the same time, highly effective instructional strategies must be paired with a thoughtfully planned curriculum. Having students learn well is of little value if what they are learning is trivial or unimportant. The combination of a thoughtful curriculum and effective instructional practices makes possible true improvement in education. (p. 37)

POLITICS, CRITICS, AND OUTCOME-BASED EDUCATION

Within the educational establishment there are critics of OBE whose reasons are based on educational desirability and workability (e.g., Furman, 1994; Schwarz, 1995). The critics within the establishment tend, as we noted earlier, to come from a certain segment of the progressive child-centered movement, and their perception is that OBE is a fixed, rigid, reductionist approach that logically applies only to training and not to education. However, these critics are few compared to the legions of parents and political and social conservative voices in society.

The history of OBE, brief as it is, is instructive to those who would understand the phenomenon that the eminent researcher Robert Slavin has called the Pendulum. Bruno Manno (1995a) observed:

Though initially a conservative idea for improving education standards, an idea bitterly resisted by the left, it is today as much championed by the left as it is decried by conservatives. . . .What happened was that the conservative effort to move the educational establishment in the direction of measuring the quality of education not by inputs (e.g., money spent on education) but by actual student achievement, or outcomes (e.g., grades and test scores), was hijacked by the left. Though conservative reformers successfully moved the debate in the direction of outcomes, they lost the battle over how to define which outcomes constitute a well-educated student. (p. 19)

In fact, what has happened is that in many states, districts, and schools where OBE has been adopted, educators have not followed Spady's limited definition of an "outcome" (see Fig. 13.3), and have indeed included values, attitudes, and beliefs as educational outcomes for the schools. Of course, Spady himself cannot expect, neither can he be expected, to control a movement once it is abroad in the land. Outcomes that focus on the "appreciation of diversity," the ability to live in a "global community," and "good citizenship" are invitations to differential interpretation at the very least. And how will they be measured even if we (1) agree on definition, and (2) agree that they are important school-based outcomes? Does appreciation of diversity mean a student must accept and be taught about the diversity that includes so-called alternative lifestyles? Must a child and the child's parents accept the idea of a "global community" in place of traditional patriotism? Even some of the more cognitive outcomes are seen by some as part of a social agenda for which they have no sympathy. For example, several critics cite the outcomes developed by a Virginia school district: "Students should become knowledgeable of various racial and ethnic cultures . . . and differences based on gender, age and physical ability." A second outcome states that students should be "good citizens who are responsible, contributing members of the local, national, and world community. . . ." This is seen by the wary as a way to open the schools to the teaching of feminism and the acceptance of homosexuality. "World community" means teaching a view of one-world government that would eliminate nationalism. And so on.

For example, Phyllis Schlafly, President of the Eagle Forum, has stated, "OBE outcomes include global citizenship, world government, population control, radical feminism, environmental extremism, and acceptance of lifestyles that most people believe are immoral" (1994, p. 27). She has seven objections to OBE: (1) the dumbing down effect, (2) a feel-good emphasis, (3) an antiphonics commitment, (4) attitudes, not aptitudes, (5) invasion of pupil privacy, (6) lack of accountability, and (7) unacceptable ambiguity.

Beverly LaHaye, President of Concerned Women for America, has cited numerous examples of stated outcomes that are affective and values-laden in character. She has written that "Transformational OBE leaves parents completely out of the learning process and attempts to restructure their children's values and emotions" (1994, p. 28).

Robert L. Simonds, President of Citizens for Excellence in Education, writes, "As a whole, OBE is a dangerous concept, capable of trashing an entire education system in a school district" (1994, p. 41).

These comments are typical of the criticisms of OBE that have come largely from outside the educational establishment. As one might imagine, Spady maintains that the critics' writings are "replete with dozens of inaccurate and misleading points, assertions, conclusions, and allegations that are extremely familiar," and that "not everything that is called OBE actually is" (1994b, p. 30). Spady's defense is typical of these situations, and there have been many in 20th-century educational history, where the opposing sides are sharply drawn and a movement has taken on a life of its own. If one were to read the chronicle of the progressive–essentialist debates from the 1920s to the present, one would have little trouble finding similar charges. The history of these battles follows a familiar litany where educators within the establishment come up with a reform of some sort, which spreads rapidly through the professional educational community, and finally a counterattack is launched by traditionalists, generally from outside the educational community. We could be talking about the child-centered movement, open education, look-say and language-experience reading approaches, or New Math. The players change with time, the innovations vary somewhat, but the plot line stays the same.

To return to OBE specifically, where the outcomes are indeed affective in nature and the critics are right, it may be as Bruno Manno (1995a) has observed: "Forcing parents to send their children to school is one thing. But for the state to declare that students cannot graduate from a school that they must attend unless they demonstrate competence in state-approved values and attitudes has all the trappings of Aldous Huxley's Brave New World" (p. 22).

A final criticism of OBE is the perception that it has a "dumbing down effect" resulting from the type of watered-down curriculum designed to ensure equal outcomes. The problem here is twofold. In the first place, spelling out desired end results seems to create a least-common denominator effect. This phenomenon plagued the competency-based education movement, and it is one that mastery learning has attempted to deal with, achieving some success, primarily through acceleration as opposed to enrichment, which might well be considered questionable. The other issue is that there is considerable difference between equal outcomes and equal opportunity. To deny a child equal opportunity to learn is unconscionable. To decide on equal outcomes prior to experience is to ignore a vast array of educational variables. In fact, it may be somewhat like fixing a basketball game so that all players play regardless of ability, perseverance, or motivation, as it will not matter because the score has been predetermined as a tie. We leave it to you to make up your own mind as to the validity of these charges.

THE RESEARCH BASE FOR
OUTCOME-BASED EDUCATION

LEVEL I RESEARCH

OBE makes few direct claims here that we were able to find. We would say, however, and this represents some interpolation and inference building on our part, that the theory of reductionism is at work here. By that, we mean that OBE defines success as increased achievement as reflected by higher standardized test scores. Given the OBE operational definition of success, and given that objectives are reduced toward alignment with test content, we can reasonably assume a reductionist world view.

There are three major premises upon which OBE is founded. Those premises are: (1) all students can learn and succeed, not necessarily in the same way or at the same rate; (2) success breeds success (just recall the old saying than nothing succeeds like success); and (3) schools control the conditions of success. A measure of OBE's own success is the set of statements found in the National Goals for America's Schools, which demand student outcomes at the center of improvement efforts.

The idea that all students can learn the curriculum traces back to the work of John Carroll who wrote a most intriguing article for Teachers College Record in 1963, titled "A Model of School Learning" (Carroll, 1963). Carroll's thesis, which in time was adopted by Benjamin Bloom, was that the issue is not whether a student can learn the curriculum, but the length of time it might take the student to learn it. Carroll suggested that we have confused time with ability, unwittingly rewarding those who are able to keep up with the daily flow of events and punishing the slower (not necessarily less intelligent) students.

Thus all, or nearly all, students can learn the third grade mathematics curriculum, for example, but they will naturally learn it at different rates. This ought not to surprise us, but apparently it does, given the way school is controlled by time. And that becomes one of the central arguments of OBE: that by reconceptualizing our sense of purpose we are able to determine what we really want to accomplish.

The second premise of OBE, that success breeds success, is something that each of us knows experientially. Some research has shown (Walberg, 1984) that the motivation to learn academic subject matter is primarily the result of prior learning. In other words, the rich get richer and the poor get poorer. OBE enthusiasts point to success for every learner as something that needs to be built into the goal structure. Who could not argue?

The third premise of OBE, that schools control the conditions of success, is depressing if one thinks of the realities of school life for many children who walk down a lonely road of failure every day. On the other hand, it is an empowering idea if one thinks of the possibilities. Again, the idea is that by reconceptualizing our very sense of purpose, we will think in terms of success for all rather than a competitive system where learning is treated as a scarce resource available only to a few.

LEVEL II RESEARCH

At Level II, some people like to point to the research base for mastery learning as evidence for the effectiveness of OBE (as we did in the previous edition of this book), but, as Slavin (1994) has stated, this is probably not correct to do. In any event, mastery learning does not necessarily show the efficacy of OBE because, as Guskey points out, the two are not really the same things. As Slavin writes, "This being the case, advocates on both sides of the debate have attempted to make inferences about OBE from other areas of research." When considered apart from mastery learning, we are not aware of small-scale experimental studies that look at the efficacy of outcome-based education, although there is no shortage of anecdotal stories and claims made about its value. Earlier, Evans and King (1994) also concluded that published research was very limited. In fact, Slavin (1994) stated, "To my knowledge, no studies directly compare students in OBE classes or schools to students in similar control schools" (p. 14). We couldn't find any either.

LEVEL III RESEARCH

At Level III, or the level of actual program evaluation re-search, we found many stories about schools and whole districts that have been "turned around" by OBE. Given the previously ad-dressed definition of success as improved test scores, we encountered claims from the far-flung outposts of empire: John-son City, New York; New Canaan, Connecticut; Red Bank, New Jersey; Sparta, Illinois; and the list goes on. The fact that test scores have improved is a hard fact to walk away from, given the manifold woes of American schools.

What is not clear is the quality of these program evaluations. They are largely unpublished and otherwise unavailable for critical review. They could range from those of excellent design and execution to mere "gee whiz" stories. Where we were able to obtain unpublished program evaluation results from districts, we examined them carefully, concluding in each case that too many unaccounted for variables (e.g., changing demographics) raised the specter of rival hypotheses that threatened both the internal and external validity of the results.

CONCLUSION

The ideas underlying OBE and its implementation remain to this day more in the realm of speculation and belief than in empirical findings. Some of them have virtually no empirical evidence to shore them up. Others have some. And most are so complicated by untoward variables as to render any attempt to "prove" them highly problematic.

OBE as such may well have run its course. This observation could raise the question of why we included it in the present volume. We included OBE because it has survived in mutated forms, particularly as Performance-Based Education. Whether this change is something William Spady and his colleagues approve of is uncertain. And whether it will be greeted any more enthusiastically than its predecessor is yet to be determined. It does, however, keep the idea alive while allowing it a kind of fresh start that may render it less controversial. To the extent that Spady's plea that the focus should be on cognitive outcomes and not on affective outcomes is heeded, it may well take hold. The problems, however, with a model that is essentially about training and not about the complexities of education still remain.

At the present time, a large number of states have moved ahead with a performance-based agenda, one which is closely tied with attempts to reform assessment protocols. One thing is certain, the idea of setting goals, objectives, competencies, performances, and outcomes for school learning seems to have considerable staying power, and we predict it will be around for a long time in one form or another.

REFERENCES

Bloom, B.S. (1984). The search for methods of group instruction as effective as one-to-one tutoring. *Educational Leadership, 41*(8), 4–17.

Burns, R., and Squires, D. (1987). Curriculum organization in outcome-based education. *The OBE Bulletin, 3.* San Francisco: Far West Laboratory for Educational Research and Development (ERIC Document Reproduction Service No. ED294313).

Carroll, J.B. (1963). A model for school learning. *Teachers College Record, 64,* 723–733.

Dykman, A. (1994). Fighting words: across the nation outcome-based education is embroiled in controversy. *Vocational Educational Journal,* November/December, 36–39.

Erickson, W., Valdez, G., and McMillan, W. (1990). *Outcome-based education.* St. Paul, MN: Minnesota Department of Education.

Evans, K.M., and King, J.A. (1994). Research on OBE: what we know and don't know. *Educational Leadership, 51*(6), 12–17.

Furman, G.C. (1994). Outcome-based education and accountability. *Education and Urban Society, 26*(4), 417–437.

Guskey, T.R. (1994). Defining the differences between outcome-based education and mastery learning. *School Administrator, 51*(8), 34–37.

Guskey, T.R. Rethinking mastery learning reconsidered. *Review of Educational Research, 57*(2), 225–229.

Guskey, T.R., and Gates, S.L. (1986). Synthesis of research on the effects of mastery learning in elementary and secondary classrooms. *Educational Leadership, 43*(8), 73–81.

Guskey, T.R., and Pigott, T.D. (1988). Research on group-based mastery learning programs: a meta-analysis. *Journal of Educational Research, 81*(4), 197–216.

Kulik, C.C., and Kulik, J. (1986-87). Mastery testing and student learning: a meta-analysis. *Journal of Educational Technology Systems, 15*(3), 325–341.

LaHaye, B. (1994) A radical redefinition of schooling. *School Administrator, 51*(8), 28–29.

Manno, B.V. (1995a). Educational outcomes do matter. *Public Interest, 119,* 19–27.

Manno, B.V. (1995b). The new school wars: battles over outcome-based education. *Phi Delta Kappan, 76*(9), 720–726.

Murphy, C. (Ed.) (1984). *Outcome-based instructional systems: primer and practice. Education brief.* San Francisco: Far West Laboratory for Educational Research and Development (ERIC Document Reproduction Service No. ED249265).

Network for Outcome-Based Schools. *Outcomes* (quarterly publication of the Network). Johnson City, NY: Johnson City Central Schools.

Rubin, S.E., and Spady, W. (1984). Achieving excellence through outcome based instructional delivery. *Educational Leadership, 41*(8), 37–44.

Schlafly, P. (1994). My seven objections to student outcomes. *School Administrator, 51*(8), 26–27.

Schwarz, G. (1995). The language of OBE reveals its limitations. *Educational Leadership, 52*(1), 87–88.

Simonds, R.L. (1994) A dangerous experiment. *Vocational Educational Journal,* November/December, 40–41.

Slavin, R.E. (1987). Mastery learning reconsidered. *Review of Educational Research, 57*(2), 175–213.

Slavin, R.E. (1994). Outcome-based education is not mastery learning. *Educational Leadership, 51*(6), 14.

Spady, W.G. (1981). *Outcome-based instructional management: a sociological perspective.* Washington, DC: National Institute of Education (ERIC Document Reproduction Service No. ED244728).

Spady, W.G. (1988). Organizing for results: the basis of authentic restructuring and reform. *Educational Leadership, 46*(2), 4–8.

Spady, W.G. (1991). Beyond traditional outcome-based education. *Educational Leadership, 49*(2), 67–72.

Spady, W. (1994a). Choosing outcomes of significance. *Educational Leadership, 51*(6), 18–22.

Spady, W.G. (1994b). An appeal to objective dialogue: a response to Schlafly and LaHaye. *School Administrator, 51*(8), 30–31.

Spady, W.G. (1996). The trashing and survival of OBE. *Education Week*, March 6, 41,43.

Spady, W., Marshall, K., and Rogers, S. (1994). Light, not heat, on OBE. *The American School Board Journal, 181*(11), 29–33.

Stallings, J., and Stipek, D. (1986). Research on early childhood and elementary school teaching programs. In *Handbook of research on teaching* (3rd ed.), Witrock, M.C. (Ed.). New York: Macmillan.

Stephens, G.M., and Herman, J.J. (1984). Outcome-based educational planning. *Educational Leadership, 41*(8), 45–47.

Tyler, R. (1949). *Basic principles of curriculum and instruction.* Chicago: University of Chicago Press.

Vickery, T.R. (1990). ODDM: a workable model for total school improvement. *Educational Leadership, 47*(7), 67–70.

Walberg, H. (1985). Examining the theory, practice, and outcomes of mastery learning. In *Improving student achievement through mastery learning programs*, Levine, D.U. (Ed.). San Francisco: Jossey-Bass.

14

DIRECT INSTRUCTION

D.I. interventions have been shown to produce superior performance with preschool, elementary, and secondary regular and special education students and adults. They have produced superior results with various minority populations, including non-English speakers.

Gary L. Adams

It's a matter of balance. . . and Direct Instruction may in fact be limiting for some people in that it doesn't allow them to be as creative as they might. . . . It prescribes, it's limiting, it's structured, it tells you exactly how it should be done. . . . Classrooms ought to be more than worksheets, ought to be more than multiplication facts. . . . It's got to be reading plus and reading for a purpose.

Bertha Pendleton

What ever you do, don't stick this state with the DISTAR program.

Anonymous school district curriculum director

"What if somebody could come up with a method of teaching children how to read that was simple and worked every time. That sounds like the impossible dream to parents and school kids. But we found such a method. And you may be shocked to find out that most schools refuse to try it." This was how Hugh Downs of ABC–TV began a 1996 episode of *20/20*, the long-running TV news magazine. During Downs' interview with Professor Siegfried Engelmann, the originator and developer of Direction Instruction (D.I.), Engelmann claimed that in his 30 years of working with D.I. he has never found a student who couldn't learn to read.

Given the problems with basic literacy that this country faces, could this be the miracle cure we have all been looking for? It sounds too good to be true. The never-ending quest for a silver bullet seems for once to have been satisfied. Advocates say search no more—it is just a matter of applying the principles of D.I. in classrooms. And yet, Direct Instruction has its detractors, critics, and opponents. Why is this so? In this chapter, we examine the evidence in support of and against D.I., and let you reach your own conclusion. We will define it, search for theory building and empirical evidence, and see whether program evaluations tend to support its use or not.

WHAT IS DIRECT INSTRUCTION?

There is some confusion over the terminology, so let us begin there. First of all, it is useful to distinguish between direct instruction (d.i.), and Direct Instruction (D.I.), although there is a relationship. D.I. refers to a range of about 60 instructional programs, developed by Engelmann and his colleagues, that set standards of learning based on specific techniques and teacher-directed sequences, whereas d.i. refers to the work of Barak Rosenshine (1979; 1986), and others, which is based on a highly organized and structured, teacher-directed, task-oriented approach to instruction. Obviously, there is common ground here, the commonality being primarily that of a basic skills, linear, teacher-directed approach to instruction. Philosophically, both are, roughly speaking, educational manifestations of a point of view known as essentialism.

Linda Darling-Hammond and Jon Snyder (1992) quote Rosenshine's description of direct instruction as occurring in:

> academically focused, teacher directed classrooms using sequenced and structured materials. It [d.i.] refers to teaching activities where goals are clear to students, time allocated for instruction is sufficient and continuous, coverage of content is extensive, the performance of students is monitored, questions are at a low cognitive level. . . and feedback to students is immediate and academically oriented. In direct instruction, the teacher controls instructional goals, chooses materials appropriate for the student's ability, and paces the instructional episode. The goal is to move the students through a sequenced set of materials or tasks. Such materials are common across class-

rooms and have a relatively strong congruence with the tasks on achievement tests. (p. 65)

Adams and Engelmann (1996) write that "the most common confusion is that Direct Instruction is simply teacher-directed instruction, the opposite of the so-called 'child-centered' approaches (such as the open classroom or discovery method) in which the teacher is supposed to act as a facilitator for students. Traditional teacher-directed instruction is not Direct Instruction; it is just direct teaching or teacher-directed instruction" (p. 1). While this statement oversimplifies Rosenshine's rather elaborate description, it does draw attention to the useful idea that direct instruction is more generic, a larger tent so to say, than Direct Instruction. D.I. is a specific instructional approach consisting of (1) "Direct Instruction techniques and sequences that set standards by documenting what students can achieve," or (2) "commercial Direct Instruction sequences and materials that are designed for use by people who have not been trained directly by Engelmann and his colleagues" (p. 2). As we shall see, commercial variants of D.I. appear under different labels applied to reading, math, and language.

It is thus safe to say that D.I. is a specific example of d.i. To return to Rosenshine's description, D.I. fits into it rather well. D.I. proponents are quick to point out that their programs are not representative of many of the aspects of generic direct instruction. Lecture, for example, is a type of direct instruction, and D.I. programs are virtually lecture-free. Wide-ranging, teacher-directed class discussions are also examples of direct instruction not found in Direct Instruction. So, like any variant of a larger set, there is commonality as well as divergence between it and other members of the set. This attempt at likenesses and differences on our part may seem laborious, but without it confusion reigns. Our focus in this chapter is primarily on D.I. because D.I.'s research claims are manageable within the constraints of a chapter, while to assess the research findings in d.i. would take us into such labyrinthine corridors as lecture, seatwork, textbooks, teacher-led class discussion, and a range of variables rather numerous to say the least.

Direct Instruction was first implemented in 1968 as part of the U.S. Office of Education's Project Follow Through and has continued in use in a variety of states, districts, and schools around the country since that time. The first series in reading and arithmetic was known as DISTAR (Direct Instruction System for Teaching Arithmetic and Reading, later changed to Direct Instruction System for Teaching and Remediation). These and other instructional programs have been published commercially and have a variety of names (see Fig. 14.1). In addition an entire series of instructional programs is available on videodisc and aimed at adult learners.

FIGURE 14.1. DIRECT INSTRUCTION COMMERCIAL PROGRAMS

Reading	Language Arts	Mathematics
Reading Mastery I, II	*Reasoning and Writing: Levels A–F*	*Connecting Math Concepts: Levels A–F*
Reading Mastery: Fast Cycle	*DISTAR Language I, II*	*Arithmetic I, II*
Reading Mastery III, IV, V, VI	*Cursive Writing Program*	*Corrective Mathematics*
Corrective Reading: Decoding	*Expressive Writing 1, 2*	*Mathematics Modules*
Corrective Reading: Comprehension	*Spelling Mastery*	
	Corrective Spelling Through Morphographs	

Source: Adams, G., and Engelmann, S.(1996). *Research on direct instruction: 20 years beyond DISTAR.* Seattle, WA: Educational Achievement Systems.

DISTAR was designed for use with K–3 children, particularly in compensatory school settings with lower achievers. It "emphasizes frequent teacher-student interactions guided by carefully sequenced, daily lessons in reading, arithmetic, and language" (Engelmann et al., 1988). The developers describe the underlying assumptions of the Direct Instruction Model: "(a) all children can be taught; (b) the learning of basic skills and their application in higher-order skills is essential to intelligent behavior and should be the main focus of a compensatory education program; (c) the disadvantaged must be taught at a faster rate than typically occurs if they are to catch up with their middle-class peers" (p. 303).

The Direct Instruction Model is guided by two major rules (Fig. 14.2) and includes carefully designed curriculums in reading, arithmetic, and language. These curriculums are basic skills, to say the least: phonics and decoding skills, grammar rules, arithmetic operations, logical processes, and problem solving. The model also stresses increased teaching time, with at least 2 hours a day devoted to these specific skills. "Efficiently teaching" means "scripted presentation of lessons, small-group instruction, reinforcement, corrections, and procedures to teach every child by giving added attention to the lower performers (Engelmann et al., pp. 306–307). Basically, there is a lot of oral drill, recitation, and memory work. The scripted lessons include exactly what the teacher will say and do during the instructional time using procedures that have been field-tested and revised for effectiveness. This also permits a supervisor to identify deficiencies quickly and to provide appropriate remedies. Critics at the time quickly labeled such approaches to education as "teacher proof," meaning that the procedures were so tightly scripted that even the worst of teachers could hardly go wrong. The idea, so critics claimed, was that "at last here is a method that even *you* can't screw up."

The D.I. model ideally requires extensive staff development and training. Teachers can, and have, used D.I. without formal training, but there is much they might miss by doing so. The equation is far more complex than merely putting a teacher in front of a group of students, even with the materials at hand, and allowing him or her to interpret along the way. Among its elaborate features, for example, is a procedure for keeping track of and coordinating all services given to an individual student, including nutrition, health, psychological, social, and guidance and counseling services. The major components of the program are presented in Figure 14.3.

FIGURE 14.2. THE TWO MAJOR RULES OF DIRECTION INSTRUCTION

I. Teach more in less time:

♦ The model uses a teacher and an aide at levels 1 and 2 of the programs, usually in kindergarten and first grade. The aides are trained to teach and function fully as teachers and, thus, increase the amount of teacher-student interaction time.

♦ Programs are designed to focus on teaching the general use of information and skills where possible, so that through teaching a subject, the whole set is learned. For example, by teaching 40 sounds and skills for hooking them together students learn a generalized decoding skill that is relevant to one-half of the more common English words.

II. Control the details of what happens:

♦ Daily lesson scripts are provided that tell the teacher exactly what to say and do. All teachers and aides use the DISTAR programs in reading, language, and arithmetic developed by Engelmann and his associates.

♦ Training is provided so that the staff knows how to execute the details of the program.

♦ Student progress and, indirectly, teacher implementation are monitored through the use of criterion-referenced "continuous progress tests" on the children every 2 weeks.

♦ Supervisors (1 for each 10–15 classrooms) are trained to spend 75% of their time actually in classrooms working with teachers and aides.

♦ Procedures for teachers, supervisors, administrators, and parents are detailed in implementation and parent coordinator manuals.

Source: Engelmann, S., Becker, W.C., Carnine, D., and Gersten, R. (1988). The direct instruction follow through model: design and outcomes. *Education and Treatment of Children, 11*(4), 303–304.

FIGURE 14.3. MAJOR COMPONENTS OF THE DIRECT INSTRUCTION MODEL

◆ Consistent focus on academic objectives.

◆ High allocations of time to small-group instruction in reading, language, and math.

◆ Tight, carefully sequenced DISTAR curriculum, which includes a task analysis of all skills and cognitive operations, and numerous opportunities for review and practice of recently learned skills.

◆ Ongoing inservice and preservice training that offers concrete, "hands on" solutions to problems arising in the classroom.

◆ A comprehensive system for monitoring both the rate at which students progress through the curriculum and their mastery of the material covered.

Source: Adapted from Meyer, L. A. Gersten, R.M., and Gutkin, J. (1983). Direction instruction: a project follow through success story in an inner-city school. *The Elementary School Journal, 84(2),* 243.

Since 1968, then, Direct Instruction programs have been used nationwide by a very dedicated, but relatively small, number of teachers and professionals who claim great success with it. The tenets have changed little since its inception 30 years ago, although it has probably become even more associated with teaching directed at low achievers and disadvantaged children than with high achievers. Its proponents say this is simply because the system works with low performers where other methods do not. They claim that it works equally well with average and high achievers, but obviously with fewer repetitions, shorter time needed for learning, and so forth.

THE CRITICS

There is surprisingly little criticism in the literature, at least that we could find, of Direct Instruction. That does not mean there are no critics. Indeed, there are many. Curiously, however, D.I. has been largely unacknowledged except by its advocates. Perhaps the old saw, "ignore it and it will go away" obtains here. The following oblique mention of the D.I. approach, aimed primarily at phonics-based reading instruction, is offered by Zemelman et al. (1993). They write: "Most children learned how to decode simple print. But we did not create a nation of mature, effective, voluntary, self-motivated, lifelong readers: on the contrary, most Americans stopped reading the moment they escaped from school" (p. 22).

There is, however, more than one way to "escape" from school. A study by Meyer et al. (1983) of high school graduation rates for three cohort groups in the New York City schools showed that the dropout rates were statistically significantly lower among students taught by Direct Instruction than were those of a comparison group. And the percentages of those applying to and accepted by colleges were statistically significantly higher among the D.I. group than among the comparison group. Interestingly, Zemelman et al. do not even mention either D.I. or d.i. in their coverage of reading research in their book, *Best Practice: New Standards for Teaching and Learning in America's Schools* (1993).

One does find in the writings of D.I. enthusiasts allusions to the objections of the critics. Critics, they say, argue that D.I. is "old-fashioned," that it is too much work for the teacher, that it is more tiring, too regimented, promotes passive and rote learning, and stifles teacher creativity. To rebut these charges, to the extent that they are even made, there is no evidence offered; in fact, one seldom finds *any* written criticism from the critics. It seems to be basically ignored, much like Brussels sprouts, primarily based on personal distaste.

The many teachers we have talked to about D.I. often point out that it is so regimented as to stifle their creativity. This is an interesting statement, to say the least. They reject it not because it doesn't work, but because it stifles teacher creativity. That is, they feel limited. But it could at least be argued that teacher creativity is not the end product of schooling, student learning is. Imagine doctors rejecting a treatment, not because it didn't work, but because it cramped their style, or stifled their creativity, or was too boring and tedious for them to use. Admittedly, this is a problem because teacher happiness and fulfillment is important. But perhaps one could put forth the scarcely novel idea that there is a time for everything—a time to be creative and a time to be didactic—especially if that didacticism is shown to work in the teaching of basic skills. As to the criticism of rote learning, there may be some degree of truth to it, although D.I. proponents say that that is only part of what is learned. On the other hand, rote learning is quite necessary in the form of number facts, letter sounds, and so on, in order to provide the building blocks of higher learning.

THE RESEARCH BASE FOR DIRECT INSTRUCTION
LEVEL I RESEARCH

The theoretical basis of both direct instruction and Direct Instruction is represented by a seemingly ad hoc mixture of behaviorism, cognitive science, and reductionism. When one peels away the layers and reaches the core, however, one encounters a clearly essentialist philosophy. Consider, for example, this ambiguity-reducing statement by Adams and Engelmann, authors of *Research on Direct Instruction: 20 Years Beyond DISTAR* (1996): "The first job of the teacher, therefore, is to teach basic skills and knowledge" (p. 27). Many, of course, would agree with this thought, but it does clearly put some distance between those who sympathize with it and those who advocate progressive education. Essentialism is largely a 20th-century phenomenon, which rose to prominence based on its drumbeat attacks on progressivism. Educational essentialists of prominence include William Bagley, Arthur Bestor, and, more recently, William Bennett. Basically, essentialism promotes fundamental skills and knowledge, standards, testing, and mastery learning, while eschewing such approaches as nondirective learning, personalized curriculum, open-concept education, and developmentally appropriate practice.

That D.I. is behaviorist in orientation is clear. Emphasis is placed on objective and observable behaviors; reinforcement theory is promoted in the form of rapid feedback; the teacher (not the student) is expected to arrange the conditions of learning; and carefully planned, sequentially-ordered teaching is carried out. Thus, one could reasonably find the theories of Pavlov, Watson, Skinner, and other giants of this movement as forming much of its backcloth. However, just as behaviorism has modified its stance against mental processes that cannot be observed, so does one find elements of cognitive science imbedded here. The type of cognitive science one encounters in D.I. is that branch related to information processing rather than to the developmental, environmental perspective advocated by Jean Piaget. Reductionism (Ellis and Fouts, 1996) suggests that learning can be broken down into constituent parts, and that simpler parts of whole complex ideas are more manageable for the learner when they are taught in some meaningful sequence that leads toward comprehension of the whole. This certainly describes D.I.

The final comment we would make in our search for Level I is that D.I. in fact represents something close to pure empiricism. In this respect, it emerges as an atheoretical model. Over the past three decades D.I. researchers have systematically sought for evidence of its efficacy, paying little attention to theory building or to matters of abstract philosophy Study after study has been conducted in such curricular areas as reading, language, and mathematics. They have asked the pragmatic question, "Does it work?" The sheer weight of the evidence published in respected journals is impressive. This is remarkably different from the many innovations that claim (often dubiously) a profound theoretical basis, but that offer little published evidence to substantiate academic or other effects. It is this very strength that may contain the elements of its weakness. Why, advocates and empirical researchers ask, is D.I. so little acknowledged and so reluctantly accepted? There may be a number of reasons, including a built-in bias toward progressive education on the part of teachers. But if that were all, how does one explain the phenomenal acceptance by teacher training institutions and school districts of such behaviorist-essentialist protocols as instructional objectives, Madeline

Hunter's ITIP, and mastery learning? Clearly, ours is a field that is more than willing to embrace eclecticism, with few qualms about a mixed progressive-essentialist agenda. Madeline Hunter was an extremely effective promoter of ITIP, an innovation that may have been more widespread and used in schools than any other was of our time. She communicated a vision of ITIP that teachers, administrators, and professors in schools of education eagerly subscribed to in spite of the fact that the empirical evidence one might wish for really never was there. We suggest that even *good* evidence is not easy to sell in the absence of a well-communicated vision. Regarding D.I., this is unfortunate, because what we seem to have here, to paraphrase Cool Hand Luke's boss, is a failure to communicate.

LEVELS II AND III RESEARCH

An impressive research agenda has been carried out over the last 30 years on D.I. instructional programs. Studies have been conducted on both small- and large-scale usage, for short periods of time and in the form of longer-term follow-up evaluations. Because of the nature of D.I. instructional programs, the research tends more often than not to be a combination of quasi-experimental and program evaluation designs, and for this reason we will discuss Level II and Level III research together.

Return with us for a moment to those thrilling days of yesteryear, to the 1960s and Lyndon Johnson's Great Society, when there seemed to be a lot more money for educational research than there is today. It was during this time that the U.S. Office of Education initiated Project Follow Through to the tune of $59 million, the most expensive education research project ever funded. The project, which involved some 170+ communities, was designed to evaluate different approaches to educating economically disadvantaged students. "A wide array of instructional approaches were included in Follow Through, ranging from open classroom models, to cognitive models based on the theories of Piaget, to highly structured programs utilizing principles of contemporary learning theory" (Meyer et al., 1983). One of these instructional approaches was the Direct Instruction Model.

The Stanford Research Institute and Abt Associates were contracted to evaluate the effectiveness of the various models in the areas of basic skills, and cognitive and affective behaviors. To make a long story short, the Direct Instruction Model produced the most desirable results in all three areas. This included results superior in the cognitive areas to those instructional programs designed specifically to focus on cognitive outcomes, and results superior in the affective areas to those instructional programs designed specifically to focus on affective outcomes (Stebbins et al., 1977). The regimented protocols of D.I. are certainly at odds with the progressive educational wisdom of the day, and as far as educational practice is concerned, these findings seemed to have been basically ignored.

Apparently convinced that there must have been a mistake, officials of the Ford Foundation funded an evaluation of the evaluation, which (not surprisingly) questioned certain conclusions drawn by the evaluators (House, Glass, & McLean, 1978). This critique resulted in several more in-depth analyses of the data generated by Project Follow Through, in which D.I. looked even better (see Adams & Engelmann, 1996, pp. 67–98, for a summary of these reports). If the research stopped at this point, we would say that the controversy surrounding the Follow Through studies could pose some reasonable threat to the research base. In the world of education, where such a premium is placed on the "new," this is, after all, ancient history. There was, however, much more to come.

In the wake of Project Follow Through, research on the effectiveness of D.I. continued at both Levels II and III. Project Follow Through itself generated numerous follow-up studies of the long-term effects, the great majority of which supported the efficacy of D.I. Having found results similar to those noted by Meyer et al. (mentioned earlier in this chapter), Gersten and Keating (1987) noted that high school students who received Direct Instruction in primary grades had lower school dropout rates, higher test scores, and a higher percentage of college applications and acceptance. Finally, Gersten, Keating, and Becker (1988) conducted two longitudinal studies on the effects of Direct Instruction and found that the results consistently favored D.I. in educational outcomes such as graduation rates, dropout rates, and college acceptance, as well as in measures of achievement, especially reading.

Apart from Project Follow Through, scores of studies were conducted during the 1970s, 1980s, and 1990s probing the effects of D.I. in the areas of language, math, problem solving and reasoning skills, reading, and spelling. A number of research reviews and meta-analyses have been conducted over the years, but we will mention just a few. Cotton and Savard (1982) reviewed 33 relevant documents that supported Direct Instruction as improving basic skills achievement and affective development, but they did not conclude that D.I. was appropriate for older students. White (1988) conducted a meta-analysis reviewing 25 studies with special education populations, which showed very favorable results for D.I., including the observation that not one research study favored the comparison group. They noted that the effects of D.I. were independent of such variables as handicapping condition, age group, or skill area. Adams and Engelmann (1996) conducted the most thorough review of the research. This very impressive analysis of the literature, Project Follow Through publications, and meta-analysis of scores of Level II and Level III studies on the effects of D.I. are very solid evidence of its efficacy, providing educators with a formidable research base.

We would add one other note on the research on D.I. Since its inception, D.I. has had a loyal group of adherents, and their names are very prevalent in the D.I. literature, including the research studies. Among those are Becker, Carnine, Englmann, Maggs, and Gersten. We are leery when the proponents of a program, and in this case a commercial program, are also the primary researchers. A conflict of interest is always a strong possibility. In this case, however, we do not believe this to be an issue for several reasons. First, there are a number of other researchers who have studied D.I. who are not connected to its commercial aspects, and their findings are basically the same.

Second, the research by prominent D.I. advocates is published in prestigious, peer-reviewed journals, an extremely important quality control point. Third, there has been no sustained or focused criticism that we could find that challenges the quality of the research.

CONCLUSION

While working on an assessment project that involved developing a list of beginning reading curriculums with Levels II and III research support, we happened to mention to a local school district curriculum director that Direct Instruction had a pretty solid research base in its favor. Her expression was one of horror, and her response is quoted at the beginning of this chapter. She was absolutely aghast at the thought of anyone using such a program. When we repeated to her our knowledge of the extensive research base that showed that it worked well with a lot of kids, she really was not concerned about that. Her reply, finally, was "I just don't like it, plain and simple."

Well, okay. We can only assume that when President George Bush said some years ago that he hated broccoli (costing him, no doubt, the broccoli growers' vote) that he already knew it contained essential vitamins and minerals. He just didn't like the stuff, plain and simple. Perhaps similar comments could be made about exercise, meditation, and adequate sleep, even though "research" has shown them to be beneficial. To stretch this thin metaphor even further, we can say with assurance that people even engage in practices that research has shown to be harmful such as smoking and excessive drinking. It is a part of the human condition that gaps have always existed between evidence of something's worth and our willingness to embrace it. Just as often, we seem to be willing to embrace claims for which there is in fact little supportive evidence.

We recommend that districts interested in a research-tested curriculum of basic skills for young learners and at-risk children should seriously consider D.I. It is, after all, one of a minority of educational innovations that has evidence on its side.

REFERENCES

Adams, G., and Engelmann, S. (1996). *Research on direct instruction: 20 years beyond DISTAR*. Seattle, WA: Educational Achievement Systems.

Cotton, K., and Savard, W.G. *Direct instruction. Topic summary report. Research on school effectiveness project*. Portland, OR: Northwest Regional Educational Laboratory.

Darling-Hammond, L., and Snyder, J. (1992). Curriculum studies and the traditions of inquiry: the scientific tradition. In Jackson, P.W. *Handbook of research on curriculum*. New York: Macmillan.

Ellis, A.K., and Fouts, J.T. (1996). *Handbook of educational terms with applications*. Princeton, NJ: Eye on Education.

Engelmann, S., Becker, W.C., Carnine, D., and Gersten, R. (1988). The direct instruction follow through model: design and outcomes. *Education and Treatment of Children, 11(4)*, 303–317.

Gersten, R., and Keating, T. (1987). Long-term benefits from direct instruction. *Educational Leadership, 44*, 28–31.

Gersten, R., Keating, T., and Becker, W. (1988). The continued impact of the direct instruction model: longitudinal studies of Follow Through students. *Education and Treatment of Children, 11(4)*, 318–327.

House, E.R., Glass, G.V., and McLean, L.D. (1978). No simple answer: critique of the Follow Through evaluation. *Harvard Educational Review, 48*, 128–160.

Meyer, L.A., Gersten, R.M., and Gutkin, J. (1983). Direction instruction: a project Follow Through success story in an inner-city school. *The Elementary School Journal, 84(2)*, 241–252.

Moore, J. (1986). Direct instruction: a model of instructional design. *Educational Psychology, 6*, 201–229.

Rosenshine, B. (1979). Content, time, and direct instruction. In Peterson, P., and Walberg, H. (Eds.). *Research on teaching:*

concepts, findings, and implications, pp. 28–56. Berkeley, CA: McCutchan.

Rosenshine, B. (1986). Synthesis of research on explicit teaching. *Educational Leadership, 43*(7), 60–69.

Stallings, J. (1987). *Longitudinal findings for early childhood programs: focus on direct instruction* (ERIC Document Reproduction Service No. ED297874).

Stebbins, L.B., St. Pierre, R.G., Proper, E.C., Anderson, R.B., and Cerva, T.R. (1977). *Education as experimentation: a planned variation model. Vol. 4A–D. An evaluation of Follow Through.* Cambridge, MA: Abt Associates.

White, W.A.T. (1988). A meta-analysis of the effects of direct instruction in special education. *Education and Treatment of Children, 11*(4), 364–374.

Zemelman, S., Daniels, H., and Hyde, A. (1993). *Best practice: new standards for teaching and learning in America's schools.* Portsmouth, NH: Heinemann.

15

ALTERNATIVE/AUTHENTIC ASSESSMENT

The only way to improve schools . . . is to ensure that faculties judge local work using authentic standards and measures. . . . [I]t means doing away with the current extremes of private, eccentric teacher grading, on the one hand; and secure standardized tests composed of simplistic items on the other.

Grant Wiggins

. . . [A]lternative assessment's rising tide has overflowed most of education's shoreline, and the schools are increasingly being flooded with calls for more direct assessment of student performance. . . . Many practitioners are unsure whether to venture into the torrents of unfamiliar assessment strategies or to drift quietly in education's backwaters, waiting to see if this movement crests and ebbs as quickly as have dozens of others.

Blaine R. Worthen

Standardized tests are still the bread and butter of statewide assessment. But in all regions—north and south, liberal and conservative—alternative assessments have been added to the menu, if not as the main course, then at least as a side dish.

Lee Sherman Caudell

THE MOVEMENT

Alternative assessment strategies have emerged as a key element of the school restructuring movement. Like so many of the varied pieces of the vast and often contradictory school-restructuring puzzle, alternative assessment represents a frontal attack on the status quo. At the energizing source of the alternative assessment paradigm is a deep and abiding dissatisfaction with traditional evaluation procedures, both standardized tests and teacher-made achievement tests. But it doesn't stop there; the alternative assessment movement has produced a number of nontraditional ideas for taking into account student learning.

As one might expect, an entire range of terms and phrases has emerged. The significant vocabulary includes authentic assessment, performance assessment, practical testing, and direct testing. Whatever the terminology, the move to alternative assessment practices is reaching epic proportions. To place this movement into some kind of meaningful context, it is necessary to develop a contrasting image of more traditional assessment patterns and their effects on students.

TRADITIONAL MEASURES

Student progress is traditionally assessed and reported along a feedback continuum which incorporates everything from daily marks and test scores to semester grades and standardized test results. These marks take on a life of their own, creating a sense of reality in the minds of teachers, students, and parents. In fact, this "reality" may or may not have curriculum content validity; that is, the tests and, therefore, the grades that flow from them may or may not be very well connected to the curriculum that is taught to students. There is, in fact, a long history of discontent with both standardized and teacher-made tests.

From another viewpoint, standardized tests furnish communities, districts, states, and the nation with benchmarks of comparative scores over time and with one another. Thus we can compare any given district with its own past performance and with other districts; we can compare Vermont, say, with Nevada, and so on. For all its perceived shortcomings, it is a relatively efficient system, one that has been around for at least 50 years. Still, the criticisms have become increasingly strident, and they cannot simply be ignored.

Thomas Toch takes standardized tests to task in his book, *In the Name of Excellence* (1991). He cites the many standardized tests that states have put in place as a means of holding teachers accountable. Thinking that such tests will lead to improved classroom performance because teachers will "know" that they have to prepare their students more adequately, state legislators have enacted legislation requiring tests in the majority of the states. But Toch sees this as nothing more than a return to "minimum competency testing," a movement that was tried and that failed in the 1970s. In a very thoughtful passage, Toch writes,

> Yet there is an immense paradox in the recent surge in standardized testing. Despite the key role standardized tests are playing in the reformers' accountability campaign, the bulk of the new tests are severely flawed as measures of the excellence movement's progress. One major reason is that the tests do not measure the sorts of advanced skills and knowledge that the reformers have argued all students should master. . . .It is largely impossible to gauge from the results of such tests whether students are mastering the intellectual skills that have been the focus of the reform movement: the abilities to judge, analyze, infer, interpret, reason, and the like. Nor do the majority of the tests gauge students' more advanced knowledge of literature, history, science, and other disciplines. Indeed, the recent surge in standardized testing amounts to little more than an extension of the minimum basic-skills testing movement of the 1970s. (p. 207)

This very vexing problem carries with it yet another twist, as though it weren't enough that the ongoing critique that standardized tests (and teacher-made tests as well) tend to measure only lower-register thinking and knowledge. In a 1973 article in the *American Psychologist*, David McClelland, a noted researcher who we would definitely categorize as a Level I theoretician, criticized standardized testing in the most basic sense. He proposed teaching people how to raise their test scores, testing abilities rather than "aptitudes," designing tests so that people's scores would rise as they learned more, abandoning multiple-choice formats—all of which is yet to happen. But his most fundamental suggestion for change was his idea that we need to stop ranking millions of people on their perceived knowledge and skills and start building tests that tap into people's motivations for learning, something that could actually be used to shape instruction for individuals (Lehman, 1994).

Teacher-made tests are yet another story. Consider this comment by Mehrens and Lehmann (1991): "Students sometimes complain that they are fed up with tests that are ambiguous, unclear, and irrelevant. Student comments such as 'I didn't know what the teacher was looking for' and 'I studied the major details of the course but was only examined on trivia and footnotes' are not uncommon. Nor are they necessarily unjustified" (p. 52). It has been noted many times over that teacher-made tests are generally of low quality, particularly with respect to their validity and reliability and with respect to the observation that they tend to assess students primarily at low cognitive levels.

AUTHENTIC ASSESSMENT

Serious students of assessment are committed to a review of the entire educational system, and this would certainly involve a close look not only at how we have traditionally evaluated students but also of the effects on students of *how* they have been evaluated. Perhaps the key to understanding the alternative assessment movement is found in a thoughtful consideration of the term *authentic assessment*. The term implies that, by contrast, it should replace assessment that is inauthentic, which means false. So, the idea of authentic assessment is to create evaluation strategies that measure more realistically and accurately those things that students are supposed to be learning.

Students proceed through their school years being evaluated on daily, weekly, and quarterly bases, taking teacher-made tests, and doing assignments such as directed readings, reports, and projects. For this, they receive semester or yearly marks, many times in the form of letter grades, sometimes supplemented by narrative teacher evaluations. In a (seemingly) unrelated process, once a year (sometimes less often) they take standardized tests in such basic skill areas as mathematics and reading, and in such content areas as social studies and science. These tests are, at best, variably connected to the curriculum that is actually taught at a given school. It is when the results are disappointing and they get in the newspapers that school people become so discouraged. In fact, a typical defensive reaction by teachers is that their students are learning many wonderful things but that those things are not effectively captured by the tests. Of course, when the results are good we all seem to take them for granted.

In a more perfect educational world (the goal of restructuring), it would be impossible to separate assessment procedures from curriculum content. If we are to do authentic assessment, it stands to reason that we should be assessing what is being taught and, one hopes, what is being learned. So, first, for assessment to be authentic, it should be as closely aligned as possible to the day-to-day experiences of the curriculum. Here there really is little argument between traditionalists and those who would change the assessment paradigm. But good alignment is not enough. It's just a place to start.

Second, it is argued that teaching and learning should be authentic. This means that learning should focus on real-life situations. "Let students encounter and master situations that resemble real life" (Cronin, 1993, p. 79). The curricular implications of this view are clearly that school activities and projects should have a real-world cast to them. This argument has been around forever, and it basically represents a philosophic divide between those who espouse an academic-centered curriculum and those who espouse a more society-centered curriculum.

The Center on Organization and Restructuring of Schools at the University of Wisconsin at Madison has developed a framework for "authentic instruction," and "authentic achievement" (Newmann & Wehlage, 1993). Newmann and Wehlage draw a distinction between "achievement that is significant and meaningful, and that which is trivial and useless." They use three criteria to define authentic achievement:

"(1) students construct meaning and produce knowledge, (2) students use disciplined inquiry to construct meaning, and (3) students aim their work toward production of discourse, products, and performances that have value or meaning beyond success in school" (p. 8). We presume that experiences that do not meet these criteria are "trivial and useless."

Not all advocates of alternative assessment procedures have such definitively articulated ideas about achievement, but the essence of their argument is the same: what we teach and what we assess are not what is important for students to learn. All too often, they are removed from the "real world" that students will face when they leave school. Therefore, they argue, it behooves us to rethink our assessment techniques, and therefore our curriculum, to provide and assess learning that is authentic, and not contrived. Such a statement presumes that school is not part of the real world.

The alternative assessment movement is obviously based on two related arguments, one that deals with curriculum and the other with assessment. First, is the ancient, abiding debate over the curriculum, and the relevance of school learning to the real world. The belief in such a dichotomy, of course, can serve as a self-fulfilling prophecy. The question becomes, "Does what students are taught in the schools apply to reality, that is, can they use their knowledge to solve problems, do their jobs, and lead their lives?" Second, "What do traditional evaluation strategies such as paper and pencil tests and standardized tests really measure, and whatever that is, is it important?"

The proponents of alternative assessment strategies have definite and predictable responses to these questions. School learning must be reality-based, and the assessment of that learning must be more natural, a logical outgrowth of the learning experiences themselves. Many of those who hope to restructure education agree and have joined the movement, seeing it as crucial. There appear to be four reasons why alternative assessment is seen as a key to restructuring.

First, alternative assessment strategies are seen as educationally superior to traditional methods. The strategies call for more formative and personalized assessment for the individual student. To do this will provide meaningful feedback to the individual, thus creating the possibilities for more significant, useful learning. The focus shifts naturally to higher level thinking skills and real-life applications that increase student interest and motivation.

A second line of reasoning is that alternative forms of assessment will provide a more adequate representation of what is actually being taught in the schools today. Current standardized tests lack validity as measures of the diverse curricular offerings. It's an interesting argument and one that has a certain elemental appeal, but the idea behind good standardized tests is that they capture students' ability to apply concepts and skills, not their narrowly defined content data knowledge.

A third point is that authentic learning and alternative assessment strategies will facilitate the type of learning that is needed by employees to allow the United States to compete internationally. Here is an example. Students who use alternative assessment procedures are more involved in assessing their own learning and are therefore more aware of their learning. This metacognitive skill (reflecting on the processes of learning) is basic to problem solving, trouble shooting, and to working one's way through difficult, unpatterned situations. Thus, assessment becomes part of the learning experience and not something that is merely tacked on and devoid of context. In the "real world," you don't take periodic paper and pencil tests to measure how well you're doing. You do your job, and that involves assessment that has to do with product quality, customer satisfaction, worker productivity, and so on.

And fourth, alternative assessment strategies and resulting accountability will force intransigent teachers to change the way they teach children. Portfolios, student record keeping, journals, reflective discussions, and other related alternative assessment procedures are themselves metacognitive learning experiences and are therefore shapers of the school day. The amount of student-to-student interaction increases, the amount of time spent in reflective thinking increases, and before teachers and students know it, they have stepped off the conveyor belt that passes for learning and have entered a more seamless world where such things as planning, activity, and assessment flow together. At least that's the argument. Ellis writes, "These are not strategies that culminate in letter grades. These are strategies to be used by those teachers and students who are truly desirous of finding out what is being learned" (Ellis, 1991).

ALTERNATIVE ASSESSMENT STRATEGIES

A number of assessment strategies for teachers (Fig. 15.1) have emerged from all this. These strategies, or activities, are thought to be useful for measuring and enhancing critical thinking skills and the application of knowledge. With the exception of portfolios, these strategies are not particularly new; good teachers are already using them extensively in their classrooms. What is new, however, is the drive to replace the dominance of standardized tests in the eyes of the public and policy makers with these assessment techniques. At the extreme edges of the argument, enthusiasts wish to replace grades and tests completely with these strategies.

IS IT WORKING?

In the first half of this decade, the alternative assessment movement proceeded full speed ahead as an integral component of the school restructuring movement. To use Robert Slavin's terms (see Chapter 2), the pendulum had started its swing. The professional literature and conference programs featured advocates who attacked traditional evaluation procedures (and rightly so), touting the reasons for needed changes and offering various alternative assessment remedies. By 1995, the alternative assessment movement had gained wide support throughout the country and alternative assessment procedures were being implemented in nearly every state. Bond and Roeber's research (1995) found that "state assessment remains a significant tool for educational reform in 45 states." They noted that, "Students are assessed most often with a combination of traditional and alternative assessments..." and that the "use of

FIGURE 15.1. ASSESSMENT ALTERNATIVES

1. **Computer Adaptive Testing**—Any assessment, other than multiple-choice questions or worksheets, that requires the student to respond to the assessment items or task with the aid of a computer.

2. **Enhanced multiple-choice**—Any multiple-choice question that requires more than the selection of one correct response. Most often, the task requires the students to explain their responses.

3. **Extended-response, open-ended**—Any item or task that requires the student to produce an extended written response to an item or task that does not have one right answer (e.g., an essay or laboratory report.)

4. **Group performance assessment**—Any assessment that requires students to perform the assessment task in a group setting.

5. **Individual performance assessment**—Any assessment that requires the student to perform (in a way that can be observed) an assessment task alone.

6. **Interview**—An assessment technique in which the student responds to verbal questions from the assessor.

7. **Nontraditional test items**—Any assessment activity other than a multiple-choice item from which the student selects one response. These items or performances are rated using an agreed-upon set of performance criteria in the form of a scoring guide or a scoring rubric or in comparison to benchmark papers or performances.

8. **Observation**—An assessment technique that requires the student to perform a task while being observed and rated using an agreed-upon set of scoring criteria.

9. **Portfolio**—An accumulation of a student's work over time that demonstrates growth toward the mastery of specific performance criteria against which the tasks included in the portfolio can be judged.

10. **Project, exhibition, or demonstration**—The accomplishment of a complex task over time that requires demonstrating mastery of a variety of desired outcomes, each with its own performance criteria, that can be assessed within the one project, exhibition, or demonstration.

11. **Short-answer, open-ended**—Any item or task that requires the production of a short written response on the part of the respondent. Most often, there is a single right answer (for example, a fill-in-the-blank or short written response to a question).

Source: Adapted from Council of Chief State School Offi-
cers/North Central Regional Educational Laboratory, *The
Status of State Student Assessment Programs in the United States.*
Cited in Caudell, L.S. (1996). High stakes: Innovation meets
backlash as states struggle with large-scale assessment. *NW
Education,* 2(1), 36.

---

alternative assessments in conjunction with traditional assessments continues to grow" (p. 9).

As is so often the case in the annals of educational innovation, there were few skeptical articles early on. However, Blaine
Worthen (1993), who provided a careful analysis of the issues,
sounded a cautionary note. We present his more salient points
in Figure 15.2. In an earlier book, we wrote about these issues
that "anyone who seriously sets out on the alternative assessment trail needs to consider these possible objections," and
that Worthen's critique "is a useful primer in what might go
wrong. The issues of conceptual clarity, standardization, public
acceptance, feasibility, and technical quality, to name a few, are
not trivial concerns" (Ellis & Fouts, 1994, p. 174).

Now, several years later, it is worthwhile to examine the
status of the movement in relation to these issues. Apropos of
this, the following headlines have appeared in recent issues of
Education Week:

"The New Breed of Assessments Getting Scrutiny"

"Even as Popularity Soars, Portfolios Encounter
Roadblocks"

"Kentucky Student Assessment Called
'Seriously Flawed'"

"New Assessments Have Little Effect on Content,
Study Finds"

"Assessment Reform at a Crossroads: A Retreat from
Performance-Based Practice May Signal the Return to
Failed Forms of Testing"

Indeed, some states that had adopted or attempted to implement statewide alternative assessment systems have begun

FIGURE 15.2. CRITICAL ISSUES FACING ALTERNATIVE ASSESSMENT

Conceptual clarity. As yet, there is too little coherence to the concepts and language being used about alternative assessment, performance assessment, authentic assessment, direct assessment, and practical testing.

Mechanisms for self-criticism. Internal self-criticism is rather scarce among proponents of alternative assessment. If voices of caution are drowned out by the clamor for more rapid adoption of methods of alternative assessment, advocates could easily forget that self-criticism is the only road to continuing improvement.

Support from well-informed educators. The success or failure of the movement will depend on the willingness and competence of the teachers in the classrooms to undertake such tasks. This implies teachers with a higher degree of assessment competencies that differs from what is required now.

Technical quality and truthfulness. What technical specifications and criteria should be used to judge the quality of the assessments, including reliability and validity? The crux of the mater is whether or not the alternative assessment movement will be able to show that its assessments accurately reflect a student's true ability that are relevant to adult life.

Standardization of assessment judgments. How to standardize criteria and performance levels sufficiently to support necessary comparisons without causing them to lose the power and richness of assessment tailored to the student's needs and achievements remains a daunting issue.

Ability to assess complex thinking skills. Do alternative modes of assessment necessarily require the use of more complex processes by students? Proponents cannot assume that students are using such skills just because they are performing a hands-on task.

Acceptability to stakeholders. The public's acceptance of alternative assessments is not a sure thing. They are difficult to use to report learning outcomes for entire classes, school districts, or state systems. Political realities demand such accountability.

Appropriateness for high-stakes assessment. Does alternative assessment provide sufficient standardization to defend high-stakes decisions based on such measures? Will ethnic minorities score better on alternative assessments than on traditional measures—or more poorly, as now appears quite possible? Will the inevitable legal challenges aimed at high-stakes decisions based on alternative assessments be more difficult to defend because of validity and reliability questions?

Feasibility. One of the most frequently debated issues is whether or not alternative assessment is feasible for large-scale efforts to assess student performance. Does alternative assessment produce sufficiently greater benefits to justify its increased costs?

> Source: Adapted from Worthen, B. (1993). Critical issues that will determine the future of alternative assessment. *Phi Delta Kappan, 74*, 444–454.

---

to temporize. And efforts in other states are bogged down. Bond and Roeber (1995) wrote, "Although there have been some successes,...the setbacks in California, Arizona, Indiana, and elsewhere indicate that widespread acceptance of performance assessment is certainly not automatic" (p. 25).

Worthen's analysis of the critical issues facing alternative assessment were right on target. Many of the issues he identified have yet to be resolved, and these problems have been pointed out by a number of writers (Neill, 1996; Caudell, 1996; Olson, 1995; Viadero, 1995; Bond & Roeber, 1995). Specifically, these concerns remain:

+ There are unresolved technical issues of reliability (basically consistency in scoring across scores and consistency in scoring from school to school or state to state) and validity (i.e., do they really reflect "higher thinking skills," "life skills").

+ As yet, there is no way to standardize the assessments for "high stakes" purposes (e.g., accountability, program evaluation, and college admission).

+ There is less than widespread public support among many parent and political groups.

+ There is insufficient funding or commitment for the needed widespread teacher training that alternative assessment procedures demand.

- There is no evidence that alternative assessment procedures are more equitable to certain groups than are traditional assessment procedures.

- The estimates of cost of various alternative assessment procedures on a large scale run from 5 to 30 times the cost of standardized multiple-choice tests, with no evidence that there is a cost benefit to them.

All of these things are embedded in Worthen's earlier critique, and, consequently, on a large-scale basis (state assessments, district assessments) the movement appears to have hit a snag, at least as it applies to school or student accountability. Still, the alternative assessment movement has encouraged many teachers to examine their evaluation or assessment ideas, and that itself is a very valuable outcome.

EDUCATIONAL RESEARCH AND ALTERNATIVE ASSESSMENT

Researchers are just beginning to address the questions of whether or not the use of such assessment strategies actually changes teacher behavior, student learning, or the curriculum. Reports from Vermont and Kentucky suggest that the strategies can have a positive effect for changing classroom activities, while reports from Arizona and elsewhere suggest that that is not necessarily so. Research done by Martin-Kniep, Sussman, and Meltzer (1995), for example, has shown that the assessment piece can be a vehicle by which teachers examine the role of the teacher and student in the learning process, but a well-designed staff development program is probably vital to make this happen.

There is only one consistent area of research that we could find that does relate alternative assessment to achievement: the updated effective schools findings. Effective schools research has been conducted for several decades, and has resulted in a variety of lists of school characteristics that distinguish "more effective" schools from schools that are less so. These charac-

teristics are thought by many to have a cause-and-effect relationship with regard to achievement, but this is a hypothesis
that has not been established empirically. Nonetheless, the effective schools characteristics do suggest why some schools
may be better than others. Recent research by Cotton (1995)
identifies the following among a long list of classroom and
school attributes:

+ Teachers make use of alternative assessments as
  well as traditional tests.

+ Administrators and other building leaders develop and use alternative assessments.

+ District leaders and staff support schools' development and use of alternative assessments.

However, these are only 3 of 59 characteristics that describe
effective schools. We believe, therefore, that this research in
isolation is not adequate evidence to suggest that alternative
assessment procedures will lead to greater student achievement.

Whether these procedures do or will actually result in
greater learning by students may or may not be the case, but
we find no conclusive evidence at this point. If and when researchers focus systematically on this question, methodological
problems will arise, namely, the determining of satisfactory
educational outcomes and methods of assessing those outcomes. Alternative assessment advocates may balk at the use
of standardized test scores as measures of achievement, with
the result that no satisfactory way can be agreed upon to compare groups. Thus, the overall effect of this movement on student learning may prove to be highly problematic. Its efficacy
would then necessarily be defended based on the belief that it
focuses teaching and learning on more purposeful pursuits.
One finds some precedent for this in the whole language
movement.

M.E. Gredler (1995) has articulated another note of caution
to researchers on the use of alternative assessments by researchers. She examined what research there is on alternative
assessment procedures and concluded that, "…at present, port-

folio assessments are not recommended as the primary source of evidence about the attainment of program goals in evaluations that compare curricula or programs. The lack of validity and reliability information makes judging a curriculum or program on the scores assigned to student portfolios problematic at best" (p. 435). She states further that, "The use of portfolios for other purposes that differ from fostering individualized student growth or demonstrating the intrinsic value of a program, leads, to no surprise, to problems and unresolved issues" (p. 436).

CONCLUSION

The alternative assessment movement is in many ways a breath of fresh air in an atmosphere gone stale over time. We applaud those teachers and administrators who continue to search for ways to involve students more fully in their own learning toward a heightened state of consciousness of purpose in learning. Traditional tests and measures have so many obvious shortcomings that we hardly need go back over that ground in the closing moments of this chapter. Still, we are equally convinced that traditional measures have value and that it would be most unwise to abandon them in spite of the allure of "authentic" approaches. Both are needed. We will make the controversial statement here that teachers and students simply do not do enough assessing in school settings. Assessment at its best is the stuff of reflection, metacognition, communication, and moral judgment. We can thank the alternative assessment movement for reminding us of that thought. In fact, the movement may be more about teaching/learning strategies than about assessment.

REFERENCES

Arter, J.A. (1995). *Portfolios for assessment and instruction. ERIC Digest.* Greensboro, NC: ERIC Clearinghouse on Counseling and Student Services.

Bond, L.A., and Roeber, E.D. (1995). *The status of state student assessment programs in the United States. Annual Report.* Washington, DC: Office of Educational Research and Improvement.

Caudell, L.S. (1996). High stakes: innovation meets backlash as states struggle with large scale assessment. *NW Education* 2(1), 26–28, 35.

Cotton, K. (1995). *Effective schooling practices: a research synthesis 1995 update.* Portland, OR: Northwest Regional Educational Laboratory.

Cronin, J.F. (1993). Four misconceptions about authentic learning. *Educational Leadership, 50*(7), 78–80.

Darling-Hammond, L. (1994). Setting standards for students: the case for authentic assessment. *Educational Forum, 59*(1), 14–21.

Ellis, A.K. (1991). Evaluation as problem solving. *Curriculum in Context, 19*(2), 30–31.

Gredler, M.E. (1995). Implications of portfolio assessment for program evaluation. *Studies in Educational Evaluation, 21*(4), 431–437.

Lehman, N. (1994). Is there a science of success? *The Atlantic Monthly, 273*(2), 83–98.

Marcoulides, G.A., and Heck, R.H. (1994). The changing role of educational assessment in the 1990s. *Education and Urban Society, 26*(4), 332–339.

Martin-Kniep, G.O., Sussman, E.S., and Meltzer E. (1995). The North Shore Collaborative Inquiry Project: a reflective study of assessment and learning. *Journal of Staff Development 16*(4), 46–51.

Mehrens, W.A., and Lehmann, I.J. (1991). *Measurement and evaluation in education and psychology.* Orlando, FL: Holt, Rinehart and Winston.

Neill, M. (1996). Assessment reform at a crossroads. *Education Week,* February 28, 1996, 33.

Newmann, F.M., and Wehlage, G.G. (1993). Five standards of authentic instruction. *Educational Leadership, 50*(7), 8–12.

Olson, L. (1995). The new breed of assessments getting scrutiny. *Education Week,* March 22, 1995, 1.

Rayborn, R. (1992). Alternatives for assessing student achievement: let me count the ways. In *Assessment: how do we know what they know?* pp. 24–27. Union, WA: Washington State Association for Supervision and Curriculum Development.

Ryan, J.M., and Miyasaka, J.R. (1995). Current practices in testing and assessment: what is driving the changes. *NASSP Bulletin, 79*(573), 1–10.

Toch, T. (1991). *In the name of excellence: the struggle to reform the nation's schools and why it's failing and what should be done.* New York: Oxford University Press.

Viadero, D. (1995). Even as popularity soars, portfolios encounter roadblocks. *Education Week,* April 5, 1995, 8.

Worthen, B.R. (1993). Critical issues that will determine the future of alternative assessment. *Phi Delta Kappan, 74,* 444–448.

EPILOGUE

*Have not the verses of Homer continued twenty-five hundred years or more
without the loss of a syllable or letter; during which time infinite palaces,
temples, castles, cities have been decayed and demolished.*

Francis Bacon

The spirit of educational reform is endowed with perennial
qualities. There seems to be a never-ending quest by educators
for better programs, better delivery systems, better ideas about
how students learn. Each year new approaches are touted, and
thousands of teachers and administrators find themselves in
meetings, taking notes while listening to some guru who
claims to have at last gotten to the heart of the matter. The
claims themselves have an enduring nature, only the topics
change.

University of Kentucky professor and writer Thomas
Guskey (1996) has likened the education profession's infatuation with educational innovations and fads with the infatuations of a young child. Guskey points out that young children
are prone to infatuations which are "passionate, totally con-
suming, and held in staunch resistance to alternative points of
view." Young children see only the positive qualities of the object of infatuation, and are blind to the faults no matter how
obvious those faults may be to others. And, what imperfections
the child does notice are "dismissed as inconsequential and
unimportant." Only later with maturity do we realize the
short-lived nature of these infatuations, and only with maturity
do we develop a "richer understanding more likely to endure
the tests of time."

Concerning education, Guskey goes on to say:

Although professional development in education certainly cannot be considered young and innocent, it
still appears to be caught up in infatuations. Ideas,
techniques, and innovations are latched on to with in-
nocence and naiveté. Devotion to these ideas is pas-

sionate and unfettered by criticism. Only positive attributes are perceived, while weakness and flaws pass
unnoticed. And as is true in the case of most infatuations, the devotion tends to be short-lived. As a result,
earnest but confused education leaders career from
trend to trend. Their infatuations compel them to invest in the perspectives and programs that are currently in vogue, even though their use may not be jus-
tified by the current state of theory or sound evidence.
(p. 34)

Few fields of endeavor are as vulnerable as ours is to miracle cures. After all, we want desperately to be efficient, to provide equality of opportunity for children, and to promote academic excellence. We want our schools to be places of good
repute. Each of us wants people to talk about our own school
with expressions of admiration. We want our students to recall
their days with us as times of hope and glory. And why not?
Why expect less of ourselves?

Those teachers and administrators who have toiled in the
vineyards of education over time come to know the rhythms of
the school year. The hope and the high expectations of a golden
September morning when the whole year lies before us and
even the most mediocre student in the most mediocre class
taught by the most mediocre teacher seems filled with the
promise of success. We learn to know the ambiguities of a cold
and dark January late afternoon when the kids have left for the
day and we're sitting at our desk wondering what's the point
and why are we doing this? And we've experienced that day in
June when it's over once more and we made it and so did the
kids and we're not sure how, and they're saying goodbye to us
and where did the year go anyway? And that kid comes up to
say goodbye, the one that everybody but us had written off,
and hands us a note that simply says, "Thank you."

Maybe there is something more to teaching and learning
than the quest for the latest program. Maybe it has more to do
with a caring teacher and a group of kids who want to learn
something than we are willing to admit in this age of innova-

tion. Maybe the real answers were there all along, and they had more to do with decency, perseverance, character, and plain old high standards than we realized in our quest for the new. Still we look for help because it's a tough job and we want to do it right. How do we know when and whether to invest our time, our energy, the public's money, and the other resources that it takes to innovate?

THE GRAVEYARD OF LOST SHIPS

To paraphrase singer Neil Diamond, there is no way to count or to measure the cost of the energy lost in the annals of educational innovation. Today's flagship is often tomorrow's abandoned shipwreck. There was the incredible new program that everyone talked about, and if you weren't up to speed, well. . . . Now the same people who touted it can barely remember it. Where are they now? All the miracle cures, all the new curriculums and methods that at long last had arrived to rescue us from the depths of mediocrity. All the answers for low test scores, for low self-esteem, for apathy and indifference to learning.

Whatever happened to Values Clarification? Whatever happened to Career Education? Whatever happened to TESA, GESA, and the other ESA's? And what of the New Math? The New Science? Competency-based Education? Behavioral Objectives? The Hunter Model? Glasser Circles? And the list goes on. It may be difficult to imagine it now, but there was a time when each of these items was the latest trend in educational circles. Some of them sank beneath the waves leaving no wake in their path. Others were forerunners of later trends and thus contributed to a certain extent to the ongoing search for better schools.

BEYOND EMPIRICISM

Much of the space in this book has been devoted to a look at the research base that supports certain educational innovations. It is our contention that teachers and administrators should demand evidence before plunging ahead into some effort that is sure to go away in time if for no other reason than that it never had a solid empirical basis. But this is not to say that everything we do in the name of learning demands evidence based on carefully controlled studies. Some things that are done, or should be done, in the name of education are not of a nature to be empirically based.

An example of a promising idea that we might assign to this category is *increased parent involvement* in their children's academic life. Researcher John Goodlad noted that where parents are involved, school tests scores are higher. We support his finding but know of no way that one could conduct cause-and-effect experiments to determine the actual driving force in the mix of variables. Rather, we must in this case be content with correlation at Level II and try to document positive academic outcomes at Level III, program evaluation. But if we were building principals or classroom teachers we would do everything we could to get parents meaningfully involved in their children's education. It not only is commonsense, it supports a larger societal goal of family togetherness. Two closely related challenges we think schools should mount include an exponential increase in the amount of reading students are expected to do accompanied by a corresponding decrease in the amount of time they spend watching television. Obviously, both of these quests would require parental support.

These ideas lead us to a closing statement that must be considered thoughtfully if we are truly serious about raising achievement levels. Schools are the direct responsibility of those entrusted to their care. We should expect good value from them. But school, it is easy to forget, is really only a subset of that something larger called education. Education is the responsibility of the society. The perspectives on the importance of learning, which our young people develop, come from all quarters of society. To the extent that the messages are uplifting, coherent, and supportive of one another, a society will do an honorable job of educating the young. Schools simply cannot do it alone apart from the larger society. A society's cultural, spiritual, and academic vision is communicated to the young through its art, architecture, music, religion, science, media, government, and social and family structures.

RESEARCH QUESTIONS TO ASK

Anyone who contemplates educational innovation should ask three basic sets of questions. These questions have been at the heart of our own assessments of the programs reviewed in this book. The questions are:

- What is the theoretical basis of the proposed program? How sound is that theoretical base?
- What is the nature of the research done to document the validity of the proposed program? What is the quantity and quality of the research done in classroom settings?
- Is there evidence of large-scale implementation program evaluation? What comparisons were made with "traditional" forms? How realistic was the evaluation? What was the duration? What was the setting?

Our strong suggestion is that as you consider innovation, you pose these questions seriously. We think you should ask them of the purveyors of innovation. And we don't think you should settle for answers such as, "The movement is so new that much of this has not been done at this point." Too much is at stake.

A CLOSING THOUGHT

We've looked at a number of highly touted educational innovations in this book. In some instances, we've been quite supportive. In others we've voiced serious reservations, especially where shaky theoretical foundations are concerned, where few or dubious studies have been conducted, and where program evaluation studies are lacking. We certainly do not wish to make cynics of you or even suggest that you not *consider* an innovation until it has "proven" itself conclusively.

What we are suggesting is caution, especially where large expenditures of funds and extensive teacher retraining are at stake. That is only prudent. But we do encourage risk taking, pilot programs, and efforts to transcend the ordinary qualities of school life. These efforts should be mounted as Level II investigations. That alone will separate your school or district from the bandwagon-hopping legions that merely think they are doing something innovative while actually practicing self-delusion. The other outcome of a commitment to Level II research is that your school or district really will become a pilot center, one that others begin to look to for leadership. When schools commit to this level of quality, we can look forward to real progress, and perhaps the era of pendulum swings will come to a well-deserved end.

REFERENCE

Guskey, T. (1996). To transmit or to construct: the lure of trend infatuation in teacher professional development. *Education Week, 16*(8) (October 23), p. 34.

INDEX